DOG
OBSESSED

DOG
OBSESSED

//

THE HONEST KITCHEN'S
—— COMPLETE GUIDE ——
to a Happier, Healthier Life
for the Pup You Love

LUCY POSTINS
WITH SARAH DURAND

Foreword by Jane Lynch
Illustrated by Natalya Zahn

RODALE

RODALE
wellness

Live happy. Be healthy. Get inspired.

Sign up today to get exclusive access to our authors, exclusive bonuses,
and the most authoritative, useful, and cutting-edge information
on health, wellness, fitness, and living your life to the fullest.
Visit us online at RodaleWellness.com
Join us at RodaleWellness.com/Join

Rodale books may be purchased for business or promotional use or for special sales. For information, please write to: Special Markets Department, Rodale Inc., 733 Third Avenue, New York, NY 10017

Printed in the United States of America
Rodale Inc. makes every effort to use acid-free ∞, recycled paper ♲.

Illustrations by Natalya Zahn
Small watercolor washes by Natalya Zahn; full-page watercolor washes
by Angie Makes/Shutterstock: pages xvi, 21, 26, 93, 118, 124, 133, 152, 209.
Photographs by Mitch Mandel/Rodale Inc.: pages 8, 40, 64, 71, 89, 130, 162, 173, 180, 184, 214, 221, 226, 230;
by Jamie Pflughoeft/Cowbelly Photography: xii, 87, 142; by Melissa Olund: xv;
by Ashley DuChene Photography: 3; by Jesse Southerland: 5; by Camilo Rodriguez: 7;
by The Honest Kitchen: 19, 67, 84, 174, 204; by Derek Call: 21; by Evan Johnson: 25;
by Kate Kober/KCK Photography: 28; by Sarah Lang: 34; by Vasi Crisan: 97;
by Julianna Hamett: 104; by Dawn Lynch: 117; by Kathleen Nahf: 146; by Wendy Gable: 167;
by Gillian Stoneback: 171; by Norm Shrout/Long Leash on Life: 188; by Ashley Roberts: 203.
Book design by Rae Ann Spitzenberger
Food styling by Lisa Homa
Prop styling by Nicole Cataffo

Library of Congress Cataloging-in-Publication Data is on file with the publisher.

ISBN 978–1–62336–748–0 paperback

Distributed to the trade by Macmillan

2 4 6 8 10 9 7 5 3 1 paperback

RODALE

Follow us @RodaleBooks on

We inspire health, healing, happiness, and love in the world.
Starting with you.

For my husband, Charlie;
my daughters, Thalia and Asha; and
the pups at the heart of my obsession:
Taro, Willow, Johnson, and Mosi

Taro

Johnson

CONTENTS

Foreword by Jane Lynch viii

Introduction: Why Being
Obsessed with Your Dog Is
Completely Okay x

Chapter 1
THE GUIDING PRINCIPLES OF THE DOG OBSESSED
The Common Traits of Those Who
Are Flat Out Nutty about Pups

1

Chapter 2
PICKING A PUP
Understanding Your New Dog's
One-of-a-Kind Personality

13

Chapter 3
IT'S A DOG'S WORLD
The Happy Home Life
of the Dog Obsessed

33

Chapter 4
FOOD, GLORIOUS DOG FOOD
Understanding Your Pet's
Nutritional Needs

53

Chapter 5
MEALTIME MISGIVINGS
Grappling with Picky
Eating, Fat Dogs,
and Food Sensitivities

75

Chapter 6
DOG HEALTH
From the Ears to the
Undercarriage (and
Everything In Between)
95

Chapter 7
THE DOCTOR IS IN
Finding and Keeping the Best
Veterinarian for Your Dog
127

Chapter 8
THE EMOTIONAL
LIVES OF DOGS
Anxiety, Jealousy, and
Other Issues
139

Chapter 9
HOLIDAYS, PLANE
TRIPS, AND MORE
The Jet-Setting Life
of the Dog Obsessed
157

Chapter 10
RUN, PLAY, AND FETCH
Easy, Essential Exercises
for a Happy, Healthy Pup
179

Chapter 11
FUN, GAMES,
PICNICS, AND PARTIES
Perfect Birthdays, Excursions,
and Make-at-Home Toys
195

MEALS FOR YOU AND
YOUR DOG—WITH WINE!
211

Recommended Reading 228
Acknowledgments 229
Index 231

FOREWORD

Like most of you reading this, I'm absolutely obsessed with dogs. I love cats, too, but it's really dogs that send me over the edge. (Please, whatever you do, don't mention this to my cat. He has claws, and he knows how to use them.)

My Dog Obsession has come out in a few ways over the years. For example, like any good pet owner, I always make sure my pups, Olivia and Benjamin, have a sitter when I go out of town for work. My 16-year-old Lhasa Apso, Olivia, only has one eye, and I have to give her eyedrops daily. I've found the best way to make sure a pet sitter knows how to do it is through a full, step-by-step, photographed demonstration.

Because of Olivia's age, I've also recently discovered that a body carrier is the best way to transport her from one place to another. It makes things much easier from a logistics standpoint, and I do like to have her close. She's adapted quite well to being in it, and luckily, my 10-year-old Belgian Shepherd, Benjamin, doesn't seem to mind having to walk. Maybe someday they'll make a carrier big enough for him?

But my Dog Obsession can best be summed up with a story concerning my early days with Olivia. I was living alone in Laurel Canyon in my very first house—the home I had fallen in love with at first sight and had started decorating almost

Benjamin

Olivia

obsessively—and I'd just adopted her. I was crazy about this little girl, whom I'd named after Olivia Newton-John. She loved it when I rubbed and cuddled her (so much so, in fact, that she'd growl if I stopped), and we'd bonded immediately. Like anyone who loves dogs, I naturally let her find her favorite place on the couch, where she'd curl up next to me anytime I sat down and made myself comfortable.

And there she lay, day after day, peeing between the cushions. I tried everything to cure her of it, and over 3 years, I bought three different couches and probably every cleaning product ever created. But did I think for a moment of making Olivia sit on a pet bed on the floor? Never. That's right. *Three years and three couches*—that's how committed I am to this dog. Finally, I bought her a doggie diaper because I couldn't bear for her to be uncomfortable anymore.

I first met Lucy Postins through my vet and friend, Dr. Patrick Mahaney, and I have been a fan of The Honest Kitchen for years. (Don't let Lucy's occasionally clipped British tone put you off; she's just got your dog's best interests at heart, and she's honestly not quite that bossy in real life.) Olivia is crazy for turkey and won't leave me alone until I feed her Honest Kitchen's Embark, her absolute favorite food in the whole wide world. Benjamin goes wild over Zeal, The Honest Kitchen's grain-free fish recipe. Lucy's company's commitment to the health and well-being of dogs comes through in the care and attention to detail it puts into every product it makes, and that commitment is reflected in how thrilled my dogs are when they get their breakfast and dinner.

Dog Obsessed speaks to people like me, who'll do absolutely anything for their dogs—even let them pee on the couch for 3 years. Lucy helps people feel comfortable being flat-out bonkers about their pets, then shows those people how to celebrate their obsession. With recipes, tips for better physical and emotional health, and terrific creative ideas for parties, traveling, and more, this is the book for any person who wants to keep their dog in tip-top shape. I've always thought that you should never be ashamed of being called a crazy dog person, and Lucy confirms that here. Being head over heels in love with your dog is really about wanting the best for them—all day, every day—and this book shows you how to give them that and more.

—JANE LYNCH

INTRODUCTION
Why Being Obsessed with Your Dog Is Completely Okay

Most people *really* love their dogs. But for some of us, the affection we feel toward our pups and the ways we show our love for them are regarded by the mainstream as a borderline unhealthy obsession. While "they" may not have even noted the date of their dog's birthday, we plan a party for ours. He may even get two birthdays per year: one to commemorate the day he was born and another for the anniversary of the day we brought him home.

When we take our dogs out to potty in the pouring rain, we shield them with a golf umbrella so they don't get soaked. We outfit them in cozy sweaters and jackets during the chilly winter months, and we monitor their moves with cameras if we've left them home alone. We take them on our road trips, think about their needs when we pick new homes and cars, and frequently snub our human friends and family to spend more time in our dog's company.

Honest Kitchen sales rep Ashley is a perfect example of someone with true Dog Obsession. When her Golden/Great Pyrenees boy, Nuke, was diagnosed with a terminal condition, Ashley decided that she wanted to show him around the country and experience a true vacation . . . just a girl and her dog. They took off together on a 3,000-mile road trip, exploring countless beaches, camping under the stars, and sharing a tiny cabin under the redwoods in Big Sur. While most of Ashley's friends and family were baffled that she chose to spend her precious vacation on a road trip with Nuke, she felt so fortunate to share that time with him. He is, by far, her favorite travel buddy!

We Dog Obsessed tolerate our dogs' mischievous escapades because, to us, they make them even more adorable, and the idea of somehow hampering their natural character simply doesn't appeal. We typically put their needs before our own, and we often prioritize their happiness over that of our human families. Witness Kim, who works in marketing at The Honest Kitchen. At her wedding she asked her husband, Dylan, to step out of a photo so she could take one alone with her dog, Gus. (You know, in case the whole marriage thing didn't work out.) My own mother, who's in her seventies, will gladly tell you of the times she's had to squish up with her knitting at one end of our sofa because one of my Rhodesian Ridgebacks is sprawled out on the rest of it. Or she'll regale you with the times she's been practically bounced out of bed in the early hours by my dogs' enthusiastic leap-and-lick morning greetings because I don't like to banish them from the guest room, fearing they'll take offense.

Many of us set varying degrees of rules and enforce them with varying degrees of commitment, but the common thread is that we're all crazy about our pups. And with good reason. There's just something inherently satisfying about doing things that make our dogs happier, more comfortable, and more included in our lives. We can't stand the idea of leaving them behind when we set off on family vacations. We find ourselves on the verge of a panic attack if we've stayed a bit too long at a party and left them home alone for longer than intended. We take them with us to run errands, include them in our Thanksgiving feasts (even if it's slightly imposing on our hosts), and make all sorts of personal sacrifices on their behalf.

Many of the things we do in our quest to provide our pups with the happy, healthy lives they deserve are regarded with polite curiosity by others. But to us, that's just a part of Dog Obsession. Take Sara, our marketing coordinator at The Honest Kitchen. Her dog, Kona, could be found perched on top of her dining room table any time she and her husband, Cale, left the house. Why? Because she wanted to look out the window by the front door and see them as soon as they returned home. At first Sara and Cale tried to make Kona stop, but every time they came back, there she'd be. They ended up putting a dog bed *on the table* because if Kona insisted on that one spot, at least they could make her comfortable. Needless to say, they could always count on visitors questioning why there was a dog bed right where they ate their dinner every night.

MY STORY

I grew up in rural England with a dog, a cat, a sister, four ducks, and two hardworking parents. My family was ahead of the times in many ways. While most people think of British meals as boring and tasteless—an endless cycle of fish and chips, Sunday roast, and mushy peas—my parents had planted an organic garden. My sister and I loved to walk outside to pick fresh vegetables and herbs and then help prepare delicious, colorful, healthy whole food meals.

I didn't really appreciate it at the time, but the older I got, the more I began to connect our good health to what was growing outside our kitchen window. I developed an interest in the medicinal and health-promoting properties of culinary herbs, vegetables, and fruits, studying up on them while helping to cook. When it was time to go to college, I enrolled in the Warwickshire College of Agriculture. After 4 years, I graduated with a bachelor's degree in equine and business studies, which I often refer to as "4 years of pony club camp" or "drinking beer while wearing wellies and reading loads of books on horses." All joking aside, agricultural college was truly a wonderful springboard to my life's calling.

Once I had my degree, I moved to Southern California with my now husband, Charlie, where I took a position as the equine and canine nutritionist for a local holistic pet food manufacturer. There I learned that most conventional pet food is made in "rendering plants"—factories that harvest the remnants of animal parts (chicken beaks, feet, feathers, innards, and bones) that are unsuitable for consumption by humans. These bits and pieces of dead animals are combined with additives like Yellow No. 5 dye and artificial flavorings to create pet foods bearing the words "Made with real chicken!" but containing no real whole food nutrition at all. To me, what the conventional pet food industry was churning out at a cost of pennies per pound wasn't healthy or honest. Instead, it felt like the equivalent of TV dinners for cats and dogs.

At the time, I had a Rhodesian Ridgeback named Mosi, for whom I'd bend over backward. He had a big, plush dog bed in our room, and I'd get up multiple times each night during the winter months to re-cover him with his blanket to make sure he didn't get cold. Around dawn, I'd hold up the duvet of our own bed so he could hop up and crawl under for a morning snuggle. He came to work with me every day (I bought a new, bigger car to make his commute more comfortable); joined us on frequent camping trips; and on outings and chilly days, proudly wore his very own bespoke fleece leopard-print jacket, custom made by his breeder, Jill.

Though Mosi was always in good spirits and great health—and despite all the pampering in the world—he suffered from ongoing ear infections. At times he'd scratch his ears and shake his head to the point of distraction, and I could tell that he was in obvious discomfort. Prescription medications for antibiotics, ear flushes, and steroids would only suppress his symptoms temporarily and never really seemed to bring about a true cure. Plus, the size of the vet bills began to rival our monthly mortgage.

I decided to get to the root of the problem.

I began thinking about the food I gave him every day. Conventional pet food was so heavily processed under such extreme heat and pressure that, to me, his dinner of uniform, slightly mysterious brown pellets felt like fast food rather than real nutrition. I wondered, *How can Mosi's body have a fighting chance to relieve his symptoms without the sort of fresh, colorful, proper food my human family enjoys?* And that's when I decided to make his dinner myself, right there in my own kitchen.

Under Mosi's watchful eye, I mixed up a few homemade concoctions of different raw ingredients. He eagerly taste-tested them to make sure they were delicious, and voilà—within a few weeks his itchy ears were gone.

The only real drawback was the mess that I'd made in my kitchen during the process. Nobody likes seeing spinach up their walls, and even the *most* Dog Obsessed might feel a bit uncomfortable by the presence of packages of bloody meat leaking in the fridge. After a lot of trial and error, I discovered that dehydration was the perfect solution—a way to create a colorful real food diet, without all the mess of raw food. I re-created my recipe with dehydrated ingredients, and Mosi's health continued to flourish.

Once I saw how eating real, nutrient-rich whole food helped him, I knew that other dog lovers would want to do the same for their four-legged best friends. That's when The Honest Kitchen's delicious meals were born. In 2002, Charlie lent me

$7,000 to purchase my first batch of human-grade ingredients. Then I talked a human food facility into producing my recipe. Tears flowed when the first test blend turned into a bag of pulverized powder, but they soon perfected the production technique. A friend helped me design the labels, another built the Web site, and after a bit of paperwork to get a legal structure and a bank account, I had a little company on my hands.

I named it The Honest Kitchen: "Honest" as a reference to some of the shady things that happen in the conventional pet food industry, and "Kitchen" to emphasize that my product was really and truly human food grade.

I had a long chat with the owner of my neighborhood pet food store and somehow convinced her that I wasn't some crazy dog-food-tasting British lady. She agreed to give my meals a shot, and to my delight, the store almost immediately sold out of the first order I sent over. It turns out I wasn't the only Dog Obsessed person in my neighborhood, or in North America.

Today, The Honest Kitchen remains a family-owned company run by foodies with a true passion for pets. Every year, we produce well over 7 million pounds of dog and cat food, supplements, and treats, all of it all-natural, non-GMO, and made from only healthy, tasty, colorful, whole food ingredients. Our FDA verification confirms that we're the first and *only* nationally distributed pet food company to be 100 percent human-grade, too. As anyone who's lucky enough to visit our office will tell you, we can often be found working at the kitchen table, taste-testing our ingredients as we dream up new recipes. Our eager office dogs can be found hovering around our test kitchen on a daily basis, eagerly awaiting the opportunity to give a bit of feedback on our latest new creation. And if one's not forthcoming, a couple of them have been known to help themselves to an unwitting staff member's sandwich instead.

WHAT YOU'LL FIND IN THIS BOOK

At The Honest Kitchen, we're experts on nutrition, but *Dog Obsessed* is about so much more than just food. Yes, what we put in our dogs' bellies affects every part of them—from their wet noses to their adorable tails to how they sleep at night—but in this book, I'll talk about all the aspects of life with your dog. I'll take you from the first moment you dreamed of picking up a puppy from a breeder or going to a shelter and bringing an older dog home—showing you the many wonderful and hilarious dog personalities you might meet along the way—through every significant milestone in your pup's life. And when I say significant, I mean the big things, like his first day at the dog park, and what the non–Dog Obsessed think is trivial, like planning a dog picnic or pulling off a perfectly executed birthday party that your pup's friends will remember forever.

I'll show you how to pick the right vet, traditional and holistic methods to manage your dog's health, and ways to deal with emotional issues like neediness, paranoia, or overexuberance. You'll learn how to ensure that he's getting the right kind of food and enough exercise, methods to guarantee that all the four- and two-legged members of your family are getting along, and tips on teaching your pup to swim. I'll show you how to create a world of fun and play for yourself and your dog with affordable, easy-to-make toys and games, and I'll provide shopping lists for must-have herbs and supplements, as well as loads of tasty, easy-to-make recipes that'll ensure your dog's getting optimal nutrition. I'll give you tips on the best ways to socialize your dog (without letting your own social life slip too much) and a 2-week program that will help get him into tip-top physical shape. I'll fall just short of showing you how to knit a sweater out of your dog's own fur, but if you wanted to do that, I'd never dream of holding it against you.

In the 14 years since I mixed up my first batch of dog food, I've made a point of really, really listening to my Dog-Obsessed customers. What they say, the things they demand, and the way they think really resonate with me and my whole team because *we're exactly the same.* We never make anything for your dog that wouldn't be good enough for our own pups to eat.

Some of our most passionate customers' anecdotes, trials, and tribulations are featured in this book, and I hope they make you smile, laugh, and rush to give your own dog a big wet kiss. At The Honest

QUIZ: ARE YOU DOG OBSESSED?

If you fancy taking this quiz, it might help you discover if you're a part of this honorable and elite group. Just count the number of times you answer "yes" to the following statements.

1. Your favorite T-shirt reads "World's Greatest Dog Daddy."

2. You and your dog have matching T-shirts (or sweaters).

3. You consider it a compliment to be called "a crazy dog lady" (just like our Honest Kitchen customer Susan Carlson!).

4. Your dog has his own Facebook page, Twitter handle, or Instagram feed.

5. You've written your dog into your will.

6. Your dog has more than one middle name.

7. Your dog has a multitude of nicknames. Possibly too many to count.

8. When you go on vacation, your dog has his own suitcase (just like the dog of our Honest Kitchen customer Lucy Meyermann!).

9. You've thought about getting (or already have) a tattoo of your dog's name.

10. You throw a party on your dog's birthday or, at the very least, make him a special birthday meal or a cake to enjoy with his dog park friends.

11. You celebrate the day you brought him home, in addition to his birthday.

12. He's allowed on the furniture, with practically no bed or chair off-limits (much to your visiting mother's annoyance).

13. You've canceled plans (or made up an excuse to tell friends or family) because you'd actually rather spend your Saturday with your pup.

Sully

14. Your dog has a collection of several different collars and leashes, and possibly some other accessories, too.

    If you answered yes to more than five of these questions, you're probably well in the Dog-Obsessed category. Congratulations!

Kitchen, we also have a staff of ambassador veterinarians on call, and they've kindly overseen all the health and nutrition advice in this book, so rest assured that the information you'll find on these pages is 100 percent veterinarian approved.

This book is for you if you consider your dog to be one of the most important parts of your life. If you're Dog Obsessed, finding the right food, toys, and treatments for him can be a full-time job, so this book is written to take a bit of the stress out of giving your pup the good life he deserves. For you, it's not just about making sure your pet is healthy; you want to make sure he's treated like royalty and isn't unduly asked to leave the couch if one's boyfriend is, in fact, absolutely fine and comfy on the floor.

Many of the recipes for treats and meals in this book don't contain Honest Kitchen products, so you can use what you have in your pantry and fridge to mix up a delicious, nutritious meal for your dog. Plus, at the end I've included some fantastic meals both humans and dogs can enjoy, with professionally contributed wine pairing suggestions in case it's a special occasion—or just one of those days when you need to take the edge off. The recipes that contain Honest Kitchen products do so because I've carefully chosen the best components to make the most nutritious and palatable food and treats possible for your pup. The texture of Honest Kitchen foods also lends a really good consistency to the finished dish. Substituting "human food" ingredients will alter the nutrition, taste, and texture of the recipe, but by all means, if you'd like to spend some time playing in your kitchen and creating your own variations with ingredients from your pantry, be my guest.

> "I spin her fur, blended with wool, and knit my barn mittens with it!"
>
> —Kris Paige, a Dog-Obsessed Honest Kitchen customer

I wrote this book out of the love—and, okay, the out-and-out obsession—I feel for my own dogs, and every word is based on our years of research at The Honest Kitchen, the feedback we've received from customers, and our own personal experiences. You don't have to be rich or have loads of free time to get something out of this book. You just have to really, really love your pup.

Chapter 1

THE GUIDING PRINCIPLES OF THE DOG OBSESSED

THE COMMON TRAITS OF THOSE WHO ARE FLAT OUT NUTTY ABOUT PUPS

often ask myself, "What is it that makes us Dog Obsessed?" Is it the fact that we've written off a prospective suitor because of our dog's lackluster reaction to him? Or because before we bought our last car, we measured the front passenger seat to make sure that our dog's bed would fit on it? Perhaps it's the fact that we might have made our husband's best friend sit on a beanbag chair on the floor because our pup was snoozing on the couch, and it just seemed too mean to wake him. . . .

Yes, all of this reflects *extreme* devotion, and to some it might seem crazy, but we know better. But Dog Obsession speaks to something much deeper.

Consider this example: On a Christmas morning many years ago, my husband, Charlie, woke up to a strange rustling sound. No, it wasn't Santa tumbling down the chimney; it was me in the kitchen, preparing scrambled eggs. Charlie sat up eagerly and thought to himself, *Terrific! Christmas breakfast in bed. What a wonderful surprise!* Then he made himself comfortable and began to anticipate my return with his breakfast feast on a tray.

Instead, I came in empty-handed. There was Charlie, sitting in his pajamas with a puzzled look on his face that quickly turned into a look of dismay.

"What's wrong?" I said.

"Were those scrambled eggs I heard you making?"

"Yes," I replied nonchalantly.

"Might they be getting cold?" he asked.

I paused. "Oh, that was Mosi's Christmas breakfast! I didn't think to make you any. And actually, now all the eggs are gone. Would granola do?"

I'd been so eager to make Mosi's first Christmas morning perfect that I'd failed to even give a moment's thought to Charlie.

That is Dog Obsession. It's not just waking in the morning thinking about your dog; it's loving him so much that sometimes you put his needs, wants, and happiness before all else.

But I think there might be even more to it than that.

Every winter one American sporting event dominates the airwaves. Millions of people eagerly turn on their televisions during prime-time hours to watch a heated contest that pits the best of the best against one another, each battling for the right to call himself the winner. The competitors train for months, and what they go through tests their emotional and physical limits. Advertising dollars pour in, and attendees flock to a stadium to witness the event live, paying thousands of dollars for seats.

The Super Bowl, you say?

Well, I suppose you could be right, though we Dog Obsessed usually tune in to the Puppy Bowl. And if we do get dragged to a Super Bowl party, we'll likely have our pooch in tow or will end up leaving early because we can't bear the thought of him watching it at home alone.

But I digress. I was actually describing something far more exciting: Westminster. Started in 1877, the Westminster Kennel Club Dog Show is the world's most popular dog breed competition and the second-longest running sporting event in the nation, just behind the Kentucky Derby. While it's garnered some criticism from organizations like PETA for promoting pure breeds and breeding over rescue and adoption (all competitors are purebred dogs and must have papers in order to have a go at the dog show circuit), no one can argue that the dogs themselves aren't beautiful.

Gorgeously groomed, with happy dispositions and pearly white smiles from ear to ear, they're pristine examples of dogs well-loved and well-raised. The swagger with which they enter the ring and the bounce in their step let you know they've got it pretty cushy, even after the show is over.

I often watch the dog show, and one thing has always struck me: While the ancestors of these dogs were bred many years ago with a very specific purpose, chances are that today's dogs aren't fulfilling it. Yes, while the Old English Sheepdog whose name is something like Percival Butterscotch

The Dog Obsessed Aren't Surprised to Hear That . . .

Seventy-nine percent of American dog owners say the quality of their pup's food is as important as the quality of their own.

BACON BERRY PANCAKES

While scrambled eggs were always Mosi's number one breakfast choice, these scrumptious pancakes were a close second. These have the added bonus of being gluten-free, so they're great for more sensitive dogs. *Makes 8 to 10 pup-size pancakes*

1 cup Love dehydrated dog food

1½ cups warm water

2 free-range eggs, beaten

2 slices bacon, cooked and chopped

½ cup millet flour

¼ cup finely chopped fresh strawberries

Safflower oil or butter for cooking

1. In a large glass bowl, hydrate the Love with the warm water. Add the eggs, bacon, flour, and strawberries. Stir to combine.

2. In a large skillet over medium heat, heat a small quantity of oil or butter. For each pancake, pour a ladleful of the batter into the pan and cook until just golden brown on the bottom. Turn carefully using a spatula, and cook until golden brown on the second side. Transfer to a plate to cool. The pancakes can be stored in an airtight container in the refrigerator for up to 3 days.

← Mosi

Little Lord Fauntleroy probably *could* herd a flock of sheep if he wanted to, on a typical Friday evening he's more likely to be found sitting in his dog bed with a slobbery chew toy, having just enjoyed a shampoo and trim, facial, and blowout.

His owner didn't buy him to tend sheep any more than you bought your dog to find truffles in the backyard or shoo rats off a ship. He shelled out thousands of dollars for his dog and continues to do so because he's obsessed with dogs, and he knows that feeding him well, grooming him to perfection, and providing him with the ultimate pampered life will bring his dog boundless joy. More than that, the show dog owner simply loves the happiness dogs bring to his world. He understands that treating his pet well helps that dog find his true purpose, which is to shine, and then let everyone around him bask in that glow.

If you're reading this, chances are you probably feel the same.

In my years working in the pet food industry, I've found that people who are flat-out nutty about their dogs share a few common principles. Everyone who works at The Honest Kitchen certainly possesses them, too. These are elevated, even aspirational notions about what it means to be a dog owner—principles you follow because doing so makes you a good dog owner and makes your dog a happy pet. Most people no longer buy dogs because they'll work for them in some professional capacity. We add dogs to our families because they say something about how we want to live our lives, and we follow these principles to create a more beautiful, harmonious world—for animals and humans alike.

FIRST PRINCIPLE
Pets Are Family

More than 90 percent of Americans consider a pet to be a part of their family. I've spoken to many customers over the years who've confessed to preferring the company of their dogs to that of their own husbands and a few who've mentioned they might serve some Honest Kitchen food to those husbands, too. (Although I'm not sure how many of them have actually followed through.) For the Dog Obsessed, pets are included in our holiday photos and greeting cards, have their own Christmas stockings, and are told "I love you" just as often as our children are. If I'm traveling for work for any length of time, I find Facetime to be a useful way to check in with my hounds. Our Pug, Johnson, was blind, so he was perfectly fine with a quick chat on speakerphone, but the Ridgebacks seem to enjoy the visuals. In some

Dog-Obsessed homes, owners have installed cameras so they can watch their pets while they're at work. Others have also installed two-way intercoms so they can speak to them during the day, in case the dogs get lonely!

Recent scientific research has shown, however, that a dog's place in the family is even more significant than once thought. Dogs aren't just sources of love; they also serve important roles in shaping the fundamental dynamics of the family structure. Dogs may serve as peacemakers, entering a room during an argument and diffusing the situation. A crying child may be comforted by a lick from a dog, cementing the dog's role as the family healer. I vividly remember being in labor with our first daughter, doubled over to get through a contraction, when Mosi came into the room and rested his chin right on the small of my back, exactly where it hurt the most. And I can't tell you how many slightly tense Honest Kitchen board meetings have been diffused by Willow putting her head up close and personal in someone's lap or Taro helping himself to one of the investor's bagels.

On the opposite end of the spectrum, if there are cracks in a family, a dog may expose them. In the same way that a couple on the brink of divorce shouldn't try to have a baby to bring them together, they shouldn't expect a dog to cure family wounds. A troubled couple may differ on what's considered appropriate behavior for the family dog, battle over how strict or lenient one needs to be, and argue about how much to spend on him. According to Dr. David Blouin, a sociologist at Indiana University South Bend, these differing opinions aren't mere skirmishes. Rather, they reveal family ideologies that are as deeply embedded as religion or cultural heritage. Essentially, your ideas about your dog reflect your ideas about how family life, society, and the world at large function.

The Dog Obsessed understand this deep in our bones.

SECOND PRINCIPLE
The Source Matters

At The Honest Kitchen, we care about where our ingredients come from. We use 100 percent natural, non-GMO, whole food ingredients that are prepared in a human-grade facility. Later in this book we'll get a little more into what those fancy terms mean—and why they should matter to you—but the main point is that our food meets the highest standards of quality, integrity, and nutrition.

The American Pet Products Association's 2014 report shows that pet owners' pet food buying habits have changed dramatically in recent years, and we're now more focused than ever on products that are gluten-free, responsibly sourced, minimally processed, and free of artificial additives. Dog-Obsessed people also seek out single-source proteins and limited-ingredient recipes made with non-GMO, certified organic ingredients that many might think of as gourmet, such as pumpkin, green beans, papayas, quinoa, parsnips, navy beans, and duck. This means we really think about how food affects our dogs, and we understand that good food is an investment that increases our chances of having a truly healthy pet who's free of allergies, skin conditions, and illnesses.

The Dog Obsessed think about more than the sources of their dogs' foods, though. Putting proper thought into the origin of the animal himself is absolutely essential. We know that dogs born in puppy mills are much more likely to suffer from terrible behavioral and health problems, so we would never buy a dog from a pet shop or online broker. The Dog Obsessed also understand that it's vital to find a veterinarian who has an open mind about holistic and alternative cures, and we know that a good vet attempts to find the root cause of a dog's condition rather than just temporarily alleviating his symptoms.

The Dog Obsessed realize that quality matters, and we seek out the best sources of food, care, and companions in order to give our dogs the finest lives possible.

You Must Listen to Your Dog

It's been shown that dogs speak a language that's comprised of three dimensions: pitch, duration, and frequency or repetition rate of vocalizations. The Dog Obsessed know this, so we really listen to our dogs to try to understand what they're trying to tell us.

Let's say your dog is in the living room, and he hears a set of footsteps coming down the path to your house. You see his ears perk up and his head lift from its resting place on the edge of your armchair. Suddenly he leaps to his feet, and . . . charge! He runs toward the door and begins barking in a deep yet frantic manner. It's the postman, and if he doesn't watch out, your dog might turn him into kibble—or at least that's the impression he's trying to convey. In contrast, a playful bark that's urging a friend to indulge him in a game of chase (or politely requesting that you throw the ball for him just one more time) has a completely different, somehow joyful, enthusiastic tone.

If you understand a dog's language, you'll know that a deep bark indicates that he's trying to appear larger than he is; short, staccato barks indicate fear. So as the wretched, much-loathed postal worker approaches the door, you can tell by listening to your dog that while he's trying to appear aggressive, he's in fact scared.

SUPERFOOD CUPCAKES

The only things that will make your dog happier than time with you are these cupcakes, which include a variety of healthy superfoods that are bursting with vitamins, minerals, and health-promoting antioxidants. They have an irresistible turkey taste, too!

Makes 12 cupcakes

1 cup Embark dehydrated dog food

1 cup warm water

½ cup shredded chard (tough stalks removed)

½ cup canned unsweetened pumpkin (not pie mix)

¼ cup fresh blueberries

1 free-range egg, beaten

⅔ cup plain yogurt

2 slices bacon, cooked and finely chopped

1 Preheat the oven to 350°F. Place paper liners in a 12-cup muffin pan.

2 In a large glass bowl, hydrate the Embark with the warm water. Add the chard, pumpkin, blueberries, and egg. Stir gently until the mixture is thoroughly combined.

3 Divide the mixture among the paper liners. Bake for 40 minutes, or until the cupcakes are just crispy on top and a knife can slide out clean. Cool completely.

4 Spoon the yogurt into a cereal bowl or onto a plate, and carefully dip the top of each cooled cupcake into the yogurt to "frost." Decorate each cupcake by sprinkling a small quantity of the chopped bacon on top, and serve as a treat between meals. The cupcakes can be frozen or stored in an airtight container in the refrigerator for up to 3 days.

If he were intending to hold his ground, his barks would be of a longer duration, yet no shallower. But the fact that he continues woofing indicates that he's interested. If he weren't, he'd only yip occasionally.

We Dog Obsessed pay attention to our dogs and intuitively understand this language. But our listening extends beyond just being able to interpret their barks. We watch for certain patterns and are exceedingly tuned in to things like fur turning a little less shiny during the hot summer months, during the winter due to central heating, or as a result of a change in diet. We'll notice emotional cues, such as our dog shivering when he senses rain or following us everywhere during our 9th month of pregnancy. We'll also pick up on super subtle indicators that all might not be well—the Dog Obsessed might notice that her dog is getting up a little later in the mornings, or is drinking more, or has a little less sparkle in his eye. We are true advocates for our pooches and proactively manage their health at all costs. The Dog Obsessed don't write off any kind of odd behavior. Instead, we know that our dogs are trying to tell us something, and we work hard to really understand them.

FOURTH PRINCIPLE
Trusting Your Gut Means Trusting Your Dog

The Dog Obsessed know how strong the connection between humans and dogs is, and we understand that if we're trusting our guts, we're also trusting our dogs.

Recent research published in *Science* concluded that the dog–human bond is so powerful that when dogs lock their gaze onto their owners or when humans pet their dog, the owners' oxytocin levels increase. Oxytocin is the "happiness hormone" you feel a rush of when you're in love. But that's just the beginning, because the more you interact with your dog, the more *his* oxytocin levels increase. So petting your dog makes you happy, which makes him happy, which makes you *more* happy. It's really a win-win for everybody (except maybe your boyfriend, who might start to feel a tiny bit left out).

All of this means that you and your dog are coupled, kindred spirits who are working together to make each other feel pleasure, much as human partners do. What's central to a good relationship? Trust. When people really listen to those little voices inside themselves, they're trying to figure out what's in their own best interests. And if you're trusting your gut (that little voice) when it comes to your dog, you're automatically working for his better good, too.

FIFTH PRINCIPLE
One Size Doesn't Fit All

The Dog Obsessed know that every dog is different. Some dogs love cats and can, on any given day, be found curled up next to one in bed. Others are simply terrified of felines or would rather forgo dinner than agree to let a lowly, uptight, or just plain snooty cat into their homes. So why treat all dogs the same? Just like beautiful little snowflakes, every dog's experience is unique, and each one needs to be understood on an individual level.

Witness Dog-Obsessed Honest Kitchen customer Michelle Ooley. Michelle adopted a most unusual dog late in his life, but she knows that patience and understanding are key to making her life—and her dog's—happy.

> I have a 15-year-old Bichon that I could describe as high maintenance and whiny. I love him dearly, but he can sure grate on my nerves at times. I adopted him when he was 12 and quickly learned that he was never taught how to play. His concept of playing was barking at me! Right away I taught him that this was not acceptable. To this day, he still doesn't understand that when I get excited about something, it's not a cue for him to go into a barking fit. I also think he has a bit of OCD. His food dish has to be in the same spot in the kitchen or he won't eat, and believe me, this is a dog that's driven by food. Up until a year ago, he would turn and walk away from me if I told him I loved him. Just 6 months ago he started letting me hold him. He's a constant work in progress, but I wouldn't change him for the world. I've learned quite the lesson in patience when it comes to Max.

Max's experience of play is very different from that of other dogs, and Michelle has had to tailor her reactions accordingly. It's not that we let the dog be the master, but we do attempt to unlock the very unique and interesting puzzles that are our best friends' curious minds.

Chapter 2

PICKING A PUP

UNDERSTANDING YOUR NEW DOG'S
ONE-OF-A-KIND PERSONALITY

Brilliant! You've made the big decision to add a new dog to your family. You took the quiz (see "Are You Dog Obsessed?" on page xvi), decided that none of these habits or traits sound at all outlandish to you, and are ready to open the door to a wonderful being who's going to change your life forever. And change the condition of your furniture forever. And forever make you scratch your head wondering where the mates for all your socks went.

If this is your first dog, you may be feeling all kinds of anxiety. Will he house-train quickly? Will the cats approve of him? (Well, probably not at first, but you still must ask yourself the question.) Will he be spunky, silly, sullen, shy, or all of the above? This chapter is here to help! If you've owned many dogs in your life and you consider yourself an old pro, you should still find this chapter useful. After all, the new puppy you welcome into your house may be extremely different from your previous dogs, leaving you baffled by seemingly simple things, such as getting him used to a crate.

DOG PERSONALITY TYPES

In general, I've found that dogs can be classified into seven personality types. If you're thinking about getting a new pup, this information may help you decide which is best suited to your family. Just bear in mind that, even with the most careful research, sometimes you just don't get what you expect. We've had a couple of absolutely lovely "butter-wouldn't-melt-in-their-mouths" puppies join the ranks at The Honest Kitchen over the years—my own beloved Willow included—who ended up turning into borderline devil dogs once they found their feet. In Willow's case, I tried flower essences, acupuncture, and sessions with two different animal communicators to try to get to the bottom of her jealous, slightly domineering behavior. In the end, a couple of weeks back with the breeder sorted her out, and I think her own mother might have had a few words with her while she was there!

If you already own a dog, you may still be trying to sort out his complex personality. This section will help! Dogs are bundles of contradictions, and what's interesting—and for many of us, all the more endearing—is that many pups will actually span several different personality types. So the puzzle of working out who they are, what they want, and what they might possibly do next is all the more fun—and sometimes all the more astounding to innocent onlookers.

Nervous Nellies

You've probably met one of these. It could be a Labrador Retriever whose former owner didn't give him enough attention, so now he follows you to the bathroom and is absolutely horrified if you shut the door and he's not allowed to gaze at you adoringly while you do your thing. Or a 15-pound Shih Tzu–Poodle mix (often affectionately called Shit-a-Poos, much to the delight of 9-year-old boys everywhere) who lunges out of sheer fear at the 90-pound Rottie who lives next door. Regardless, a dog in this lovable yet anxiety-ridden class has a complex, a chip on his shoulder, and an irrational set of fears you worry you'll never be able to untangle.

We have our own Nervous Nellie on staff at The Honest Kitchen. Gracie is a 10-year-old rare breed Glen of Imaal Terrier who belongs to Jerry, our director of production and food safety. For some reason, in her senior years, Gracie's become afraid of wood floors, and if she accidentally runs onto the hard flooring in Jerry's kitchen, she'll freeze in place and literally walk backward to the carpeted area. Luckily, Jerry and his wife have an incredible amount of patience and empathy and loads of unconditional love to give Gracie, which makes them the perfect match for

HALLOWEEN PUMPKIN GINGER NIBBLES

Even if it's not Halloween, you can make your new dog feel at home with these delectable treats. They're grain-free (which means they're suitable for pups with gluten sensitivities), and pumpkin and ginger are both incredibly soothing to upset tummies, which could be caused by the anxiety of moving. *Makes 12 to 24 treats, depending on the size*

1 cup Love dehydrated dog food

1 cup warm water

1 cup lean ground beef

½ cup mashed, cooked pumpkin

2 tablespoons honey

¼ cup cream cheese

½ teaspoon ground ginger

1 free-range egg, beaten

1 Preheat the oven to 375°F. Lightly coat a baking sheet with olive oil.

2 In a large glass bowl, hydrate the Love with the warm water. Stir thoroughly. Mix in the ground beef. Add the pumpkin, honey, cream cheese, ginger, and egg. Stir well to combine.

3 Using your hands, scoop out small quantities of the mixture and shape it into balls. (Depending on the size of your dog, these could range in size from marbles to golf balls.) Place the balls on the prepared baking sheet and flatten them gently. Bake smaller treats for 30 minutes and larger treats for up to 45 minutes.

4 Allow the treats to cool and store them in an airtight container in the refrigerator for up to a week, or freeze them, if you'd prefer. For a crispier version, try making tiny treats and leaving them in the oven for several hours after switching it off, which will allow the treats to dry out more.

this kind of dog. Having a lot of time on your hands helps with a Nervous Nellie, too, but with enough love and encouragement, this pup can become fearless in no time. Or at least he can succeed in training his owner on how life needs to be, as was the case for Honest Kitchen customer Brooke L.:

> *Payton is a Chow, Boxer, and Shar-Pei mix. When we adopted him as a puppy 5 years ago, we quickly realized that something was wrong with him. He was very nervous. We started calling him Houdini because when we left, he would escape his cage! We had to videotape him to see how he got out. He ate my couch and mattress and even chewed my door handle and swallowed a door lock! (It did pass in a few days.) After trying all kinds of treatments to help him, we finally decided that his separation anxiety is just too bad to leave him. So everywhere I go, he goes.*

Ruff-n-Tumble

The dog park is no match for this wild and crazy hound. No time for agility training or hours outside? No problem. Your beloved high-energy pup will just run circles around the house, jump on the couch, inadvertently knock over your elderly great aunt, and make your home the eye of his own personal hurricane.

My two rambunctious Rhodesian Ridgebacks, Taro and Willow, aren't necessarily in this category all of the time, but they certainly know how to tear it up and go a bit loco when the mood takes them. For some reason, weekend morning Skype sessions with our families back in England and sunset drinks with friends on our front porch are two activities that have a knack for setting them off on boisterous wrestling sessions. One of them will start things going with a bit of flirtatious tail wagging, followed by some play bows, while the other starts to leap and spin around. The next minute they're off, whizzing round the house, boxing up on their hind legs, and generally causing a ruckus. It's a standing joke with our neighbors that I spend all my spare time straightening out our area rugs after these sessions occur.

If you're not sure how to deal with this sort of rough-and-tumble behavior, a companion animal can help absorb your dog's excess energy. Unfortunately—as is the case with my dogs—there might be even *more* household chaos if the new chap ends up being drawn into the mayhem instead of acting as a calming influence. You could also hire a trainer for a bit of expert help, try herbal remedies or flower essences to calm him, or take him for extra walks throughout the day. Or maybe you can appreciate him for who he is, just like Honest Kitchen customer Jennifer Coleman.

My girl Ruckus is also known as Run A Muckus Ruckus! Her name may imply total chaos, but her personality encompasses so much more. While she's always up for play and crazy fun, and her bark is full of joy, she is loving and sensitive and has an amazing heart for those who need affection the most. To me, the name Ruckus fully embodies reckless abandon and living life to the fullest.

The Emo

He's moody and expressive and might as well be singing confessional lyrics in a '90s indie band. If you own this kind of dog, you know he has deep feelings that come out in two ways: plaintive howls or lying sullenly with his chin between his paws. He's also perfected the art of giving you the most incredible stink-eye.

Very sensitive people who crave deep connections often do especially well with this kind of dog. Even if your personality's a bit more on the happy-go-lucky side, you may still end up with an Emo Dog. You can tailor activities to meet his needs by taking long walks on cloudy days or listening to The Smiths or Nirvana together in a dimly lit room.

Ollie, a Pit Bull mix who belongs to Christin, our corporate sustainability manager, has mastered the art of displaying his many moods. Hers since she rescued him as a pup, he has the most unbelievably cushy life at our dog-centric office every day. He sleeps in any one of our many beds; eats nutritious, gourmet meals twice a day; and gets pedicures, cupcakes on his birthday, and trips to the dog park practically whenever he pleases. He also has a rain jacket for when it sprinkles and a sweater for when the weather's cool. But somehow, it just never seems to be enough. He looks permanently disdainful, as though someone could be doing just a little bit more for him. Even when he starts his daily 11:00 a.m. rounds of the office to remind everyone it's time to go for his morning walk, his whimpers and low-angle tail wagging tell everyone that if they don't start making a move, his world just might end.

Ollie

SUMMER SEAFOOD NIBBLERS

Dogs will love these tiny bite-size fishy treats in the summer—or at any time of the year! My favorite dolphin-safe, eco-friendly tuna is made by Wild Planet, a company wholeheartedly committed to looking for ways to maximize the health and resources of our planet and, thus, to boost its food production and its ability to sustain harvesting.

Makes up to 36 tiny bite-size treats

1 cup Brave dehydrated dog food

1 cup warm water

1 can dolphin-safe tuna in water or olive oil

½ cup shredded kale (tough stalks removed)

¼ cup finely chopped fresh papaya

1 free-range egg, beaten

1   Preheat the oven to 350°F. Using a paper towel, lightly coat a baking sheet with olive oil.

2   In a large glass bowl, hydrate the Brave with the warm water. Gently stir in the tuna, including most of the oil or water. Add the kale, papaya, and egg. Stir until thoroughly combined.

3   Using your hands, gently roll the mixture into marble-size balls and place them on the baking sheet about ½" apart. Bake for 20 minutes. Turn off the oven but leave the treats inside to crisp up and dry out a little more. These treats can be frozen (use parchment paper to separate layers, if needed) or stored in an airtight container in the refrigerator for up to 4 days.

Trouble Is My Middle Name

You might have lost your favorite cashmere sweater to this rowdy, unruly, rambunctious pup. Worse than that, you may almost have lost your boyfriend, too. Little Miss Trouble is one of those hounds who just can't help being naughty.

Many dogs will go through the normal "troublesome" phase as youngsters, but if your dog has this personality type, the behavior goes well into adulthood. He might unravel your loo roll when you're out of the house, help himself to your sandwich if you glance away, devour an entire box of donuts while everyone's in a meeting (like Honest Kitchen co-woofer Felix, picured below), or spend long afternoons trying to work out how to infiltrate the fence to your chicken run.

Being Dog Obsessed doesn't mean you let your dog run all over you. (One of the Cardinal Rules of Dog Obsession, described on page 21, is that *you*—not your dog—are generally in charge.) But if you're absolutely fine with a dog whose idea of a delicious snack is your neighbor's pygmy goats' droppings, far be it from me to tell you otherwise. You're the best judge of how much you can take.

We asked our Honest Kitchen customers to tell us about the worst things the Trouble Is My Middle Name canine criminals in their lives have eaten.

"My glasses! Ground to powder . . . in fact, I thought it was sugar or salt on the floor instead of my lenses!" —Linda MacKinnon

"I had a Chihuahua who ate and passed a used tampon. This was way back in the '70s, when they were a lot bigger than today's compact items. YUCK." —Caroline E. Macpherson-Mueller

"My girl killed my beta fish 2 weeks ago. My middle son found him in the couch cushions." —Vanessa Peloquin

"Elvis Costello tickets." —Mary Louise Rifkind-Vitulano

"My bathroom wall." —Julie Granlund Meehan

Bossy Britches

While the Dog Obsessed should always remember that they make the rules, the bossy dog may not always acknowledge this. As long as he doesn't overstep his bounds, though, this type of dog is perfect for a house overrun with unruly cats (as in the story below) or a yard full of irritating chipmunks who need to be chased up a tree.

Bear in mind that the bossy dog's behavior may sometimes border on the obsessive-compulsive. Some dogs will fetch their leashes to remind their owners when it's time for a walk, or they may plant their bottoms in the middle of the kitchen floor lest you forget that mealtime's approaching. My blind, senior, rescue Pug, Johnson, was a perfect example of this. We adopted him at the age of 8 and, gosh, was he all about the routine! He knew precisely what should be happening when, and his days were totally governed by the rumblings of his tummy. If he was expecting something like a bedtime biscuit after his evening wee, it really needed to happen when he thought it should, or he'd sit and make the most incredible yodeling noises in the middle of our kitchen, wagging his tail (often facing the refrigerator because his blindness meant he sometimes lost his bearings) until he got exactly what he wanted.

If you live with Mr. Bossy Britches, just trust that he knows what he's doing, and all will be well (for him, even if not for you or the other pets!). That's what Honest Kitchen customer April Pilz has realized and accepted.

> *My dog Dingo is known in my house as the Manager. She's a Jack Russell/ Australian Cattle Dog mix who is not-so-large but definitely in charge. She "manages" my other six pets by keeping the cats off the counters (or alerting me when they're on them) and breaking up any rough play between my other dogs. When we go out for walks, she walks right behind me while the other dogs are out in front, keeping her "herd" in order. She's also been known to herd people at family gatherings!*

The Baby

A part of me hesitated to even mention this category because really, most dogs are babies in one way or another. But some dogs play the part just a bit more, content to let others lead while they sit back and act frisky, cute, or otherwise like the beloved youngest child they are. This type of dog is perfect if you have a bit more time on your hands, because he may need more love, care, and hands-on attention than the

THE CARDINAL RULES OF DOG OBSESSION

One thing to note is that these imperatives are very different from the Guiding Principles of the Dog Obsessed, which we talked about in Chapter 1. Principles are the warm, fuzzy beliefs that originate in our ever-loving hearts. They're the philosophies that guide us in a world that doesn't always believe it's appropriate for a person to consult their dog through a psychic when making important life decisions. Rules are much more straightforward; they're hard and fast and should never, ever be broken by an unruly dog or his overly permissive dog owner.

1. **YOU'RE THE BOSS.** Not your dog, no matter how much he begs, pleads, or rolls on his back and exposes his adorable belly. You make the rules, and it's up to you to enforce them.

2. **THE RULES ARE UP TO YOU.** As long as you comply with the basic state laws on dog ownership and have a proper regard for general safety, the household rules you come up with can be entirely your own. If you make a rule (like I have) that your pooch isn't allowed on your bed until 5:45 a.m.—and then he can hop up and snuggle by your feet until the alarm goes off—that's up to you. (By the way, it still amazes me how many dogs have the most incredible body clocks. Willow knows to the minute when it's 5:45 a.m. and time for her morning snuggle with me in bed, and it takes her only a few days to adjust after daylight saving time changes!)

3. **LET NO OTHER DOG OWNER JUDGE.** We're all smitten with our dogs in our own peculiar way, and as such, the Dog Obsessed must respect each other and understand that their rules really are a matter of "live and let live," to each his own.

4. **SPOILING IS TOTALLY OKAY.** In fact, it's expected. So if you're thinking of preparing a special holiday or birthday meal for your pet, there's no need to feel you're going overboard.

5. **LOVE YOUR DOG.** Above all, remember this. The love he feels for you is unconditional, so yours for him must be, as well. It's just all about choosing the ways you're going to show it.

BEEF AND BANANA MUFFINS

Baby your baby with these muffins, which are a tasty combination of savory and sweet flavors. With their beef, bananas, and yogurt, they're incredibly hearty, too.

Makes 12 muffins

1 cup Verve dehydrated dog food

1 cup warm water

6 ounces ground beef

1 free-range egg, beaten

2 bananas, peeled and sliced into coins

⅔ cup plain yogurt

1 Preheat the oven to 375°F. Place paper liners in a 12-cup muffin pan.

2 In a large glass bowl, hydrate the Verve with the warm water. Add the beef, egg, and half of the bananas. Stir until thoroughly combined.

3 Divide the mixture among the paper liners. Bake for 40 minutes, or until the muffins are just crispy on top and a knife can slide out clean. Cool completely.

4 Spoon the yogurt into a cereal bowl or onto a plate, and carefully dip the top of each cooled muffin into the yogurt to "frost." Decorate the muffins with the remaining banana slices and serve them as treats between meals. These muffins are also great for puppy parties and other special gatherings.* They can be frozen or stored in an airtight container in the refrigerator for up to 3 days.

*Note: To prevent squabbles, please use common sense when offering treats to multiple dogs at one time. You may need several people and a large area to keep the dogs spaced far enough apart that slower eaters can enjoy their treats without being rushed or intimidated by jealous onlookers.

average dog. And he's perfect for children because he'll rarely complain if (as my sister and I did with our Irish Setter, Holly, when we were probably old enough to know better) they try to put him in a dress and cart him around in a pram.

Bear in mind that The Baby may also be a bit naughty, as with Honest Kitchen customer Megan Moberly's incredibly lovable pup.

> *I would describe Ame as the youngest child, spoiled and mischievous. We have seven dogs total, and she's the baby of the pack. Picked on by her older sister, best buds with one of her older brothers, she likes to play pranks on the adults and pretend as if she didn't do anything. She definitely fits the youngest child role well.*

The People Pleaser

While every sane and sensible dog thinks his owner is wonderful, the People Pleaser is especially concerned with making you happy. As he lies in his dog bed, snuggling the socks you left on the floor, you may wonder whether he's doing that to keep them warm for you or if he just misses the delicious scent of your feet. He showers you with wet kisses when you come home from work, takes great care to hang out near you if it looks like you might be going on a trip (even if it's only a quick one, to the loo), makes you laugh if you're feeling stressed, and perhaps even brings you your slippers in the morning.

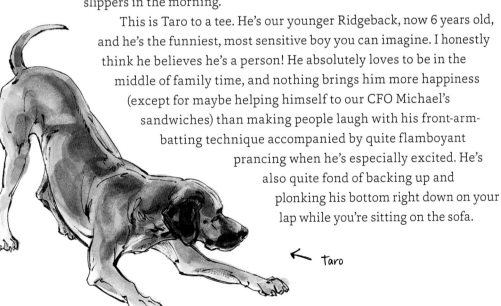

This is Taro to a tee. He's our younger Ridgeback, now 6 years old, and he's the funniest, most sensitive boy you can imagine. I honestly think he believes he's a person! He absolutely loves to be in the middle of family time, and nothing brings him more happiness (except for maybe helping himself to our CFO Michael's sandwiches) than making people laugh with his front-arm-batting technique accompanied by quite flamboyant prancing when he's especially excited. He's also quite fond of backing up and plonking his bottom right down on your lap while you're sitting on the sofa.

← Taro

HOW MUCH IS THAT DOGGIE IN THE WINDOW?

When you've decided you want to add a dog to your family, there are several places you can find one. While some people inherit dogs or decide to take one off the hands of a friend or neighbor, most of us go to one of three places: a breeder, a shelter, or a pet store.

It's time for me to get a little serious. If there's one kernel of wisdom I can impart to you in this book, it's this: Please, please don't ever even *think* about buying a puppy at a pet store. I've actually felt very strongly about this for many years, and despite a couple of threats of lawsuits from displeased pet shop proprietors, ever since the company began, I've refused to allow The Honest Kitchen's products to be sold in stores that sell puppies. The true cost of that doggie in the window—in terms of animal welfare, health concerns, and other problems—is unbelievable. Some people find it next to impossible to resist picking up that adorable puppy who's rolling around in shredded newspaper behind a wall of glass. But if you buy one of these dogs, you're doing more harm than good on many different levels.

Practically all dogs sold in pet stores come from puppy mills—hideous places that raise animals in terrible conditions without the proper socialization or health care that's so essential to the making of a good long-term pet. These irresponsible breeders mass-produce purebred dogs with no concern for genetic quality, instead focusing on profit. Puppy mill dogs are notorious for having a host of chronic conditions including epilepsy, kidney problems, and diabetes. A responsible breeder would ensure a sick dog is removed from the husbandry pool, but that's not the case with a puppy mill operator who's mass-producing dogs to be sold like any other inventory in pet stores.

Puppy mills are downright inhumane, with deplorable conditions that cause dogs to suffer and die prematurely. Can you imagine letting your precious pup live outside in the dead of winter, or forcing him to live in a wire cage with no padding for his tender paws? Puppy mills do this on a regular basis. Unlike most happy puppies from responsible breeders, these dogs aren't in the kitchen surrounded by things like children, cats, and normal daily activities and routines. This lack of socialization to people means they don't have well-developed manners, which essentially sets them up for failure as house pets.

Most puppy mill puppies are taken away from their mothers by 6 weeks of age—a time when they are still learning their way in the world and desperately need a mother's affection. Then they're shipped like freight on trucks, and many perish on the road to their temporary shop-window homes. Chances are that the store makes little to no effort to ensure that the right animal is placed with the right family, and if you end up with a problem with the puppy later in his life, neither the store nor the breeder is going to help you out.

Finally, puppy mill pets are not sufficiently socialized to normal everyday situations—like going out into the yard to pee and poop—which causes them to suffer various behavioral problems like nuisance barking or difficulties with potty training because they've had no choice but to live in contact with their own urine and feces. Frustrated owners then give up on them, sending them off to shelters, where they may be rendered unadoptable.

You might believe that you're "saving" a dog if you buy him at a pet store, but in actuality it perpetuates a huge, long-term problem. So please, end the sad cycle of abuse started by puppy mills and channel your energy into buying or rescuing a dog responsibly.

Breeder or Shelter?

Now that you've eliminated pet stores from your search list, you have to decide between a rescue dog and a dog from a breeder. No choice is wrong or right, and it's not my place to tell you what's more appropriate for you or your family. I've gone both routes; I've owned a rescue Pug and three Rhodesian Ridgebacks from a responsible breeder that I've been close friends with for more than 15 years, and I've loved all of my dogs equally.

As you weigh the pros and cons of each option, bearing in mind the following things and consulting a few handy resources may make your choice a little easier.

HYPOALLERGENIC DOGS

Imagine you've always dreamed of getting a dog, but then you discover that your new boyfriend explodes into a coughing and sneezing fit every time he's near one. You want to keep the boyfriend, but Dog Obsession may lead you to kick him to the curb. Wait! Don't chuck the man just yet. There's a solution.

- **AFGHAN HOUND:** You may be surprised that a dog with this much hair doesn't shed, but it's true.

- **AMERICAN HAIRLESS TERRIER:** The name says it all. No hair, no allergies.

- **BEDLINGTON TERRIER:** If you saw one in a field, you might mistake it for a sheep. Instead, it's a lovely, fluffy dog who won't make you sneeze.

- **BICHON FRISE:** The AKC describes this as a "powder puff of a dog," and I can't think of a more apt description.

- **CHINESE CRESTED:** Another hairless breed, but technically not hairless. He has a Donald Trump–esque wisp of hair on his head, a hair-tipped tail, and hairy boots for feet.

- **COTON DE TULEAR:** This beautiful dog's fur resembles a cotton ball. And he's about the size of one, too.

- **GIANT, MINIATURE, AND STANDARD SCHNAUZER:** While these are three distinct breeds, all are perfect for allergy sufferers.

- **IRISH WATER SPANIEL:** A relatively rare breed whose rich brown coat has an almost purple hue.

- **KERRY BLUE TERRIER:** Don't let the name deceive you—he's actually gray.

- **LAGOTTO ROMAGNOLO:** Hailing from Italy, he has a coat with the consistency of wool. He's also been known to enjoy drinking limoncello on warm afternoons.

- **MALTESE:** His long, silky, white hair may remind you of Gandalf in *The Lord of the Rings*, but his magical powers extend only to his ability to not make you sneeze.

- **PERUVIAN INCA ORCHID (HAIRLESS):** No hair, no explanation needed.

- **POODLE:** Poodles are often bred with other types of dogs, so while these hybrid breeds aren't 100 percent hypoallergenic, they are good choices for many people with mild allergies.

- **PORTUGUESE WATER DOG:** Made famous by Bo and Sunny Obama. Since their arrival, the White House has been dog hair–free.

- **SOFT COATED WHEATEN TERRIER:** These dogs are wonderful for allergy sufferers, but sadly, I do know one who's allergic to humans.

- **SPANISH WATER DOG:** A close cousin of the Portuguese Water Dog and Irish Water Spaniel.

- **XOLOITZCUINTLI:** Hard to pronounce but easy to love, especially if you have allergies.

BREEDERS

If you have a specific breed of dog in mind, look up the breed club in your state or local area; they will probably have a registry of approved breeders that you can connect with via e-mail or phone. There may be a waiting list for dogs that are particularly popular, so be sure to ask the breeder about this. Most will also have Web sites where you can "meet" your prospective puppy; ask lots of questions about the breed and the breeder's philosophies on nutrition, vaccination, and so on; and see the setting in which the puppy you have your eye on has spent his formative first few weeks. Most breeders will also welcome the opportunity to share their knowledge and passion.

Responsible breeders ensure that you're getting a pet who's fit and genetically sound. They invest in robust genetic testing to make sure their breeding stock has healthy hips, eyes, and hearts and doesn't suffer from any other problems that their breed may be genetically prone to. Unfortunately, they can't promise that your dog won't steal the sheets or lie in the middle of the hallway, but good genes are a start.

Breeders want to help you throughout your dog's life. For example, some breeders will specify what sort of food you should feed your pup, give guidance on vaccine protocols, and even refer you to a vet they love. If for some horrible reason it doesn't work out—say, you lose your job and have to relocate to a place your dog can't come to—a responsible breeder will take back your dog and help find him a new home. My own dogs' breeder had cause to do this a few years ago; she had sold a Rhodesian Ridgeback puppy to a local gentleman who sadly passed away 13 years later, remarkably outlived by his dog. Although the owner had specified quite clearly in his will that his sister was to take in the dog, she declined, and the dog ended up being dropped off at the shelter. Fortunately, the shelter contacted Ridgeback Rescue, which put out the word among its member breeders, and the dog was recognized right away. The breeder who'd lovingly reared him in her kitchen many years before drove 60 miles the same day to pick him up, and she brought him home before he even had to spend one night at the shelter. She was even able to find him a new loving home until the end of his days.

Bebe

BACKYARD BREEDERS

These unregistered breeders are typically small-scale operations, hence the name "backyard." They may post classified ads in the newspaper, or they might be your next-door neighbor who decides to breed his Golden Retriever every year just to make a few bucks.

Backyard breeders typically don't adhere to standards for the breed, may inbreed, don't perform genetic screenings, and often don't provide adequate veterinary care for their pets. Because they're unlicensed, there's no way to ensure that you'll be bringing home an animal who's free of illnesses and genetic conditions, nor will you be able to return a dog if there's a life event that means you aren't able to keep him.

The ASPCA and animal welfare organizations across the country are, under all circumstances, opposed to backyard breeders. If you do decide on a purebred dog, be sure to check that the breeder is licensed and registered with the American Kennel Club and meets the criteria described above.

SHELTERS

According to the ASPCA, approximately 3.9 million dogs enter shelters in the United States every year. Of these, 1.2 million are euthanized, which is more than the entire population of Montana. If you adopt a dog from a shelter, you're not just providing a wonderful home to an animal in need; you may also be saving his life.

But how can you find the right dog for your family, when there are so many shelters—and so many dogs in them? Petfinder.com is an absolutely terrific resource. You can search based on your area code, the type of dog you're looking for, their age, their sex, and more. Most shelters include photos of their dogs, so you can fall in love with them before you even have a chance to meet them.

If you're only interested in a purebred dog, you can also contact your local pure-breed rescue. A responsible breeder will almost certainly be able to put you in touch with one, and he might even have an older dog that he's working to re-home. Don't discount shelters, however, as many former purebred puppy mill dogs are in them, waiting for loving homes.

As a service to you and your dog, many shelters will vaccinate, deworm, and microchip your dog before you take him home. Because no-kill shelters don't want to spread sicknesses from dog to dog, they'll work with local vets to address any preexisting illnesses, as well as to rehabilitate injuries. Finally, if you adopt from a shelter and are asked to pay an adoption fee, your purchase is considered a donation, so it's tax deductible. Thank you, Uncle Sam!

READYING YOUR HOUSE . . . AND YOUR LIFE

Bringing a new dog into your home isn't just about making sure you have the right kind of dog food in the pantry. It's also about mentally preparing yourself and the other members of your family—human and animal alike—for a full-on emotional and physical invasion.

Yes, a new dog is a wonderful thing, but the change in routine, the inevitable jealousy from your other pets, and the damage that may soon be done to your soft furnishings, shoes, wallet, and various other possessions can be quite shocking to some people. How can you prepare? Use these handy lists, which I've tailored to several kinds of Dog Obsessed individuals, to make sure you have everything you need.

Must-Have Products for Welcoming a New Puppy into Your Home

- ☐ Bowls, one each for food and water
- ☐ Crate (optional)
- ☐ Healthy, wholesome dog food
- ☐ Dog bed* (well padded, with enough room for him to curl up)
- ☐ Collar
- ☐ Leash
- ☐ Harness (I like the Sense-ation harness, which has a front attachment for the leash and discourages pulling)

---

* Some dogs like a nice, flat bed that's not too squishy and lets them sprawl out. Others like one that's deep and cushiony, with bumpers on the sides for curling up against. I love a company named Molly Mutt, which makes lovely "duvet cover"–style dog beds that you can stuff with your own old clothes or bedding if you're feeling especially eco-friendly.

- [ ] Dog grooming products:
    - [ ] *Shampoo (our Honest Kitchen Sparkle shampoo bars are an eco-friendly, no-spill option that's surprisingly easy to use)*
    - [ ] *Conditioner*
    - [ ] *Brushes and combs*
    - [ ] *Nail clipper (choose one that has a stopper or guard to reduce the risk of accidentally clipping your dog's nails too short)*
- [ ] Chew toys and treats, such as Beams pure fish skin chews
- [ ] Soft/plush and interactive toys, such as those made by Planet Dog and Kong

EXTRA! For the Outdoorsy Dog

- [ ] Long leash, so that your dog can run ahead on strenuous hikes
- [ ] Harness, such as the Sense-ation, which makes steering and general control much more manageable in the face of on-trail distractions
- [ ] Leash with a built-in carabiner for tethering to trees during breaks (optional, but handy).
- [ ] Water bottle (of course, you can opt to share a water bottle with your dog, but it's worth bringing him his own dedicated drinking bowl if he's an avid deer-poo connoisseur and you're not)
- [ ] Bandana, because a dog really needs to look the part on-trail
- [ ] Small backpack (optional, as you, rather than your dog, may prefer to carry the dog treats; I especially like the ones from Ruffwear)
- [ ] Booties, for the truly outward-bound hound (Ruffwear makes these for general terrain as well as snowy conditions)

EXTRA! For the Dog Who Lives in a Cold Climate

- [ ] Warm sweater, preferably wool
- [ ] Rain or snow jacket
- [ ] Blankets (optional: Knit a blanket yourself, so it's infused with your love)
- [ ] Rubber boots (many dogs find that their pads become irritated by salt and icy conditions)

DOGS VS. FLOORS

If your house has hardwood floors, bringing home a new dog can be a bit traumatic, at least until the first few scratches have found their place and your standards begin to lower. While your puppy never means harm, his excitement over your coming home may cause him to slide across a shiny wood floor like Tom Cruise in *Risky Business,* leaving scratch marks everywhere. How can you cope? Bear these things in mind.

- The love you feel for your dog is meant to be eternal. Hardwood floors aren't.

- If you call your floors "antique," "vintage," or "shabby chic," perhaps no one will notice.

- Area rugs can help to protect some areas, cover scratches you can't live with, or at least slow your dog's speed as he whizzes through.

- Consider this a chance to pamper your pet. Give him weekly pedicures, or indulge in fashionable booties.

- Think of these scratches as badges of honor, something only the Dog Obsessed can be proud of. They are, after all, a sign that you're fortunate enough to share your house with a dog.

At my house, we have some excellent scratches on the reclaimed timber wooden floor at the top of the steps from our den to the kitchen. This is the midway point of the Ridgebacks' racetrack through our house!

EXTRA! For the Dog Who Loves to Travel

- ☐ Travel harness and dog seat belt for car trips
- ☐ Travel bowls for food and water (the flexible canvas kind like those made by Kurgo take up minimal room in the car)
- ☐ Extra bed and/or blankets for the car
- ☐ Pet carrier
- ☐ Tiny luggage (optional; Although dogs typically refuse to carry their own suitcases, most Dog-Obsessed owners are fine doing double-duty and acting as their dog's porter)

Chapter 3

IT'S A DOG'S WORLD

THE HAPPY HOME LIFE OF THE DOG OBSESSED

Bringing your new dog home is a terrifically exciting time. There's so much preparation and anticipation in the weeks leading up to this momentous occasion that it's sometimes hard to believe it when Dog Day finally comes!

You may be so overwhelmed that you don't know which way is up, so it's best not to head into this wonderful new adventure alone. Before I adopted my first beloved Ridgeback, Mosi, his wonderful breeder suggested I take a friend with me on the mountainous drive to collect him, and I'm so glad I did. As my friend Ellie steered the car back toward home and I soaked up the euphoria of our first proper cuddle, it was my own heartbeat he heard, and my lap—mine alone—that he snuggled on and then, unfortunately, got carsick on. As I wiped his vomit off my sweater and jeans, I knew that our first moments of true bonding had begun!

Having a designated driver for Dog Day is also much safer; it's practically impossible to concentrate on the road when you've got a brand-new pooch to gaze at in the car. If you have to make the drive alone, though, take a crate to prevent him from getting stuck under your seat, or worse, your pedals. A blanket and some old T-shirts that smell of you will also help him get comfortable en route to your house.

Once you're finally home, it's time to begin getting settled in. The first order of the day is to take your new dog outside to potty. Lavish him with an inordinate amount of praise—and maybe a treat—when he does the deed. You can also begin to put a name to the act as a very first step in teaching him to go on command. (More on this later in the "How to House Train" section on page 35.)

After that, it's time to start setting boundaries. Your new canine roommate has no idea how you run your house—and unless he's a well-socialized senior, he probably won't know that dining room table legs have nothing in common with his favorite treats—so the key is to work out the rules you'd like him to live by, and then be absolutely consistent in enforcing them so he has the best possible chance of success.

Settling in can take time and lots of work, but through it all, remember to have fun. There's no reason to feel stress or pressure to make things "perfect." Having a happy, well-settled pup is not about how much money you spend or how beautifully appointed your home is; it's really about the love you give him. Obviously a lovely plush dog bed is far preferable to a pile of dirt in the backyard, but we also know that sometimes, a dog just likes to lie in dirt (or, unfortunately, in horse poop or dead things). So sometimes it's all right to let your dog have his moment in the dirt pile. Allow him to run, play, and be the silly, messy creature he loves to be, and then give him lots of love and kisses when he comes back inside. After all, affection and attention are the things that will make him feel most at home. (And there are so many lovely pet shampoos and conditioners to choose from nowadays.)

HOW TO HOUSE TRAIN

If you've brought home an adult dog or a puppy who's already house trained, there's a good chance you'll be able to skip this section, you lucky thing. But if you have an untrained puppy, just know that this too shall pass, and your dog will soon be using your shrubs as his own personal urinal.

In general, a puppy is ready to learn to pee outdoors when he's between 12 and 16 weeks of age. House training him doesn't have to be complicated, and while there are many ways to go about it, the experts agree on a few strategies. And, no, none of them involve constructing a small fire hydrant in your living room or rewarding your dog with cupcakes each time he doesn't have an accident. Save those for his birthday party!

- **Stick to a routine.** At a minimum, take your dog out first thing in the morning, after eating and playing, at midday, and before bedtime. A puppy can hold his bladder for an hour for every month of age, so unless you enjoy stepping on wet carpet, don't let a 4-month-old puppy wait 6 hours to pee. Be consistent with mealtimes, too.

- **Have a key phrase for potty-time.** Much as you say "sit" when he should sit, say something like "potty" when he should go to the bathroom. Dogs respond well to commands, and it won't be too long before he begins to associate the word with the act. I use "tiddle tiddle" as the potty command for all my dogs, and it seems to work well, although I do still have to remind pet sitters to say it in a singsong voice with a British accent for best results.

- **Reward him.** If your dog successfully goes to the bathroom in the appropriate spot—and it's best to pick one designated spot outside, at least to begin with—give him tons of praise and a small treat to show him how happy you are.

- **Ban drinking before bedtime.** Putting away the water bowl 2½ hours before bedtime will help eliminate nighttime accidents.

- **Privacy, please!** Even puppies need their own personal space. When you leave the house or go to bed, keep your dog in a crate or in a gated-off space with his bed. Just as you probably don't like to nap on the bathroom floor, your dog will try to resist going to the bathroom in his sleeping spot.

- **Never get angry.** Puppies aren't mature enough to understand anger and will just become frightened, so don't be upset if your dog has an accident. Instead, try clapping once or twice to signal that he's done something wrong.

- **Above all, be patient.** The Dog Obsessed understand that dogs want to make you happy, so with consistency, love, and understanding, your dog will be house trained before you can say "potty-time!"

The Pros and Cons of Crating

Crates aren't for every dog—or for every owner. Some pets feel too confined and will whine to get out, and some Dog Obsessed people will balk at the idea of having their dog sleep anywhere but on a temperature-regulating silk dog bed lined with lamb's wool and stuffed with the hypoallergenic fibers from seed pods of sustainably harvested kapok trees. The decision is up to you, but bear in mind that crates can be an excellent way to house train, give your dog a sense of safety (many dogs view the crate as their "den"), safely transport your dog, or just keep him out of trouble. If you still need convincing, perhaps these easy fixes will make the idea of a crate more palatable.

- A wooden or steel crate can double as a side table.

- A crate with your dog's name on it may make him (or rather, you) feel more at home.

- It's quite nice to stitch curtains for your dog's crate to give him a sense of security, and it's also a great way to help your crate blend in better with your décor.

- A few companies now make really lovely crates that double as pieces of furniture. More on this in the section on apartment living (see "Pets and the City" on page 49).

Just remember that the crate should be a positive place, so don't use it for punishment. And never leave your dog crated for more than 4 hours.

VALENTINE'S SUPPER TREATS

When you have a new dog, every day feels like Valentine's Day! These savory treats are unbelievably simple to prepare and are a really special way to show your pup just how much he means to you. Makes 12 large or 24 small treats

2 cups Love dehydrated dog food

1 cup warm water

½ cup grated Parmesan cheese

½ cup fresh ground beef (preferably grass-fed)

¼ cup grated carrot

2 free-range eggs

1 Preheat the oven to 350°F. Lightly coat a large baking sheet with olive oil.

2 In a large glass mixing bowl, hydrate the Love with the warm water and stir thoroughly. Add the cheese, beef, carrot, and eggs, and stir to form a thick batter.

3 Carefully mold the batter into patties and flatten them gently. Place the patties on the prepared baking sheet. Bake for 30 minutes, or until slightly crispy on the outside.

4 Cool completely before serving. The patties can be stored in an airtight container in the refrigerator for up to a week.

YOUR FIRST VETERINARIAN VISIT

Just as you might find a trip to the dentist to be terrifying, your dog might find his first veterinarian appointment a bit panic inducing. Whether you're visiting a new (to you) vet or someone you've been seeing for years, every dog comes with a different set of issues to tackle, and every doctor is different.

We've asked our fabulous veterinary consultant, Dr. Patrick Mahaney, to answer a few common questions that should apply no matter what your dog is like or which vet you visit.

Q: I just brought home a new puppy. What should I expect on my first trip to the vet?

A: First and foremost, it's crucial that you schedule an examination with a veterinarian within the first 24 hours that your pup's at home. Whether or not the vet's office asks you to, bring a fresh sample of your puppy's feces for parasite testing. If he has worms, you want to nip the problem in the bud as quickly as possible! Depending on your puppy's previous medical history (since many breeders take care of initial testing), there may be a need for deworming, vaccinations, antibody titer testing (blood tests to assess the body's response to previous vaccinations), or other procedures.

Make sure that your vet discusses the following topics with you: parasite prevention, nutrition, training, exercise, lifestyle issues (housebreaking, settling in at home, etc.), and licensing. Finally, you should schedule a follow-up evaluation before you leave the vet's office so that you can maintain a schedule for wellness appointments.

Q: Which vaccinations are necessary for my new dog?

A: Good question! First, here's a little background about what vaccinations entail. Vaccines stimulate the production of antibodies (blood proteins), which help the immune system fight viruses, bacteria, or other pathogens upon exposure. When your immune system can combat these, you reduce your chance of contracting certain illnesses. There are multiple vaccinations that puppies and adult dogs may receive throughout their lifetimes, but it's most crucial that "core" vaccines are given to help prevent infection by potentially life-threatening or zoonotic diseases. The life-threatening diseases that are part of a core vaccination protocol for a puppy include distemper, parvo, and rabies. Rabies is also a zoonotic disease, which means it can pass among species (dog to person, raccoon to dog, etc.).

Starting at 6 to 8 weeks of age, puppies receive a series of multivalent (combination) vaccinations that include canine distemper virus (CDV), canine parvovirus (CPV), infectious canine hepatitis virus (ICH or adenovirus), and canine parainfluenza virus (CPIV). This combination is known as a DAPP vaccination and is administered every 3 to 4 weeks until three DAPP vaccines have been given. In my practice, I perform antibody titers (tests to determine antibody levels) for CDV, CPV, and ICH after completing the puppy's DAPP vaccination series to ensure that his immune system has responded sufficiently. This bolsters my confidence that my patient is appropriately vaccinated and will be able to fight off an infection.

Q: I just brought home an older dog. What will my first vet visit be like?

A: When you bring home an adult or senior dog, the first trip to the veterinarian involves a more extensive evaluation than what's needed for a puppy. There are many health issues that may crop up during the adult and senior years, including periodontal disease, kidney and liver malfunctions, hypothyroidism, osteoarthritis, obesity, allergic skin disease, cancer, and more. A thorough assessment of an adult or senior dog's health includes pairing the veterinarian's physical exam findings with a baseline evaluation of internal organ function, including blood and urine testing and a fecal evaluation to check for parasites. Additionally, if a dog is in pain during a physical evaluation or if there are obvious mobility challenges, I take radiographs (x-rays) of the affected limbs or other body parts (vertebral column, pelvis, etc.). If I become concerned about the health of the organs in the dog's chest or abdominal cavities, I'll order radiographs, an ultrasound, or other diagnostics.

TEETHING (or, What Are Those Tiny Knives in My Puppy's Mouth?)

Who knew teeth so small could wreak such havoc in your life? You thought you brought home an adorable 10-pound ball of fluff, but judging from the holes in all your clothes, you might as well have purchased a starving piranha. Getting these tiny, needlelike teeth *really* hurts, so your dog will want to chew on everything in sight—including you and your family members.

While nibbling is a natural response to the discomfort he's feeling, it's important to be consistent about *not* allowing your pup to teethe or gnaw on your hands or clothes, because this can become quite painful as he grows and gets stronger. Houseguests, children, and members of the general public almost certainly won't appreciate being used as a chew toy, and it can be terribly difficult to change the rules later. Better to start off by not allowing him to chew on you at all, rather than trying to "untrain" him later on.

Puppies usually have a full set of baby teeth (also called milk teeth) by 6 to 8 weeks, and that's when the problems tend to start. By 8 weeks, permanent teeth begin to come in, and by 7 months, he'll have a full set of 42 teeth. Sorry to break it to you, but that's 7 months of teething. Seven months of a nibbling dog whose teeth function like tiny razor blades. Don't think you can take it? Here are some tips to help you *and* him.

- **Pup in pain?** Hyland's Teething Tablets—a homeopathic remedy for children—are an excellent option. Because they're designed for nighttime relief, they'll also help calm your uncomfortable, irritable dog. They can be given several times throughout the day, and they dissolve on the tongue almost instantly, so they're extremely difficult to spit out.

- **Support healthy teeth.** The homeopathic remedy calcium phosphate may help. This is a mineral salt that supports the healthy growth of bones and teeth and also provides pain relief.

- **Try good ol' chamomile.** Many people take chamomile tea when they are sick or just need to unwind, but it can also help a restless puppy (see Chapter 6 for a couple of additional uses). Simply steep a chamomile tea bag in boiling water, cool the tea in the fridge or freezer, and mix it with a little broth to make a soothing drink. You can also use some brewed chamomile tea to hydrate Honest Kitchen food. Better still, stuff the chamomile-infused food into a Kong toy and pop it in the freezer. Serving his meals this way will help to keep your pup occupied for longer, cool and soothe his gums, and satisfy his innate need to gnaw.

FANTASTIC FIRST-TIME TOYS

What dog doesn't like a new toy? These creative toys will make every dog—puppy and old-timer alike—feel comfortable in a new home.

1. **STUFFED KONGS, RAW MEATY BONES, AND "INTERACTIVE" PUZZLE TOYS FILLED WITH TREATS.** These can be useful management tools for a nervous dog. Not sure what kind of "stuffing" to use? Dehydrated food works really well. Or if you use a conventional pelleted pet food, block the ends with cream cheese or peanut butter.

2. **OLD TENNIS BALLS.** Not at all creative, but no dog can resist! Never mind that your tennis balls will be permanently coated in a thick layer of slobber. It's a happy reminder of how much your dog loves them.

3. **BALL AND ROPE TOYS.** These toys will never roll away—the rope attached to the ball prevents that. But what puppies really love is that when the ball does roll slightly, a new side is exposed. More space to chew!

4. **VIDEO CAMERAS.** Is your dog a budding photographer? There's a mount you can put on his collar that will allow him to film his day-to-day activities. This *should not* by any means be used as a chew toy and he should never be unsupervised with a camera, but it will provide fodder for your social media feed.

FEEDING YOUR NEW PUPPY

The nutritional needs of puppies are a bit different than those of older dogs. So while you may be tempted to start feeding your puppy the high-quality adult dog food you already have stocked in your pantry or to cook him a special meal to make him feel at home, don't rush into anything. Keep him on the same diet the breeder or shelter gave him for at least a few weeks. Moving into a new home is already a stressful experience, and switching to a new food right away will only add to the stress.

When you're ready to give your puppy the food of your choosing, bear in mind that because they're growing, puppies generally do need more calories than older dogs, and those calories should mostly come from protein and fat.

Just like their human counterparts, dogs need vitamins, minerals, and an array of amino acids in their diets, so be sure you're giving your pup the highest-quality nutrition you can find (or cook!). The canine diet should contain between 1:1 and

2:1 parts calcium to phosphorus, and while puppies generally require more calcium and phosphorus than adult dogs, be careful not to go overboard with calcium for large and giant breed pups because they have an increased propensity to develop bone and joint problems. Puppies also have slightly different daily requirements for nutrients such as copper and vitamins A and D, as well as several amino acids, so be wary of feeding them adult dog food.

Never overfeed a puppy, particularly one who's a large breed. You should be able to see a puppy's slender waist. Being overweight can put an unnecessary strain on the delicate developing skeleton, which can lead to bone and joint problems later in life, so keeping a lean figure starting early on is vital.

Think your puppy is eating too much? Fret not. Most puppies need to eat more for their body weight than older dogs do. Puppies younger than 8 weeks eat four times a day, and from around 8 weeks until about 6 months of age, a pup will eat three times a day. From then on two daily meals will do.

Finally, the time it takes to move from puppy food to adult food depends on the type of dog you have. Large-breed dogs can transition more quickly, often at 4 to 5 months old. Smaller-breed dogs can continue eating puppy food for up to 2 years!

Above all, remember to feed your dog high-quality, nutrient-dense food, ideally made with real, whole food ingredients whose names you can recognize and pronounce. It's not necessary to load him up with supplemental vitamins unless your veterinarian recommends it, and it's certainly not mandatory to calculate every calorie or milligram of each nutrient in his food. You can achieve nutritional balance over the course of a few meals rather than in each individual bite.

> "I made meatloaf cupcakes with mashed potato frosting for her birthday pool party with all her dog friends. She gets sleepy-time cookies every night before bed."
>
> —Honest Kitchen customer Lynne Larson, who has her older dog on an appropriate diet—for special occasions and every day

Transitioning Your Puppy to a New Food

After he's spent 2 or 3 weeks getting settled into his new home, you may decide it's time to move your puppy over to a new food. Don't do it suddenly! Instead, changes in diet should be made gradually, over a period of 4 to 7 days, depending on your dog's sensitivity.

You can start by adding just a small amount of the new food to your dog's current meals for a couple of days. Gradually increase the amount of the new food while decreasing the amount of your dog's original diet so that you're at a 50/50 mix for a few days, and then phase out the old food completely. This will allow the natural "friendly" gut flora in your dog's intestines to get accustomed to the new diet and become more efficient at digesting the new food.

For pups that have very sensitive gastrointestinal (GI) tracts, it may be a good idea to try adding in some of our herbal digestion aid, Perfect Form, during the transition. You might also consider our Pro Bloom instant goat's milk, which contains five billion active culture digestive enzymes and probiotics.

YOU'RE HOME TOGETHER. NOW HOW DO YOU *LIVE* TOGETHER?

We Dog Obsessed are really only happy when our dogs are happy, and we'll go to the end of the world to ensure their comfort and security. But others may see things differently. Your husband may become upset when you plan your puppy's first birthday party after forgetting his, or your elderly mother may be appalled when she's relegated to a cushion on the floor while your puppy makes himself comfortable on the couch.

I remember the early years of The Honest Kitchen, when my days were absolutely consumed with getting the company up and running. While I was working hard to prepare documentation for the Department of Agriculture in support of our use of the term *human grade* on our product labels, I became vaguely aware of my eldest daughter, Thalia, who was a toddler at the time, saying "Mummy? Mummy?" to me as I finished typing the paragraph I'd been working on. Before I could look up, she got down on all fours and began with "Ruff? Ruff?" to see if that might garner attention. It was a tiny bit shocking, but it did do the trick because she succeeded in getting my full focus. Unfortunately, it also started me wondering whether I'd have taken as long to see to Mosi's or Willow's needs. . . .

Just how can you prevent someone from feeling slighted by your new dog? There are many inappropriate and ultimately self-defeating ways to tackle the problem—such as by simply not allowing other humans who might be offended inside your house. But from talking to other Dog Obsessed individuals, I know that there are three primary strategies for making others (besides the dog) feel at home in your home.

1. Communication

Make it abundantly clear right at the outset that everyone in your home is equal. It's true that they might not always *feel* equal, especially when you offer the dog a snack before you offer one to your children (but that's only because your dog has a bit more trouble controlling himself when he's hungry). Be straightforward about the fact that you have plenty of love to give everyone, and then act on that intention. It's also helpful to let others know that the dog is a member of the family and will be treated as such; if you do that, no one will be shocked when you hire a massage therapist to tend to your dog because he's been a tad bit anxious lately.

> *"I have five grandsons whom I love dearly, but I have more pictures of my dog and two cats than I have of them."* —Honest Kitchen customer Jackie Brewington, who avoids any jealousy by being abundantly clear that she loves her grandkids very much, even though she admits she's currently framing pictures of her pets to hang in her living room

2. Boundaries

If you have enough room in your home, it's helpful if everyone can select their own designated areas. The dog has his chosen spot on the couch, and no one else should sit there. No one should be offended by that if they have space of their own choosing, and if they are, simply refer to point number 1 above. There is plenty of love to go around, and ideally, plenty of room in the house. And if you have a small apartment, there's a section on page 49 just for you!

> *"How am I obsessed with my dog? It could be the car seat, stroller, playpen, and several front carriers designed for infants. It could be her extravagant birthday parties, or it could be as simple as her day-to-day feeding routine (this pup eats way better than I do). But I tend to think it's her closet, which holds more clothing than anyone else's in my home!"* —Honest Kitchen customer Monroe Diamond, who allows each person in her home to have their own space for their clothing, thereby avoiding unnecessary jealousy

3. Patience

Welcoming a new member into your home is never easy, and you must always bear in mind that it takes time for everyone to get along and fall into a new routine. Your teenage son may balk at the idea that he has to walk your dog at night, but try to refrain from losing your temper. He'll fall in love with the dog in no time at all and will begin to look forward to taking him out. Likewise, you should ask others to be patient with you. Making dessert for your dog from scratch does take time, after all, and no one should be offended if it delays dinner.

> *"My father used to tell me that, when he died, he wanted to come back as one of my pets because I take such good care of them."* —Honest Kitchen customer Jan Rose, whose family was patient and soon realized the virtues of her Dog Obsession. Your family may eventually do the same!

BEDS AND SOFAS. WHO'S THE BOSS HERE?

The Dog Obsessed love sharing their beds and their sofas with their dogs. Many report that it's been years since they've had a proper snog with their partner in bed that didn't involve the dog attempting to get a snuggle in, and a few have even bought a bigger bed to accommodate everyone. Is there anything wrong with this? Not if it doesn't bother you!

Some people do worry—and with good reason—that if they let their dog on the bed or sofa once, it will become a habit. Most trainers agree that it's easier to cement good habits rather than break bad ones, so if you don't want your dog to treat your furniture as his own, it's best never to let him on it. Buy a dog bed or a crate (or four) that he'll learn to love, and if he does jump on the bed, use positive reinforcement (like treats or praise) to lure him off of it. Teach him to associate the dog bed with happiness and love, which you can do if you refrain from punishing him or shaming him for climbing on the couch.

While sleeping with your pup can be wonderful, there are a couple of minor downsides, so before you welcome your dog up on the bed or sofa, just remember that any number of irritating—and sometimes, slightly shocking—things may occur.

Dogs are pack animals, and co-sleeping is hardwired into their psyches, so sometimes you might find them sleeping just a wee bit too close for comfort. If you've ever been lucky enough to visit a litter of puppies, you'll have noticed that as soon as naptime rolls around, they wriggle their way into the most adorable puppy pile, literally on top of one another, with somebody's tail over someone else's nose in a mountain of snoring, snoozing cuteness. Grown dogs, too, think it's normal, and preferable, for everyone to sleep in a big pile in close proximity to the rest of the pack, so that's why they're bed hogs. They may start off curled in a neat ball at your feet, but as the night goes on, they start to spread out and can be practically impossible to move. My Rhodesian Ridgebacks could win a gold medal in stretching out, and they have great big, strong limbs that can jettison even the most determined bedmate. If you have a big bed without too many other pups (or people) in it, it can sometimes be easier to get out and go around to the other side to find some space. If you can't do this, be prepared for leg cramps, back complaints, and other aches and pains that result from sleeping in unnaturally contorted positions, as well as cold limbs that may end up being unwillingly squeezed out from under the duvet as your dog takes over every inch of space in the center of the bed.

Sometimes worse than being pushed out of bed by your pup, though, is the predicament of waking up in close proximity to a part of your dog's body that's best left undiscussed in proper company. Many of us Dog Obsessed have had the misfortune of waking up with bottoms in our faces, and I'm not referring to the human kind.

On par with this (or perhaps worse) is the fact that co-sleeping with your pup may result in mysterious damp patches on your sheets. My dog Taro loves to nibble very delicately with his front teeth on the sheets of our bed. (Someone once told me this is a sign of contentment, but I'm not sure if that's true.) This can cause small

areas of dampness that those who aren't Dog Obsessed could find unsettling. I promised Willow a few years ago that I'd no longer speak publicly of the urinary incontinence she suffered as a pup, so I won't include anything about that here, but that sort of thing does happen and can become more frequent in senior dogs, too.

Some dogs are also impossible snorers. My Pug, Johnson, was in this category and had a snore that would just about shake the walls, so for that reason he had a choice of dog beds elsewhere in the house, but not in our bedroom. Even those dogs who don't snore too often can whimper, whine, quiver, and run in their sleep, and many of these slumber-based activities can be sleep-disturbing for human bedmates.

If you like a lie-in (and even if you don't), remember that dogs naturally tend to become quite playful in the mornings. Allowing multiple dogs to be bedmates can lead to your bed being used as a trampoline-slash-play-structure for morning (and sometimes evening) wrestling sessions or an obstacle in games of chase; at the least, you can expect an almost certainly ruffed-up duvet.

When you co-sleep with your pup, certain adjustments also have to be made in the romance department. Ideally, it's better to socialize puppies to the sounds of any grown-up bedroom activities you might indulge in. That way, they won't become alarmed, overexcited, or jealous if and when you've got company in the boudoir.

While your dog may find this type of nighttime behavior highly unusual, I can promise you that the sleepy-time routines of some dogs are even worse. Carmen, our marketing director at The Honest Kitchen, has awoken a number of times with her adorable white mixed-breed dog, Abba, standing over her on the bed, simply staring at her face. Until you get desensitized to your particular dog's idiosyncrasies, be prepared for some sleepless nights.

When they finally *do* sleep, they're never quite out, either. Many dogs' senses remain on high alert even while they're sleeping. Sounds of neighbors returning from the pub, predawn grocery deliveries, and even spouses leaving the house to catch crack-of-dawn flights can mean you're all up and barking, no matter what time

The Dog Obsessed Aren't Surprised to Hear That . . .

The American Pet Products Association recently reported that nearly half of all dog owners sleep with their pups. Thus the Dog Obsessed wonder, "Why did I buy that $100 dog bed?"

it is. But this sort of response can be a bonus if anyone ever tries to break in, so it's best to let it slide so they can keep their instinctive guard-dog reactions sharpened.

Finally, a word on dog toys in your bed. Once you start allowing them into it, many dogs start to adopt the position that your bed is actually their own. Most of us draw the line at allowing things like raw marrow bones to be chewed on our duvets. You may, however, still on occasion wake up snuggling with a slightly spitty plush platypus or be stirred from your slumber by a sharp chew toy prodding you in the back.

DEALING WITH PROBLEM CATS

While humans typically have the emotional capacity to deal with new roommates, cats may not. And as any cat owner knows, felines are rarely humble, so instead of being downgraded to second place, they may resort to urinating on your dog's bed, swatting at him when he passes, or worse, taking it out on you.

You love your cat, but this behavior can't be tolerated. Bear in mind that many cats take months or even *years* to become accustomed to a new dog, so strange behavior is the norm. Your dog may see the cat as prey rather than a playmate, so when your cat swats at him, he's only defending himself. Be sure to monitor your pets closely if things escalate. A dog will often react strongly to a cat's claws, lunging at him, and if you don't break up the fight, one of them could be injured or killed (likely the cat).

Introducing a cat to a new dog can be time consuming to do properly. But it's worth it not to see your dog's nose scratched to bits, or worse, to have to talk a friend into giving a home to dear old Fluffy. Here are a few steps you can take to make the first introduction go swimmingly. Start with the first step and proceed on.

1. Trim your cat's claws.

2. Warm up your cat by rewarding her with treats when you call her name. She'll begin to associate her name with a reward, and she'll start to trust you a bit more.

3. Separate the cat and dog with a baby gate.

4. Call your cat. Anticipating a treat, there is a slim possibility she will come to you. If she does, make sure your dog is restrained, then reward the cat *and* give your dog a treat when he reacts calmly to your cat. If he doesn't, separate them.

5. Repeat this exercise as necessary until your dog reacts calmly in your cat's presence.

I can't promise that your dog and cat will be best friends for life, but if they can at least behave civilly toward each other, you'll have a happier home. And time will tell if they'll become friends, despise each other, or remain somewhere in between, as frenemies. Things may change at any point, too. I've heard of some pets who've hated each other for years being found one day—much to their obvious shame—curled up in the same bed!

PETS AND THE CITY

Tiny apartment? Your problems can be equally tiny. Many people are surprised to realize that a dog doesn't need a huge house with a yard to feel perfectly content. You just need to bear a few things in mind to ensure that your dog stays active and well socialized—and that you don't alienate your fellow city-dwellers.

First and foremost, know that a tired puppy is a good puppy: Frequent visits to the park are essential to help your dog blow off steam and stay fit. Unfortunately, not all dogs are comfortable in a dog park; it may be too chaotic, there might be too many dogs, or your dog may just be one of the shier types who prefer being alone. When you can, treat yourself and your dog to a trip to the beach or the country so he can exercise without feeling anxious or bullied.

When you've figured out what and where your dog likes best, try to stick to a daily routine so that your dog's natural cycle of circadian rhythms sets in. If it does, he'll be able to take regularly timed trips outside to go potty. If you can't make it home at precise intervals, consider a pet sitter or dog walker, and failing that, try puppy pee pads. When you get home and can take your dog outside, never forget that you should *always* pick up your dog's poop. This is a *must,* especially in an urban environment. In Paris, few people used to pick up their dogs' poop, and every year hundreds of deaths from poop-related slips and falls were reported. As the French say, *"Merde!"*

To save space in a small apartment, you can make equipment do double duty. For example, a nice wooden crate can double as a side table. (I especially like those made by DenHaus.) There are also many beautifully designed beanbag-style pet beds on the market today. Choose one that coordinates with your décor, and keep a small hand vacuum nearby so you can give it a quick cleanup when you use it as guest seating—as long as your dog doesn't mind sharing, of course. Baskets or small boxes can be used to contain leashes, poop bags, keys, and towels by the door so everything is handy to grab as you come and go.

Being a good neighbor is key in apartment buildings, where thin walls and big hallways may cause noise to travel far and fast. Make your dog use his "indoor voice" by training him with the command "Quiet!" to silence barking. Area rugs over hardwood floors can also deaden noise that could upset people living below. If your dog is prone to barking when you're away, leave the radio on when you're out and about to combat the lonely silence of being home alone. (My two enjoy the dulcet tones of NPR or the BBC World Service.) Also consider an interactive puzzle toy or Kong stuffed with food to help prevent boredom.

Finally, teach your dog good manners. A well-behaved dog who knows to lie on his mat on command is especially important when you live in more confined quarters and don't have a spacious yard in which he can blow off steam.

WHEN HOME LIFE IS *TOO* GOOD

Most dogs love the outdoors; some even love it a little too much. Some of us have taken our dogs to the beach and watched with dismay as they ran toward the water so fast we feared they'd kick sand in their own eyes or, worse, be carried away by the tide. Others among us cringe, recalling the times we've stood aghast as our calls were carried off on the breeze, utterly ignored by a dog who'd taken off in hot pursuit of a fast-moving squirrel.

But what if your dog just doesn't want to leave the house? This is unusual for a dog, but it does happen. First, know that this behavior will likely change sooner rather than later; few dogs want to stay indoors too long. But if the behavior persists for longer than you're comfortable with, there are steps you can take.

First, figure out if there's a pattern. Does your dog want to stay inside when it's raining? Then he probably fears thunder—or just hates getting wet. Have the neighborhood kids been shooting off fireworks every night? He probably associates the outside with what he can only assume are bombs going off. Give your dog a break here. He'll probably want to start going out as soon as the rain or fireworks end.

You can also make small adjustments in your life to get your dog outside. Taro and Willow are simply dreadful about going out in the rain. Even walks in the drizzle can be quite upsetting for them, and I'm certain Taro has been ready to call the SPCA on me for making him spend a few minutes at the beach on rainy mornings before we go into the office. Luckily, it's not a frequent problem because we live in San Diego, but if we're having an El Niño winter (or even a light sprinkle), I keep my husband's extra-large golfing umbrella by the back door and take them out to the yard one by one on the leash to do their business without the horror of getting wet.

If there's not a pattern, check your dog to make sure there are no bites or scratches that may have been caused by another animal or an insect. Something outside may have spooked him, and his refusal to go out may necessitate a trip to the vet. Once he's feeling better, he should be his old playful, outdoors-loving self in no time.

If all else fails, you may need to work with your dog to help him associate the great outdoors with something positive. Place his favorite chew toy outside and call his name to lure him to it. When he's out, reward him with treats. Don't grab his collar and pull him—he'll view that as an aggressive move. Instead, gently take him outside using his leash, preferably in conjunction with a harness like the Sense-ation, which provides an added sense of security.

You may need to allow your dog to use pee pads inside when he's feeling particularly housebound, and you might need to refer to Chapter 7 to learn about methods to reduce anxiety. But that's okay. Again, this behavior is likely temporary, as dogs are, by nature, rarely hermits.

Chapter 4

FOOD, GLORIOUS DOG FOOD

UNDERSTANDING YOUR PET'S NUTRITIONAL NEEDS

Frequently we Dog Obsessed can be found huddled in our kitchens, mixing up homemade meals for our families. Or maybe just our dogs. We naturally worry about whether we're feeding our pups the right sort of food, asking ourselves: *Can we trust the brand, and are the ingredients wholesome? Should my dog be taking in a few more milligrams of phosphorus to ensure proper skeletal development? My dog's fur is looking a little shabby—will a different diet help? And just what is a beef by-product?*

Other people might assume that a dog can and will eat anything, but we understand that it's hard not to hover nervously at our puppy's side during mealtimes, fearing that the fare we've served isn't good for him— or that he just won't like it. This chapter will teach you the nuts and bolts of what to look for in a dog food, how to cut through the jargon on food labels, and exactly what's necessary to offer your pup the best possible chance at long-term good health. Whether or not we've served it is really up to him, but chances are that if he's a dog, the food will be gone before you can say, "bone appétit!"

WHAT EXACTLY *IS* THAT IN HIS BOWL?

Old-fashioned dog food is brown and mostly solid, and you'd probably be hesitant to eat it, even if it were the only food left on Earth.

But dog food doesn't have to be frightening. In fact, a dog's needs are remarkably similar to a person's in that dogs really should eat a well-balanced diet of colorful, minimally processed, high-quality whole food nutrition. Variety is the spice of life when it comes to your dog's diet. Even most wild animals enjoy the benefits of a varied diet, and there's nothing about the domestication of *Canis familiaris* that says he's better off eating monotonous meals of hard brown pellets every day. If you don't have good food, your health will deteriorate, and you won't live as long. Most of us have experienced that slightly disturbing feeling of inner wooziness and lethargy that arises after eating a processed, artificial-additive-laden meal like a hot dog or a TV dinner. Dogs are no different. Yet the thousands of dog food brands on the market—many of whose ingredients labels are a mile long—all proclaim to be healthy, wholesome, and delicious. What should you be looking for?

Filet mignon and truffles are certainly nice, but you can save those for special occasions. Instead, a dog's diet should be constructed from a few essential building blocks that I describe ahead. As for how to go about feeding him—raw meals, home cooked, or dog food from the store—it's really up to you. The key thing to bear in mind when it comes to nutrition is that every animal is an individual. What works well for one dog may trigger food sensitivities in another. Keep an eye on your dog, and if he's sensitive, keep track of what you're feeding him each day so you can determine if there are connections between certain ingredients and health problems such as an upset stomach or itching. Whole foods are always better than ingredient fractions, and the less processed the food you offer, the better off your dog will be.

Top Signs of a Happy, Healthy, Well-Fed Dog

1. His bowl's so clean at the end of each meal, it could practically skip the dishwasher.

2. His fur no longer resembles Donald Trump's comb-over.

3. At the conclusion of every mealtime, you get a big, wet kiss.

4. Bathroom breaks are so regular that you refer to noon as "poop o'clock."

5. You're starting to wonder if *you* should be eating dog food.

Protein

Protein is essential for building up and maintaining a dog's muscles, so meat or fish should form the lion's share of most canine diets. They're both concentrated, easy-to-assimilate sources of protein that are full of amino acids, which are the building blocks of cells, muscles, and connective tissues throughout the body.

Many people choose not to make their own dog food, and there's honestly no shame in this, because cooking from scratch can be incredibly time consuming and laborious. I know, because I did it myself many years ago! If you choose to buy your dog's food, be sure to look for a type that contains real meat rather than meat by-products. By-products are used in many well-known, poorer-quality brands of commercial food, and unfortunately, they lack decent nutrition, may be difficult to digest (the amino acids in feathers, for example, are more difficult for the body to assimilate than those in muscle meat), and are often laden with chemical preservatives. Animal or meat by-products may include beaks, feet, hide, dried blood, feathers, and viscera freed of their contents in quantities that occur unavoidably in good processing practices! All of these sound foul to almost any Dog-Obsessed owner worth his salt. In my opinion, these slaughterhouse leftovers, which have no place in the human food supply, are much better suited to an afterlife as fertilizer (in the case of blood and viscera) or stuffing in someone's duvet or sofa cushions (in the case of the feathers).

If you do choose to be your dog's short-order cook, always try to feed pastured, free-range, or grass-fed meats, even if you can't find organic. It's generally best to look for wild-caught fish over farm-raised fish, too, although there is an argument to be made for buying a mix of both in order to take some of the pressure off the ocean's delicate ecosystem and avoid depleting wild stocks. Finally, selecting natural and non-GMO alternatives is simply better for your dog and the planet.

A dog's teeth and jaws are built for gnawing on meaty bones, which essentially means he's designed to be a protein-chomping machine. That said, the domestic dog's saliva has adapted through the process of evolution and does contain the enzyme amylase, which is used for carbohydrate digestion. Many plant-based foods are loaded with essential vitamins and minerals, and it's much better to provide these nutrients in the form of colorful produce than in a man-made premix. Bones

should *never* be fed cooked; they're more prone to splintering and have the potential to cause intestinal damage. So toss out that T-bone you didn't finish at your nephew's wedding; unfortunately, it's just not good for your dog. Instead, many owners offer whole, raw, meaty bones such as chicken backs, while others prefer to feed the bones ground. (Many commercial raw dog foods also contain finely ground bone and cartilage.) Again, this is a matter of preference. Your dog will surely appreciate whatever kind of bone you give him!

In addition to muscle meats, many owners incorporate organs such as liver and kidney into their dogs' diets, and many dog foods contain these. Organ meats are rich sources of nutrients that aren't present in muscle meat, but most holistic vets recommend feeding them only a couple of times each week, especially in the case of liver, which could lead to vitamin A toxicity if fed in excess quantities. If possible, try to feed only organic organs, since nonorganic varieties may be contaminated with toxins from pesticides, medications, and other chemicals. This is especially true of the liver, which is essentially a filtration system for toxins.

> "We eat vegan, but I cook chicken for Maizy."
>
> —Honest Kitchen customer Stephanie Burnett Horne

What about eggs? They're a great source of protein and can be added directly to your dog's food, raw or lightly scrambled. What dog doesn't love a fluffy omelet on Sunday mornings, and what Dog Obsessed owner doesn't enjoy making one?

Many pet owners prefer to feed only one kind of protein at each meal, which may help to uncover food intolerances in more sensitive pets. Single-source proteins in each meal are also more biologically appropriate because they tend to better emulate the way a dog might eat in the wild. However, most dogs will benefit from a variety of different proteins throughout the week. Some holistic vets believe that nonstop consumption of one single type of food may actually make a dog more predisposed to food sensitivities over the longer term. Variety is the spice of life!

Fats and Oils

Your dog's diet should be about 8 to 20 percent fats and oils. Dogs with certain health conditions, such as pancreatitis, should consume diets containing a percentage of fat near the lower end of this range. Fats and oils are important sources of fuel and energy, and they supply essential fatty acids, which do everything from inhibit the development of cancer cells to aid in brain development.

Dietary fat may be provided in the form of meat and raw, meaty bones, as well as some types of oily fish, such as salmon and sardines. Some people also supply extra fat in the form of a supplement such as evening primrose, flax, borage, or fish oil (which many pet owners and holistic vets prefer), because the omega-3 fatty acids from fish can be assimilated more readily than those from plant sources. Fish body oils are preferable to fish liver oils, since—again—the liver may be contaminated with toxins.

Carbohydrates and Fiber

In general, carbohydrates should not be the major component of canine diets. Carbohydrates provide energy and help to maintain a healthy body weight in many dogs who seem to become too skinny on a very low-carb plan. The key is to feed nutritious carbohydrates in the form of whole vegetables; fruits; and whole, organic grains that are rich in vitamins, minerals, phytonutrients, and soluble fiber, which is essential for healthy digestion. In stark contrast, refined carbohydrates are heavily processed, lacking in their most nutritious components, and laden with sugar.

Grains should be completely eliminated from the diets of dogs who have sensitivities to gluten, which can cause ear infections, diarrhea, itching, and a host of other problems. I'm pretty sure Mosi's ear problems were linked to eating an excess of refined carbs, because his ears improved tremendously when I began serving him less processed meals made from whole foods. But not all grains are bad, and grains do have their place in the diets of some dogs. I found Mosi was able to tolerate organic whole grains much better than the refined grain products in his previous kibble diet.

Which types of grains should you avoid?

- **Wheat, corn, and soy.** They're thought to be the top three carb-derived allergens for dogs.

- **Rice and beet pulp.** These also trigger reactions in many dogs, although they do provide a source of fiber and help keep down food costs.

It's also worth noting that 80 to 90 percent of the corn, soy, and beet pulp in the United States is now genetically modified. In the United Kingdom, there was a 50 percent increase in reported allergies to soy products in the human population after the law there was changed to allow genetic modification of soy. I've long held the theory that genetic modification could

BEEF, FLAX, AND HONEY BARS

Not only are these bars delicious, but the flax, beef, and eggs also offer a good variety of the dietary fats and essential fatty acids that your dog needs. Makes 12 to 18 bars, depending on the size

1 cup Verve dehydrated dog food

1 cup warm water

1 cup ground beef

½ cup ground flaxseed

3 tablespoons runny honey

2 free-range eggs, beaten

1. Preheat the oven to 350°F. Using a paper towel, lightly coat the bottom and sides of a 9" x 9" baking dish with olive oil.

2. In a large glass bowl, hydrate the Verve with the warm water and stir thoroughly. Add the beef, flaxseed, honey, and eggs. Stir until thoroughly combined.

3. Transfer the mixture to the baking dish and flatten it out using a large spoon or spatula. Bake for 30 minutes, or until slightly crispy on top. Cool completely, and then use a sharp knife to slice it into individual bars that are sized appropriately for your dog. These bars can be frozen or stored in an airtight container in the refrigerator for up to 3 days.

play a big role in the rising rate of food allergies in both pets and people. What's more worrying is that there are absolutely no laws here in the United States governing the safety of GMO foods, and there's no requirement that they be labeled. Early studies have shown developmental problems in butterflies that live on GMO crops and a 70 percent increase in intestinal inflammation in hogs who are fed a GMO diet, compared with those fed non-GMO feed.

Fruits and vegetables provide healthy soluble fiber, some carbohydrates, and—most importantly—vitamins and minerals, so they can be excellent sources of the small amount of "good" carbs your dog needs. Many of the brightly colored pigments in fruits and vegetables are actually phytonutrients or antioxidants (such as carotenoids), which help to slow the signs of aging. Phytonutrients can also help to protect against cancer, heart and eye problems, and other age-related diseases. Later in this chapter, you'll learn more about their powerful, health-promoting properties, as well as which foods contain which phytonutrients.

> "They have two freezers and a fridge, and I spend more money on their food than I do my own."
>
> —Honest Kitchen customer Jennifer Kleinman-Mackey

If you're cooking from scratch, how should you prepare fruits and vegetables? To assist with digestion, root vegetables should be pulped or steamed and pureed before serving, while leafy vegetables can be fed finely diced and raw or lightly steamed. Dogs with certain preexisting arthritic conditions should eat nightshade family vegetables (such as peppers, eggplant, and potatoes) only in moderation, since there is some evidence that they can aggravate the problem. Onions, grapes, and raisins are toxic to dogs and should not be fed to them at all.

Dairy, Nuts, and Seeds

Dairy products, nuts, and seeds form a relatively minor component of most doggie diets, but they do provide valuable fats and proteins. Live-culture plain yogurt is an excellent addition to the diets of most dogs, even those who are sensitive to milk, because live yogurt is unpasteurized and contains the "good bacteria" necessary to facilitate its own digestion. Goat's milk is an even better option since it contains less lactose than cow's milk. Many pet specialty retailers and health food stores now carry raw goat's milk, and The Honest Kitchen's Pro Bloom, which is an instant goat's milk powder, is bolstered with five billion active culture probiotics plus digestive enzymes.

For dogs who do well with dairy, cottage cheese can also be added to meals occasionally to provide extra protein and calcium. Kefir (similar to drinking-style yogurt) is a fermented milk product that's very popular among many raw feeders.

Finally, nuts and seeds such as sesame, flax, chia, and quinoa provide protein, essential fatty acids, and fiber. However, macadamia nuts are toxic to dogs and should never be fed to them.

FOODS THAT ARE TOXIC TO DOGS

- Alcoholic beverages
- Apple seeds
- Apricot pits
- Avocado skin and pits
- Candy (particularly chocolate—which is toxic to dogs, cats, and ferrets—and any candy containing the sweetener xylitol)
- Cherry pits
- Coffee (grounds, beans, and chocolate-covered espresso beans)
- Grapes
- Gum (can cause blockages, and sugar-free gums may contain the sweetener xylitol, which is toxic to dogs)
- Hops (used in beer brewing)
- Macadamia nuts
- Moldy foods
- Mushrooms (certain species)
- Mustard seeds
- Nutmeg
- Onions and onion powder
- Peach pits
- Potato leaves, shoots, and green parts of the skin (we only ever use properly stored, peeled potatoes when they're called for in an Honest Kitchen recipe)
- Raisins
- Rhubarb leaves
- Salt (in excessive quantities)
- Tea (because it contains caffeine, although moderate amounts of green tea are okay)
- Tomato leaves and stems
- Walnuts
- Xylitol (a natural sweetener found in many gums and some peanut butters)
- Yeast dough

Adapted from a list by the Humane Society of the United States.

THE IMPORTANCE OF COLOR

It doesn't matter what kind of dog you have—if his food is always brown, the health benefits he's gaining from his food are similarly ho-hum.

Phytonutrients, the pigments that give fresh foods their vibrant hues of red, green, purple, yellow, and orange, do more than just make a pretty meal; they also possess powerful antioxidant properties that can have a profound effect on total health. While it's true that some produce enjoyed by humans isn't necessarily biologically appropriate—or even safe—for canines (see "Foods That Are Toxic to Dogs" on the opposite page), many fruits and vegetables are suitable for dogs to eat and contain compounds that can provide protection against many ailments and diseases.

Despite the fact that most phytonutrients are officially considered "nonessential nutrients" because their consumption isn't essential for survival, phytochemicals are vital for deep-seated good health, well-being, immunity, and—probably— longevity. Some of the health benefits of consuming phytonutrients include enhanced immune system activity, protection against cancer, eye and heart health support, improved communication between cells, and repair of DNA damage. Antioxidants also help slow down the signs of aging.

The study of phytonutrients is one of the most exciting areas of nutritional research being undertaken today. It's extending our knowledge of the health benefits of food far beyond the macronutrients (protein, fat, carbohydrates, and fiber) and micronutrients (vitamins and minerals) that we've historically studied. Researchers have identified hundreds of different individual phytonutrients, and it's estimated that one day we may have discovered as many as 40,000. While the majority of the research on phytonutrients is being done on humans, it's likely that most of the benefits being demonstrated apply to numerous animal species, including domesticated pets. Read on to discover which colorful foods are best for your dog.

Red and Pink Foods

Tomatoes, pink grapefruit, watermelon, and papaya are rich in the antioxidant lycopene, a carotenoid. In addition to its antioxidant activity, which slows down aging, lycopene has been shown to suppress the growth of tumors in both laboratory and animal experiments.

Purple, Reddish, and "Black" Foods

Blueberries, cranberries, blackberries, eggplant, and plums contain compounds called anthocyanins, a class of flavonoids. These have been found to help reduce the risk of cancer, stroke, and heart disease; improve memory function; promote healthy aging; reduce inflammation; and treat diabetes and ulcers. It's also thought that anthocyanins possess antiviral and antimicrobial properties. Cranberry proanthocyanidins have been shown to reduce the binding of *E. coli* bacteria (the most common cause of UTIs) to the bladder mucosa, thereby helping to prevent infection.

Dark Green Foods

Spinach, kale, bok choy, and cabbage contain lutein, another free-radical-quenching carotenoid antioxidant that's especially important for skin and eye health. Lutein is also present in egg yolks. Dark green foods also tend to be good sources of vitamin K (which is important for blood clotting), as well as the B vitamin folate (which helps produce and maintain new cells). Folate is essential for the formation of DNA and RNA, the building blocks of cells, and it helps to prevent the types of DNA changes within cells that may lead to cancer.

Orange, Yellow, and Green Foods

Sweet potatoes, carrots, mangoes, spinach, and pumpkin contain beta-carotene, which can be converted by the body into retinol, a source of vitamin A. This potent antioxidant is beneficial for eye health, immune system function, and a healthy heart. Zeaxanthin, which is also found in yellow and green foods such as spinach, collard greens, and egg yolks, is beneficial for the eyes and immune system. Many foods that are rich in beta-carotene, such as oranges, papayas, bell peppers, and kiwifruit, also contain vitamin C, which helps to protect cells from free radical damage as well as promote skin and immune system health. Unlike humans, though, dogs can actually manufacture their own vitamin C in the liver and therefore have less nutritional demand for it.

White Foods

Bananas, parsnips, and potatoes take their color from pigments called anthoxanthins. These contain health-promoting chemicals such as allicin, which may help lower blood pressure. Additionally, their role in reducing the risk of stomach cancer and heart disease in humans is under study. Some white foods, such as potatoes and bananas, are also good sources of potassium, which is needed for nerve and muscle function, as well as maintaining blood pressure.

What's the bottom line? Most dogs just aren't getting enough colorful foods in their diets. When you think about conventional pet food, it's predominantly brown, which shows just how heavily it's been processed, to the extent that the natural health-promoting phytonutrients that were in many of the ingredients have been obliterated. Our dogs have been domesticated for thousands of years, but they still need a varied, colorful, healthy, whole diet just like their wild counterparts enjoy. A simple hike in the country will reveal the red- and purple-stained scat of coyotes who've supplemented their mostly meat diets with colorful berries. Refined and processed food that has turned brown from extreme heat or pressure (like the brown stuff in your dog's bowl) is missing the magical nutritional properties that phytonutrients provide. So even though meat should make up the majority of a canine's diet, the value and health benefits of the pigments present in fresh, dehydrated, or other gently prepared produce shouldn't be overlooked.

Foods to Stock Up On

Even if you aren't making your dog's food from scratch, it's good to have these foods around the house so you can add them to your dog's bowl from time to time. As a general guide, add-ins like these can make up about 10 percent of your dog's total meal. Or you may run out of dog food one busy week, and mixing something up using these ingredients will take no time if you're in a pinch.

- ☐ Ground meat: Can be served cooked or raw.
- ☐ Eggs: Scrambled, poached, or raw, your dog will lap them up.
- ☐ Instant or quick white rice: Terrific for settling the stomach.
- ☐ Frozen peas or carrots: A great source of phytochemicals.
- ☐ Unsweetened applesauce: A perfect dessert!

(continued on page 66)

TURKEY AND ZUCCHINI LOAF

The zucchini in this recipe provides just enough good, healthy carbs and soluble fiber for your dog, balanced out by healthy servings of dairy and protein. Zucchini is also a super source of antioxidants and vitamins A, B_6, and C, and potassium.

Makes 1 loaf, about 12 slices

2 cups Marvel limited-ingredient dog food

2 cups warm water

½ cup cottage cheese (at room temperature)

½ cup fresh ground turkey

¼ cup grated zucchini

2 free-range eggs, beaten

1 Preheat the oven to 350°F. Lightly coat a loaf pan with olive oil.

2 In a large glass bowl, hydrate the Marvel with the warm water and stir thoroughly. Add the cottage cheese, turkey, zucchini, and eggs. Stir to form a thick batter.

3 Transfer the batter to the loaf pan and bake for 45 minutes, or until slightly crispy on top. Cool thoroughly before slicing and serving. The loaf can be stored in an airtight container in the refrigerator for up to a week.

- ☐ Yogurt: Add this to your dog's food if he's prone to digestive upset.
- ☐ Unsweetened, canned pumpkin; like rice, this will help stave off diarrhea.
- ☐ Fresh fruits, such as melon, blueberries, and pitted peaches (not grapes or raisins), as well as dried fruits, such as cranberries or pitted dates. Feed in moderation, as too much fruit may cause diarrhea.
- ☐ Plain cottage cheese: An excellent source of added protein.
- ☐ Parsley, dandelion leaves, or nettle leaves: These are loaded with antioxidants and possess wonderful medicinal benefits, too.
- ☐ Honey: Helps stimulate the appetite after illness and may combat diarrhea.
- ☐ Ground nuts, such as almonds (but never macadamia nuts or walnuts): Tasty and an excellent source of protein!

If You Have a Bit More Time to Prepare Food

- ☐ Raw, meaty bones: Start by grinding them so you can introduce them to your dog slowly.
- ☐ Organ meat: ½ cup added to food once or twice a week is a healthy treat.
- ☐ Raw or cooked fish, such as cod, mackerel, sole, and haddock: An excellent source of fatty acids. Note that salmon should always be cooked.
- ☐ Kale, pumpkin, yams, and parsnips: Lightly steam or pulp them to aid digestibility.

KIBBLE, CANNED FOOD, AND MORE. WHAT'S WHAT IN THE PET FOOD AISLE?

It's dizzying how many brands and categories of pet food there are. Not sure what to pick? Bear in mind that the less processed a food is, the better. If cost is an issue, remember that you can always beef up your dog's food with some basics you can find around the house (see the list above).

Kibble

Best known as dry food, this simple and convenient food is baked or pressure cooked, then extruded into brown pellets. On the plus side, kibble is extremely quick to serve—

and is complete and balanced—for those who like a "scoop and go" type of product. Unfortunately, it's very heavily processed, so your dog won't get all the nutrients he needs. Some holistic vets attribute the continuing rise in kidney problems in pets to kibble consumption because dogs become chronically dehydrated due to the lack of dietary moisture in these pellets. Low-quality kibble can be unbelievably cheap—in fact, alarmingly so—and along with canned food, it tends to be a receptacle for all sorts of unpleasant, health-jeopardizing by-products from other industries.

Wet Food

This food is soft, moist, and found packaged in cans or flexible pouches. Higher-moisture foods are generally better for your dog's total health, but canned foods are produced at very high temperatures, which can destroy most of the natural nutrients. Most canned food also has chemicals like BPA in the plastic lining, which can leach into the food. The other important point to remember is that a big part of the price you pay for a can of wet food is tied up in the cost of the individual packaging, as well as the freight, because canned food is incredibly heavy and bulky to transport.

Frozen, Raw Food

Now available in many natural pet stores, this is a great choice because it's natural and undergoes almost no processing at all. The main inconvenience with raw food is the storage; some people end up buying a new freezer to accommodate their supplies. It's also important to note that once raw food has been thawed, it can't be refrozen.

Dehydrated and Freeze-Dried Food

Foods made by The Honest Kitchen are dehydrated, so I'm partial to this newer, emerging segment of health food for dogs. These foods are made gently, at low temperatures and under low pressure, which maintains most of the natural goodness in the ingredients. When hydrated with water, these foods provide a good-quality, minimally processed, high-moisture source of nutrition. This moisture really helps to prevent

Dehydrated food is naturally colorful, which shows that the phytonutrients have been retained.

CHICKEN AND CRANBERRY MUFFINS

The cranberries in these muffins are a great source of flavonoids, but your dog doesn't need to know that. Just tell him they're delicious! *Makes 12 standard or 24 mini muffins*

1 cup Thrive dehydrated dog food

1 cup warm water

½ cup dried cranberries, divided

6 ounces ground chicken

1 free-range egg, beaten

⅔ cup plain yogurt

1 Preheat the oven to 375°F. Place paper liners in a 12-cup standard or 24-cup mini muffin pan.

2 In a large glass bowl, hydrate the Thrive with the warm water. Add ¼ cup of the cranberries, the chicken, and egg. Gently stir until thoroughly combined.

3 Divide the mixture among the paper liners. Bake for 40 minutes, or until the muffins are just crispy on top and a knife can slide out clean. Cool completely.

4 Spoon the yogurt into a cereal bowl or onto a plate, and carefully dip the top of each cooled muffin into the yogurt to "frost." Use the remaining berries to decorate, placing one on top of each muffin. The muffins can be stored in an airtight container in the refrigerator for 2 to 3 days.

chronic, low-level dehydration and its associated health problems, such as urinary tract infections, crystals, and kidney disease. As a bonus, they're shelf stable (they don't need refrigeration), and they're quick and easy to prepare.

READING A PET FOOD LABEL

What you choose to feed your pet can be influenced by many factors. Is it nutritious? Will he turn his nose up at it in disgust? And will I still be able to afford all the toys, sweaters, and treats I know he loves? If you turn on the TV or log on to Facebook, you're also bombarded by advertisements that may influence the way you shop. If a dog food is made by a brand you haven't heard of, is it good?

The three things you should look for when buying a food are ingredient quality and sourcing, the integrity manufacturer, and the wholesomeness of the finished product, which will depend in part on how heavily it has been processed. So, just as we become educated about what's healthy for ourselves—counting carbs and calories, choosing whether or not to buy organic ingredients, and understanding that "natural" may not always mean what you think it does—it's very important to be able to interpret what a pet food label is saying.

Let's start with ingredients, which form the basis of what you should look for when you feed your dog. The ingredients list is ordered by weight, with those ingredients that make up the majority of the blend listed first. Try to look for a product that has meat as the number one ingredient unless you're feeding a premix or there are special circumstances (for example, if your dog is on a restricted diet).

> "I feed my dog from a spoon for every meal."
>
> —Honest Kitchen customer Sheri Couture Davis

An ingredient is nothing without quality. Meat can show up in dog food in a number of different forms, but the actual quality of those forms can vary greatly. Meat meals are a common ingredient in dry foods, and they consist of meat from which the moisture has been removed, making a dried product that can be ground into powder. Chicken meal, lamb meal, and other specifically named meat in a meal form is okay. "Poultry meal," "meat meal," and "meat and bone meal" that are from unnamed or unidentified animal sources are highly questionable in my opinion and should be avoided at all costs. These are generic terms that encompass a mishmash of meats of all sorts of dubious origins and in some cases might even include roadkill, supermarket waste, or other dead-on-arrival meats that are unfit for human consumption. My motto is, if I can't bear to eat it, then my dogs shouldn't, either.

There are pros and cons to a dry food that lists "fresh meat" in its ingredient list. Fresh meat undergoes less processing than meal, but the fact that the listing is ordered by weight means a fresh meat will invariably be listed as the number one ingredient. But in fact, after kibble processing is complete, the fresh meat's moisture will be entirely gone, so the actual equivalent amount of meat protein in the finished product is less than if a meal had been used in the first place. Basically, while you may assume more meat equals more protein, in this case, it doesn't.

Integrity refers to just how honest a company is in its packaging and labeling. Sadly, some pet food companies employ a number of tricks to mislead and confuse consumers, or at least to make their products look better than they really are. Have you seen bags of dog food with beautiful illustrations of plump fresh veggies and fruits? Be wary. The veggies and fruits may appear toward the very end of the ingredients list, meaning they don't actually make up much of the final recipe. Some pet food labels may also advise you never to add any homemade or fresh ingredients to your pet's food. These companies are trying to ensure that you feed their food alone, which will inevitably make you buy more of it! The truth is that many pets will benefit from added healthy extras. The average domesticated canine's digestive system is not so primitive that it can't tolerate a variety of ingredients throughout the week, so don't be brainwashed into thinking you should only feed the same commercial food for every meal, day after day.

Some manufacturers indulge in the shady practice of "ingredient splitting." Stay away from them! By law, the ingredients in a pet food have to be listed in order of predominance by weight. A food label may list chicken as the number one ingredient, but if the manufacturer lists a less-appealing ingredient like corn in each of its individual components throughout the ingredient list (e.g., corn meal, corn gluten meal, corn flour, corn germ, corn bran, etc.), there could be more total corn in the formula than chicken. When you see this type of food, you may assume that the kibble will be sprinkled with fresh, delicious corn kernels—or taste like a buttered cob! But in fact, the ingredient is overprocessed, quite poor in quality, and couldn't be further from what you imagine corn to be. Corn is frequently genetically modified, its production is heavily subsidized in the United States, and it's used by many pet food manufacturers as a cheap filler.

Finally, be wary of products marketed by major conventional dog food manufacturers touting their wares as "natural" or "holistic." Including a picture of some carrots on the front or one or two herbs in an ingredients list does not make it a natural product. The recipe may still be overprocessed, be full of additives, or contain so few nutritious ingredients that they don't add much anyway. Just because the packaging looks natural and earthy doesn't mean the product is inherently healthy.

So just what *does* make a food wholesome? The nutritional content of the ingredients used. A company's "vitamin premix" is listed in the lower portion of the ingredients list and shows what the company had to add in order to make their dog food "nutritionally complete." A very long list of vitamins and minerals indicates that the raw ingredients the company started off with were probably pretty devoid of nutrition or that the extreme heat and pressure the food underwent destroyed any nutrients the ingredients contained. Stay away from these long lists. Instead, try to

find a food with lots of real, recognizable food ingredients and a premix with just a few added vitamins and minerals.

What we in the food industry call the "guaranteed analysis" is the breakdown of percentages of nutrient content in a food. This is typically listed in a chart on the label. In pet food, the list consists primarily of protein, fat, fiber, moisture, and sometimes ash. Keep in mind that the percentage of protein listed in the guaranteed analysis is not the same thing as the amount of meat that's actually in the recipe. Meat itself isn't 100 percent protein; it's made up of protein, fat, and moisture, plus some vitamins and minerals. Even a cup of 100 percent pure ground beef is only about 18 to 24 percent protein, on average. A recipe could contain 40 percent meat but show only, say, 27 percent protein on the guaranteed analysis.

Some foods contain ingredients such as "poultry by-products," which might include beaks, feet, and feathers. These will add to the total protein content of the finished product but will likely be highly indigestible and of little nutritional value to your dog. They may even put an additional strain on his liver, kidneys, and other systems as his body tries to digest them. Try to steer clear of all by-products.

A guaranteed analysis that shows a high fat content is not as detrimental as it might sound. Dogs are very capable of utilizing quite high levels of fat and do not suffer with cholesterol as humans do. Beware of added animal fat in the ingredients list, though; it may be loaded with chemical preservatives. Ideally, animal fat should come from the meat that's already in the food.

Conversely, a super-high fiber content, which humans may seek for themselves, isn't necessarily the best option for our animal companions. A lot of fiber may also be indicative of a lot of carbohydrates, and as I mentioned before, a mounting wall of research shows that high levels of carbs are neither natural nor desirable for pets. The type of fiber (soluble versus the refined carbohydrate kind) is more important than the quantity, in many regards.

Finally, the "ash" that's sometimes listed as part of a guaranteed analysis relates to the total mineral content of the food. While it shouldn't be excessively high (lower than 8 percent is preferable), it doesn't in fact mean that the manufacturer added real ash to its finished product.

Whatever kind of food you buy, be discriminating. No amount of research is too much when it comes to your beloved pet. After all, his life and health may depend on it, and if you're Dog Obsessed, that means yours will, as well.

TUNA FISH CAKES

These tuna fish cakes use our gluten-free, grain-free Zeal dog food, which is perfect for dogs with food sensitivities. You can use these cakes as snacks between meals or as meal replacements, and as with anything from The Honest Kitchen, you can eat them yourself.

Makes 8 to 12 fish cakes, depending on size

1 cup Zeal dehydrated dog food

¾ cup warm water

1 free-range egg, beaten

1 can (5 ounces) tuna in water or olive oil (no salt added)

2 tablespoons chopped fresh parsley

2 tablespoons room-temperature coconut oil

1 Preheat the oven to 375°F. Lightly coat a baking sheet with olive oil.

2 In a large glass bowl, hydrate the Zeal with the warm water. Add the egg and stir to combine. Drain most of the excess liquid from the tuna, leaving a small amount with the fish, and add the fish and remaining liquid to the egg mixture. Stir in the parsley and coconut oil until the mixture is thoroughly combined.

3 Using your hands or 2 tablespoons, transfer portions of the mixture onto the prepared baking sheet and flatten them gently to form round cakes sized appropriately for your pup. Leave about ½" between the cakes. Bake for 20 minutes, or until the fish cakes are slightly crispy on top. Cool before serving. Store in an airtight container in the refrigerator for up to 4 days, or freeze for later.

Chapter 5

MEALTIME
MISGIVINGS

GRAPPLING WITH PICKY EATING,
FAT DOGS, AND FOOD SENSITIVITIES

So what if you spent so much time grilling your local pet store owner about dog food that you took it outside and discussed it over tea? You're even forgiven if your veterinarian was in your wedding. You've *finally* made a decision about what food to feed your dog, and now he's having second thoughts about eating it. Or maybe your senior dog has become a little chunky, and while you still think he's the most handsome pup on the planet, you worry he won't be able to fit into his favorite Christmas sweater. Or somehow, the food you thought was good for your dog is giving him some trouble. What do you do?

Few dogs go through life without any issues related to food. Sensitivities, weight problems, general fussiness, or difficulty transitioning to a new kind of food are common complaints, but there are others that may be more severe. Obviously, if the food he's eating is making your dog truly sick, it's essential to see your veterinarian without delay. If not, let this chapter be your guide to some of the food-related issues your pup may encounter at one point or another.

TRANSITIONING TO A NEW FOOD

Consider yourself lucky if you brought home a new dog who instantly lapped up the food you gave him and begged you for more. While some dogs are quick to transition to a new food, others protest with a hunger strike. Before you rush off to the vet—or your neighborhood pet specialty store for the 17th time—fretting that your dog isn't getting the nutrition he needs, try taking a step back and transitioning him super-slowly to his new food. The way you switch him over depends on his age, the type of food he's been eating, and any number of factors you may not be able to determine, so I've laid out two different strategies that you can follow.

Plan A is for the average dog, while Plan B is for the especially challenging pup. If you follow both of these and your dog is *still* having trouble, you should consult with a vet, but there's absolutely nothing wrong with slipping him a treat or two to ease him through this rough patch. Just as getting a lollipop after a trip to the pediatrician is a wonderful reward for a frightened child, a snack or two is perfectly appropriate for a troubled eater who finally takes a bite of food.

Seven Signs Your Dog's a Finicky Eater

1. He takes so long to eat that you'd think he'd been served in courses.

2. In the words of Jerry Seinfeld: "She eats her peas one at a time."

3. You find yourself putting down his food dish with a sense of trepidation, and you hover nervously at his side for the duration of every meal.

4. You feed him by hand or from a teaspoon more often than just on his birthday.

5. Mealtime involves an elaborate sniffing ritual.

6. The cat has become his taste-tester.

7. You're beginning to suspect that he might have *you* trained because now you actually make people food "scraps" for him, from scratch.

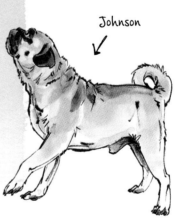

Johnson

Plan A: Easy Transition

This plan should work for most dogs, provided they don't have excessively sensitive tummies. Just bear in mind that a pup's digestive tract typically needs a few days to get used to a new food, so above all, be patient. If your dog has been eating a varied diet, he'll likely become accustomed to a new food in 1 or 2 days. If his diet's been mostly processed kibble, the changeover may take 4 to 7 days. Just keep a close eye on your dog and watch for signs of gastrointestinal upset (refusing food altogether, diarrhea, gas, or general crankiness).

1. Think about how you've structured your dog's eating habits. If he's always been free-fed, with access to food 24/7, now's the time to get him used to a bit of structure and fixed, regular mealtimes.

2. Begin by adding just a small amount of the new food into your dog's current food. This will allow the natural "friendly" gut flora in his intestines to grow accustomed to the new diet and become more efficient at digesting the new food. How much you start with will depend on the size of your pup and how sensitive he is to change. A good place to begin would be with one-part new food and three-parts old. After a day or two, you can gradually adjust the ratio to equal parts new food and old, and then you can phase out his original diet completely over the course of a few more meals. Feel free to adjust the amount and schedule to suit your pup's individual sensitivity.

3. If you notice that your dog is still struggling or resisting, he may have an extra-sensitive tummy and need a digestive aid. The Honest Kitchen produces an herbal formula called Perfect Form that should do the trick.

Plan B: Transitioning an Especially Fussy, Finicky, Sensitive, or Snooty Dog

If you've tried Plan A and it's not working, it may be time for a different approach. Perhaps a slower transition will do the trick: Start with 5 percent to 10 percent of the new food and transition over 7 to 14 days. It may be the case that your dog simply enjoys his old food a little too much. The sad truth is that most highly processed dog food tastes like junk food—and is just as addictive. It's flavor-enhanced; loaded with refined carbs, excessive salt, and sugars; and probably sprayed with an unsavory coating of poultry fat. Moving a dog off it is akin to taking potato chips out of a child's lunch box and replacing them with apples. A little complaining or sulking should come as no surprise! But you *can* get your picky dog on a new food, and the delicious mix-ins your dog will enjoy in Plan B should help.

1. Combine a small amount of ground meat (chicken, turkey, beef, etc.) with your dog's new food.

2. Offer the food for just 30 minutes, and if he still shows no interest, put whatever he hasn't eaten in the fridge. Serve it again at the next meal. Some dogs prefer food at room temperature, so you'll have to experiment to see what yours likes.

3. If that fails, add a low-sodium broth, a spoonful of plain yogurt, cottage cheese, or a sprinkle of shredded cheese to help him warm up to his new food.

4. Once your dog laps up his dinner, feel free to reduce and eventually remove the additions over the course of a few meals. Or keep them forever! Contrary to what many conventional pet food companies will tell you, adding healthy whole food extras is absolutely fine. I recommend limiting them to about 10 percent of a total meal. In fact, I encourage it!

Obviously, it's important to check that the food you're offering isn't out-of-date or spoiled, so give it a good sniff. If it smells even faintly like chemicals or paint thinner, that's a big red flag. Or if you have more than one dog and several are refusing it, it's worth listening to them. But if the food's fresh and pleasant smelling, others in the pack are enjoying it without a problem, and you're still having trouble after implementing both plans, it's either time to visit the vet to see if there's an underlying health issue causing his appetite woes or time to try a different recipe. Just like people, some dogs simply don't like certain foods. A good place to start is with the protein. So if, say, you've been trying to get him to eat chicken and he won't, it's worth having a go with beef or fish to see if that makes any difference. If even that doesn't work, start over with the original food and try again in a few days.

Again, don't get too worried if things are tough. A dog *has* to eat, and he wants to please you, so never fear—he will most certainly transition to his new food in due time. And as long as he has access to fresh water, a healthy pup can fast for a day or two with no long-term harm.

COD AND POTATO OVEN FRITTERS

When your dog's back on track and eating well, reward him with these wholesome fritters, which can be served as an occasional meal replacement or as a topper to his regular meals.

Makes 8 to 12 fritters, depending on the size

8 ounces boneless cod or other whitefish, such as haddock or pollock

1 cup Zeal dehydrated dog food

1 cup warm water

¼ cup instant mashed potato flakes

2 free-range eggs, beaten

2 tablespoons cottage cheese

1 Preheat the oven to 400°F.

2 Place the fish in a shallow baking dish and bake for 15 minutes, or until just flaky. Remove the fish from the oven and flake it gently with a fork. Reduce the heat to 375°F.

3 Meanwhile, in a large glass mixing bowl, hydrate the Zeal with the warm water. Stir in the potato flakes. Add the eggs and cottage cheese and stir to combine. Add the flaked fish to the Zeal mixture and stir to combine.

4 Use a paper towel to generously coat a baking sheet with olive oil. Using 2 tablespoons or your hands, transfer small quantities of the mixture to the baking sheet and flatten it to form fritters the right size for your pup. Bake for 20 minutes, or until the fritters are slightly crispy on top. (Smaller fritters will require less baking time than larger ones.) These fritters can be stored in the refrigerator for 2 to 3 days, although they'll lose a little of their crispiness if they're not eaten right away.

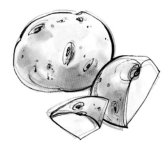

ESSENTIAL FOODS FOR HEALTH AND HEALING

Those of us who are Dog Obsessed may have a shelf in our pantry set aside to hold the ingredients for healthy meals and treats for our dogs. Or we may have cleared space in our closets for special shampoos, dog brushes, and conditioners that will make our pup's fur oh, so soft. But don't forget that some foods actually have wonderful medicinal properties and are worth keeping in your pantry or fridge at all times.

- ☐ **Honey.** A terrific digestive aid that can help to combat appetite problems, especially in puppies. A small amount of honey (about 1 teaspoon for a medium-size dog) can also be added to his food once a week for general nutrition and health support. Use only raw honey because heat processing destroys its natural health-promoting properties, but be aware that raw honey does pose a very slight risk for botulism.

- ☐ **Parsley.** This herb can be tremendously helpful in combating episodes of gas. Add a small amount of fresh parsley directly to your dog's food. As a bonus, it will also freshen his breath.

- ☐ **Apple cider vinegar.** Apple cider vinegar can be used in a solution to clean the ears (see Chapter 6 for details). It can also be added to dog food occasionally, as it has natural antibacterial properties and is purported by some to help support healthy digestions and improve energy levels. I'm such a fan that I often take a couple of tablespoons mixed with a glass of water. It tastes like the wine we sometimes drank in college, but unlike that stuff, I always feel a bit better for it.

- ☐ **Chamomile tea bags.** Peter Rabbit's mother gave him chamomile tea when he was feeling unwell after a mischievous day out, and for dogs, it can help with a variety of problems, from upset tummies to crusty, debris-filled eyes. To use, brew a cup of hot tea using a chamomile tea bag and boiling water. To soothe digestive upsets, pour some tea over some simple food, such as plain boiled rice with a little boiled chicken. For sore eyes, make the tea, cover, and let it stand for about 15 minutes. Ensure that the tea is cool enough to handle. Dip a cotton ball or gauze into the tea and squeeze until it's slightly damp. Holding your pup carefully, dribble a small amount of the tea into his eye.

☐ **Sea salt.** I don't recommend that you add salt to meals—it can be dangerous for heart and kidney function—but using it in a sterile wash can clear up goopy eyes or skin wounds in no time. Add 1 teaspoon of sea salt to 1 cup of boiled water. After the salt dissolves, allow the solution to cool, and then apply it to the eye or wound by letting it drip from a cotton ball or sterile dropper.

☐ **Pumpkin.** Pumpkin is absolutely packed with antioxidants, beta-carotene, and soluble fiber. Add a tablespoon to canned pumpkin to your dog's regular meal during times of tummy upset; it's incredibly soothing to the whole GI tract, can help to firm up loose stools in a matter of hours, may stop diarrhea, and eases digestion.

☐ **Ginger tea bags.** Ginger is wonderful for nausea, and adding a little ginger tea to a light meal or some chicken broth and serving it before road trips could help save the upholstery in your car for those dogs who suffer from the dreaded travel sickness. You can also slice a few strips of fresh ginger and add them to lightly boiled water.

EATING DISORDERS: HOW TO DEAL WITH APPETITE WOES

You've transitioned your dog to a new food, and everything is going swimmingly. But suddenly, your once ravenous dog has stopped eating. For the Dog Obsessed, witnessing a normally hungry dog's refusal to eat—whether it's skipping a meal now and then or just eating less than usual—can be unnerving. The main thing is to identify what's causing the problem. Occasional fasting can be entirely normal, but more often than not it signifies something.

A dog who suddenly starts refusing meals is different than one who's always been a bit picky. The latter is just a little bit eccentric; the former makes you bite your fingernails with worry. If the issue continues for more than a couple of days, there could be a problem with the food itself, or dental issues or food sensitivities may be developing. Sometimes, a serious underlying health concern can make a dog reluctant to eat; he may be trying to send a message to you that something's wrong.

And if a dog flat-out refuses to eat *anything* (often very suddenly), it could be the result of trauma, grief, or serious illness.

Some dogs are predisposed to eating less—for example, smaller breeds generally have less ravenous appetites—but others are just picky. Other very perceptive dogs may be trying to tell you that they just can't abide by your constant hovering during mealtimes.

What should we do when our beloved pet just isn't himself around the food bowl? Some Dog-Obsessed parents resort to hand-feeding or spoon-feeding their dogs or offering a selection of food alternatives and unhealthy additions (ketchup and grated Parmesan, anyone?) if he doesn't finish his dinner. It's better *not* to give an eating disorder too much charge by maintaining a low-key approach to meals. Some dogs are born attention seekers and love the fact that you'll sit there and keep them company at dinnertime if they act sheepish about it. Pandering to a picky pup can cause greater anxiety and self-consciousness, and you may even unwittingly train your dog that if he doesn't gobble up his whole meal right away, something better is sure to come along. In short, an eating disorder is usually a whole lot of worry for no reason, and there are several easy solutions for turning the problem around.

> "I shop at thrift stores looking for lovely china for Delta's dining pleasure. The smallest piece is Spode!"
>
> —Honest Kitchen customer Sue Brockman-Zeigler, who gives her dog the kind of tableware that makes every mealtime a five-star experience

First, your dog may just be bored. Some pups have been fed the same food for so long that they'd rather go hungry than face another bowl of cold, hard, brown pellets. And who can blame them? Boredom in dogs is very common, and it's no wonder when so few of them experience any dietary variety whatsoever. A varied diet of minimally processed, colorful whole foods can help. You could try mixing things up a bit by adding some freeze-dried or dehydrated food to his regular fare. Primal and Small Batch both make freeze-dried foods that work well for this, and The Honest Kitchen's Proper Toppers are also perfect, with the added bonus of having superfood goodness built right in.

In some cases, grief or some other upset can cause a dog to fast, and if this happens, lots of patience and the use of complementary therapies such as flower essences or homeopathic remedies can help with the emotional aspects of the problem. While not to be rushed into, if the grief is for another pet, introducing another new puppy to the home when the time is right can provide a bit of much-needed competition for food, which usually helps to improve consumption. See page 133 for some additional remedies to consider during times of grief.

It may be that your dog just wants everyone to stay away from his bowl, thank you very much. Some dogs actually become nervous and distracted when there are multiple animals—or a micromanaging owner—in the household. You can experiment by feeding your dog in a crate or another isolated environment, versus in a group setting, to determine if this is your dog's issue.

While most of us don't expect our dogs to be discerning about tableware, sometimes, the bowl itself is the issue. Some dogs can't stand the jangling noise their tags make when they bump against the side of a steel dish. Others are averse to plastic and the taste that leaches from it. A tough Pyrex bowl may help, and the novelty factor of feeding meals temporarily from a china "people food" plate can be enough of a temptation to spur a fussy pup into mealtime action. It's a bit of a mind game, but when he consumes his supper from a plate he thinks is yours, he might believe he's eating the forbidden fruit (or forbidden bone). Lastly, bowl issues may be a matter of biology. Some dogs with flatter faces find that any sort of bowl is awkward to deal with, and for them, a plate is more comfortable.

You may just be pushing your dog too hard, too often. Food should be offered for 30 minutes. If there's no interest, it should be removed. Give the next meal approximately 8 to 12 hours later in the same manner. These timed feedings improve metabolism and promote a healthier appetite, and most dogs adjust to them in 3 days or less.

Finally, your dog could be suffering from a case of "too much of a good thing." Offering much smaller portions can help a sensitive dog feel less overwhelmed than he does when you give him a giant bowl of food. Spoon- or hand-feeding should be avoided, however.

Just remember that there's a fine line between pandering to a picky pet and paying attention to a situation that actually needs some corrective action. As long as major weight loss isn't occurring, it's generally better to stand back and allow your pet to regulate his own intake *without* outside interference.

DEALING WITH FOOD "ALLERGIES"

A pet food allergy may not be exactly what you think. A true food allergy is defined as an actual immune system or inflammatory response that's triggered by eating certain foods, and the incidence of this type of reaction—such as the throat-swelling, hives, or vomiting that occurs in an allergic person who eats a peanut—is actually quite uncommon in pets. Most dogs who are described as having "food allergies" only have a food intolerance—a less severe, low-grade reaction to something in the diet, but troublesome all the same.

A food sensitivity may present itself as generalized itchiness, hair loss, digestive upset, or ear infections. Hot spots (pyoderma) and chewing of the feet are also classic responses to food sensitivites. If hot spots and other skin irritation occur suddenly, you should think back to whether there was a recent dietary change. Not sure? I've outlined a simple program below that will help you figure it out.

But first, what causes food allergies and sensitivities? There are lots of different theories. Most holistic practitioners agree that *true* allergic reactions are usually the

result of an underlying health problem or system imbalance. Dogs don't actually develop allergies as a result of exposure to allergens, but rather because they have suddenly become susceptible or vulnerable in some way.

Bad-quality food may deplete the immune system over time because this inferior food is laden with toxins and other substances that place an unnecessary burden on the body's organs and immune system. Or it could be because it lacks the vital phytonutrients, antioxidants, or enzymes that are abundant in fresh and gently prepared foods but killed by high-heat processing. Stress and genetics can predispose a pet to food allergies as well.

Certain ingredients are much more likely to cause allergic reactions than others. Some of the top food reactors are wheat, corn, soybeans, rice, white potatoes, peanuts, and milk. By-products, colorings, preservatives, and cheap fillers can also deplete the immune system over time (but are often used in low-quality pet foods). Many pets have problems with lamb, which is a "warming" (yang) food in traditional Chinese medicine (TCM) and can cause a pet to feel hot, red, and itchy and thus exacerbate "yang" hot spots and skin and coat problems, especially when it's consumed over the long term. For the dog with excess yang energy, better alternatives to lamb are "cooling" or "neutral" meats such as duck, fish, or turkey.

Don't fall for gimmicky marketing, and remember that pets are individuals! Both food allergies and food sensitivities are *entirely* specific to the individual animal, and for this reason it's very important to be wary of commercial pet foods labeled "allergen-free," "hypoallergenic," or "nonallergic." There's no such thing as a one-size-fits-all diet for dogs, and this is even truer when it comes to dogs with food sensitivities. A supposedly "hypoallergenic" diet that's made from turkey, say, will be no good at all for the dog who's intolerant of poultry.

Steps to Take for Pups with Food Allergies or Sensitivities

For many lucky pets, eliminating wheat, corn, soy, rice, and beet pulp and then identifying the single proteins that they are able to tolerate is all that's needed to manage pet food allergies—for life. In other cases, cutting out all grains from food and treats brings about a dramatic improvement.

Feeding a whole food diet that's very minimally processed and that contains a single protein source can also make a huge difference. Many dogs seem sensitive to beef in the form of a beef-flavored kibble but can actually tolerate lightly cooked hamburger, beef marrow bones, or a piece of raw steak very well. That's because the high heat and pressure processing used to make kibble can alter the amino acid structure of proteins, making them unrecognizable to the body and increasing the likelihood of a food allergy. This possibility vanishes when the human food equivalent (fresh, raw, or minimally processed) is fed to them.

But sometimes, an elimination diet or "feeding trial" is needed to uncover the cause of a pet food sensitivity. This involves feeding an extremely simplified diet—say, fish and sweet potatoes or bison and millet—for a few weeks, until the allergic reaction subsides, and then gradually adding in additional ingredients while observing your pet for any signs of intolerance (such as itching or diarrhea). Bear in mind that an elimination diet should consist of all new ingredients. For example, a dog who has previously eaten turkey must not be fed it during the elimination trial. It's also critical that no other foods be served to your dog during the period before additional ingredients are added.

Below, I've laid out an easy-to-follow elimination diet that even a finicky dog won't mind. Just be sure to document what you feed each week and what reactions occur or subside, so that you can start to identify patterns.

Week 1

Feed a diet of 50 percent cooked ground turkey (hormone- and antibiotic-free, no nitrites) and 50 percent cooked mashed sweet potatoes. Some reduction in itching and/or diarrhea should be observed over the course of this week.

Week 2

If itching and/or diarrhea persists, replace the cooked ground turkey with an alternative protein such as cooked ground beef or bison.

If conditions are improving, replace some of the sweet potatoes with kale, parsley, or other greens.

Week 3

If itching and/or diarrhea persists, replace the cooked ground beef with cooked white fish (for example, cod or haddock), and replace the sweet potato with a green vegetable such as pulped celery, broccoli, or kale.

If conditions are improving, replace some of the sweet potatoes and greens with a small amount of chopped banana, pureed melon, or other soft fruit (not grapes), to a maximum of about 5 percent of the total diet.

Week 4 and Beyond

If conditions are improving, you may continue adding one or two new ingredients every couple of days. Continue observing for any reactions.

If a flare-up or recurrence of previously improved symptoms occurs at any point, this probably indicates that an ingredient the dog can't tolerate has been introduced. Remove any new ingredients from that week and try something different. Some dogs are intolerant of ingredients like eggs, alfalfa, and flaxseed, so these may be best left until later in the elimination diet period.

Finally, if itching and/or diarrhea persists, consider laboratory-based allergy testing to help accurately pinpoint what foods your dog can and cannot tolerate. If you wish to feed grain to your dog, a seed such as quinoa or millet, or gluten-free grain such as organic oats would be your best choice.

Keep in mind that, sometimes, itchy skin and other problems can be related to the environment and are not, in fact, due to diet. If an unexpected flare-up occurs or systematic changes in diet do not yield any improvement, think about your surroundings: Molds, dust mites, and pollen are the leading causes of environmental allergic responses. Laundry detergent, household cleaners, or yard products may also be culprits.

In many chronic cases, real commitment is necessary to uncover what is causing a pet food sensitivity. Scrutinizing the label of every food that passes your dog's lips—including snacks and treats—is essential. Patterns often emerge where, for example, diarrhea occurs every week after a dog returns from day care, and the cause is the cookies he receives there (or the adrenaline from all the excitement of seeing his friends).

SUMMER NO-COOK PROBIOTIC CUPCAKES

Good digestion is made easy with these cupcakes, which your dog and his friends will love! They have a slightly sweet taste and offer the added benefits of active digestive enzymes and antioxidant-rich blueberries. *Makes 12 cupcakes*

¼ cup Pro Bloom instant goat's milk powder

1 cup Force dehydrated dog food

¼ cup fresh blueberries, plus additional for decorating

2 free-range eggs

3 tablespoons honey

1 cup unsweetened applesauce

1   Place paper liners in a 12-cup muffin pan.

2   In a small bowl, combine the Pro Bloom, Force, and blueberries. The blueberries will break apart slightly.

3   In a medium bowl, combine the eggs, honey, and applesauce. Stir thoroughly with a wooden spoon. Add the blueberry mixture to the egg mixture and stir to combine.

4   Divide the mixture among the paper liners. If desired, decorate each cupcake with a couple of blueberries before serving.

The Benefits of Digestive Enzymes

Sometimes determining what foods your dog can't tolerate—and making a commitment to avoid them over the long term—isn't enough. Detoxification and supporting the immune system with herbs, probiotics, and digestive enzymes can be immensely helpful in getting your dog's body back on track and ensuring proper absorption of any food he's eating.

Enzymes such as amylase, trypsin, chymotrypsin, and lipase are made in the pancreas and found in fresh, raw foods. The more processed a dog's diet is, the fewer natural enzymes it contains, so the more work the body has to do to produce its own. When there's a shortage of digestive enzymes in the body, enzymes will be "borrowed" from other functions, such as immune system activity. Digestion is also impaired, which can adversely affect the absorption of important nutrients.

What kind of health conditions might your dog expect when he can't digest his food correctly? They aren't pretty—for you or for him. He may experience gas and vomiting, hallmarks of gastrointestinal upset. Food sensitivities may also arise, and worst of all, his aging process may speed up.

Adding digestive enzymes to meals can *really* help. These enzymes enable the proper digestion of food without depleting the body's own limited supply of metabolic enzymes. Supplementing between meals allows enzymes to circulate in the bloodstream; supports normal immune system function, cell growth, and detoxification; and gives the pancreas a much-needed break. A few very good-

Beware of Heat Exhaustion, Especially in Unfit Dogs

General disorientation or excessive panting, sitting, or lying down mid-walk can all be signals your dog has overdone it. Give him rests in the shade if your dog needs to, and take a small amount of water with you to prevent overheating or dehydration. Just don't allow him to gulp large amounts of water during or right after vigorous exercise, as it can increase the risk of bloat. This is especially important in larger, barrel-chested breeds. Try pouring the water onto your dog's head, neck, and back if he'll tolerate it without getting overly upset. Many dogs love this, but others really don't like to get their hair messed up!

quality supplements include Prozyme (available from reputable pet specialty retailers) and Pro Bloom, an instant goat's milk (made by The Honest Kitchen) that's fortified with five billion active culture probiotics and digestive enzymes—and tastes delicious, too! Recent studies show probiotics improve not just intestinal immunity but also systematic, whole-body immunity.

Just remember that cells, organs, and tissues can't function properly without good digestion, which in turn can't happen without enzymes, so giving your dog a supplement isn't over the top. It may just be essential.

THE DOG WHO RESEMBLED A COFFEE TABLE: FOUR FIXES FOR FAT DOGS

Nobody really enjoys seeing a grossly overweight animal, and it's unlikely the animals themselves feel very good, either. Obesity is one of the most prevalent health problems affecting dogs in the United States, and being overweight can shorten a pet's life expectancy and increase the risks of all sorts of problems, including diabetes, bone and joint pain, and arthritis.

Some people may find it hard to acknowledge that their dog has become fat. We love our animals and don't want to hurt their feelings by calling them chubby. But the fact is that it's likely *your* feelings that are more hurt than theirs; animals generally don't become an emotional wreck about this sort of thing. It may be a friend, your vet, or a complete stranger who alerts you to the fact that your Chihuahua's a little too thick in the middle, or it may just dawn on you one day. Try not to lash out if someone does make mention of the fact that there's a little junk in your pup's trunk. They're probably just trying to help, so it's better to face the facts and come up with an action plan than to bury your head in the sand.

Once you've accepted that you live with a fat dog, just what do you do? Follow these four tips.

- **Cut down on treats!** Many dogs will gaze at their owners and lay on all the tricks and emotional blackmail they can conjure to try to acquire a treat, but it's important to do your best to resist their advances. You might get a dirty look or some other devastated reaction, but once you get used to the sight of your pet skulking off in disappointment, you can build up your own reserves of determination to stick with the program. Long term, you'll be doing your pup a huge favor if you can stay strict about calorie intake. If you do feel it's absolutely necessary to dole out a daily treat, provide it only as a reward for expending a few calories beforehand; maybe just give him treats after long walks, or make him fetch a ball a few times before the cookie comes out.

- **Start rationing.** Besides the treats, of course, it's important to ration your dog's food correctly. Use a measuring cup if you have to, and refrain from giving him extra food, especially if you're inclined to do so to make up for a lack of attention. Rather than putting more food in the bowl, try adding some water to create a "soup" that will help fill up your pet without supplying extra calories.

- **Beware a too-big bowl.** If it's a real emotional struggle for you to keep your dog's meals small, invest in a smaller food dish. You can fill his bowl to your heart's content if it's petite enough, and you'll make yourself feel much more magnanimous in the process. Your pet may or may not catch on to what's occurring, but if you serve each meal with confidence and a heartfelt smile, he's less likely to become suspicious.

- **Work it out.** We provide a detailed exercise plan in Chapter 10, but here's a primer for you. Plenty of exercise is key to achieving and maintaining a healthy body weight, of course. You can't start off too enthusiastically if you have a dog who's very overweight; it's important to build up gradually to avoid injuries that could land you back at the vet. Start off with a gentle stroll and work up to 20 minutes a day; the time it takes to get to this level will depend on how diligent you are and what shape your dog is in. It's really essential to stick to it on a daily basis, too. Ultimately, two brisk 20-minute walks every day will be sufficient to keep most dogs in top shape. Some dogs require more and others less, though, so pay close attention to how your dog reacts to exercise.

Losing weight may take some time, but believe me, it's hugely beneficial for your dog in the long term. He'll feel better, look better, and live longer, and, if you're Dog Obsessed, that means *you'll* feel better, too.

BODY CONDITION SCORE

You can determine if your dog is over- or underweight just by looking at him. This chart can help.

VERY THIN
Body Score = **1**

THIN
Body Score = **3**

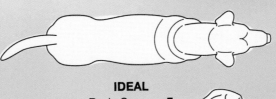

IDEAL
Body Score = **5**

OVERWEIGHT
Body Score = **7**

OBESE
Body Score = **9**

Chapter 6

DOG HEALTH

FROM THE EARS TO THE UNDERCARRIAGE
(AND EVERYTHING IN BETWEEN)

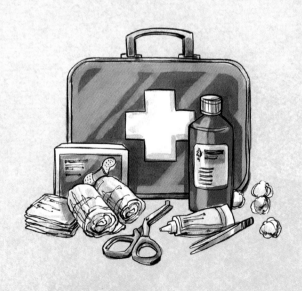

You can't imagine loving your dog any more than you already do. From his wet nose, to the adorable way he woofs under his breath when he's having a dream, to the fact that he wakes you up every morning demanding breakfast—irritating to some, but not us Dog Obsessed—he makes Lassie seem like an amateur to you. You'd do *anything* for your dog—except, perhaps, express his anal glands yourself.

From time to time, a nagging health problem comes between you and the pup you love. Maybe you can't approach that dog modeling agency you've exhaustively researched because your dog's teeth are looking a little less than pearly white. Or perhaps you're forced to postpone investing in that gorgeous new Oriental rug because your dog has a bit of an oozy hotspot or deposits a trail of his fluff everywhere he goes.

The previous chapter touched on some of the common health concerns that stem from a mediocre diet or food sensitivities, but this chapter will expand into areas beyond gut upset and food avoidance. It's true that many health issues stem from food, but others may not have such an obvious cause, and I'll describe those in detail. So whether it's oily fur or scabby ears, this chapter will help you turn your dog back into the handsome prince you know him to be.

HOW TO DO A HOME HEALTH CHECK

First things first! You may be able to tackle some health problems at home—or prevent them entirely. Checking over your dog at home can help you identify possible health problems early. Because more moderate—and less costly—treatment options are usually an option during an ailment's earlier stages, you may be able to nip a health issue in the bud and save thousands of dollars in vet bills in the process.

Try to get your dog used to being checked over from an early age. Otherwise, he's likely to be completely taken aback if you suddenly start looking at and feeling body parts you've never paid any attention to before. Depending on your pup's temperament and willingness to be fussed over, you may have to work up to a full-body check.

Before you do anything, give your dog a gentle massage to relax him. This also doubles as a way to feel for any unusual lumps, bumps, or sore points. You can check your dog's torso while he's standing up or lying down, and you can gently feel for any unusual lumps and bumps during grooming or petting sessions. Pay special attention to his neck, armpits, and abdomen, where a number of lymph nodes are located. Also look for any areas of hair loss, redness, or irritation.

You can check his limbs and paws the same way during a home health check or just through general observation when he's out and about. Make sure you're familiar with your pup's normal gaits, and pay attention to any unusual signs of stiffness, difficulty getting up or navigating steps, or limping.

Then tackle his mouth: Start off by gently putting your fingers inside and touching your dog's teeth and gums. Once he's comfortable with that—which may be in the first or second sitting, or months later, depending on the individual animal; the number, size, and relative sharpness of his teeth; and your level of confidence with the task—gradually pry his mouth open for a brief moment and take a quick look inside.

Checking his ears is comparatively easy after you've tackled his mouth. With some dogs, it's possible to peek into the ears without them even noticing your doing so—you just have to catch them when they're sleepy or distracted, or sneak a peek in between bouts of rubbing them while you're casually watching *Game of Thrones*. With others, you may have to hold them quite firmly or enlist a strong, confident adult family member to help you. Larger dogs can be secured between your knees.

Your pup's tail and undercarriage should be free of any signs of redness, irritation, or unusual secretions. Impacted or leaky anal glands are never fun to deal with; ask your vet or groomer for help before problems cause embarrassment or discomfort for either you or your pup.

It should go without saying that anything you find that seems even remotely serious warrants a trip to the vet. Don't try to treat a real issue at home; your dog's health is of paramount importance.

DEALING WITH DOG EARS

Picture it: One day you're scratching your beloved dog behind his floppy, soft-as-a-bunny's-cotton-tail ears, and he seems to be enjoying it just a little *too* much. So you lift up his ears, only to discover the swamps of Middle Earth growing inside. You rush to the vet, and she prescribes a laundry list of prescription medications—including steroids and antibiotics—and then writes an invoice that may prevent you from ever eating out again. Your dog has an infection, and you've got a big problem.

Characterized by a yeasty-smelling, dark, disgusting, tarry buildup, ear infections can quickly become chronic and impossible to clear up. They may come one after the other with all-too-brief moments in between during which everything seems to be okay, but then something as apparently innocent as a quick swim at the beach will bring them roaring back.

Some breeds have a genetic predisposition to developing ear infections, and dogs with long, floppy ears like setters, spaniels, and retrievers are among the most susceptible. One very dangerous sign of an ear infection is hearing loss, which is not to be confused with failure to listen to instructions. Less serious signs include shaking

BEEF, PUMPKIN, AND QUINOA BURGERS

These treats are quick and easy to make and are a great choice if your pup has sensitivities to gluten and common grains, which I discovered Mosi had. Quinoa is technically a seed, not a true grain, and it's not used in most pet foods because it's more expensive than other grains. At The Honest Kitchen, we use it in Thrive, our minimalist, limited-ingredient diet. *Makes 12 to 18 burgers*

2 cups uncooked instant quinoa

½ cup canned (unsweetened) or fresh cooked pumpkin

¾ cup ground beef

2 tablespoons chopped fresh parsley

1 free-range egg

1　Preheat the oven to 350°F. Lightly coat a baking sheet with olive oil.

2　In a medium bowl, combine the quinoa and pumpkin. Add the beef, parsley, and egg. Stir until well blended.

3　Use your hands or 2 tablespoons to shape the mixture into balls sized appropriately for your dog. Place them on the prepared baking sheet and gently flatten them into "burgers." Bake for 15 to 20 minutes, or until slightly golden on the outside but still soft in the middle. Cool before serving. These treats can be stored in an airtight container in the refrigerator for about a week.

or cocking of the head, scratching obsessively, or holding one ear slightly higher (or sometimes lower, it can be hard to tell) than the other.

Sometimes the problem isn't *inside* the ears, either. Before I started The Honest Kitchen, my Rhodesian Ridgeback, Mosi, had chronically itchy ears that were made worse by his robust dog-park social life of rough-and-tumble wrestling. He had fun, but he ended up with tiny abrasions on the ends of his ear flaps. Periodically the scabs at the tips of his ears would go flying when he shook his head to try to relieve the itching, spattering dots of blood up my beach cottage walls. I tried all sorts of remedies, lubricating ointments, and even a couple weeks' worth of Civil War–style head bandages to try to stop his ears from swinging about, to no avail. Eventually my homemade diet of real, whole foods and a bit of Vaseline topically (and regularly) applied to the tops of the pinnae did the trick; the shaking stopped, and his pinnae were returned to their former, furry glory. (I've since discovered that calendula ointment is one of the most fantastic products for promoting healing. I like the creamier or oil-based versions better than the clear, water-based gel because they stick where you want them and are much more emollient.) Bear in mind that ointments should never be applied to open or infected wounds as they'll trap bacteria and make the infection worse.

Unfortunately, many people don't connect itchy ears or the buildup of dark, yeasty, tarlike stuff in the ears with food sensitivities. Often the culprit is the grain—a common proinflammatory for dogs and humans alike—in your canine's kibble. Try feeding your dog a grain-free diet and avoiding any sugary treats for just a few weeks, and there's a good chance you'll marvel at the results. Grain contains sugar, and sugar is a quick and easy fuel that helps stuff like ear yeast to grow. In order to properly manage the situation and prevent the problem from recurring, you should also avoid feeding your dog wheat, corn, rice, beet pulp, and soy; stock up on fresh food; and aim to stick with a minimally processed diet for him for the long run.

Healthy ears don't start and stop with a good diet, unfortunately; they require vigilance and care, and they may result in you getting a little bit dirty (but hopefully not too much). Once you've modified your dog's diet so that it's no longer aggravating his condition, it's time to do a bit of spring-summer-fall-winter cleaning. Begin with a trip to the vet for a thorough ear cleaning, followed by washing at home every couple of days to allow healing to take place from the inside out. Sure, taking care of a dog's ears may be difficult, but it's necessary to keep the yeast at bay. Here are some tips to help you do it the easy way.

How to Clean Your Dog's Ears

1. Take a deep breath. Turn on gentle music. Continue breathing steadily till the worry passes.

2. If the weather's nice and you can avoid distractions, consider going outside. What goes into your pup's ears must come out, and when your dog starts shaking his head in response to having his ears cleaned, you'll end up with the contents being expelled all over your couch, your new sweater, your walls, and your irate husband. It would be much better for this waxy, yeasty discharge to be deposited in your garden than on your walls.

3. Speak to your dog in a soothing tone. Reassure him that this will be over in just a little bit. Whatever you do, don't mention squirrels or cats or dinner. Sudden movements are to be avoided.

4. You'll probably have to hold your dog pretty firmly or enlist an unsuspecting adult family member to help you hold him. If your pup has any tendency to nip when he's anxious or in pain, consider using a soft

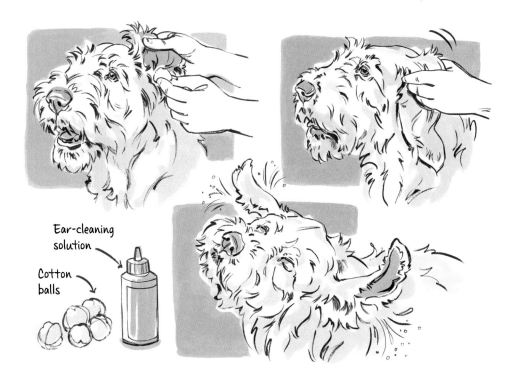

Ear-cleaning solution

Cotton balls

muzzle during this procedure, to avoid any mishaps. You can hold a large dog in a standing position between your knees. Again, don't be afraid to grip quite firmly, especially for squirmier dogs; I've been riding horses since I was 5 years old, so my knees are like nutcrackers and quite difficult for a dog to escape from, but if you're weak at the knees or timid in your approach, be prepared for a bit of a workout, which may include pursuing your dog around the house between very brief cleaning sessions. A smaller dog can be swaddled quite firmly in a towel to restrict his movement and held in your lap for the procedure. The key is to try to keep the whole event as calm and stress-free as possible.

5. Gently pour some ear-cleansing solution into the first ear. You can use a solution from the vet or make your own. (I like to use a blend of 1:9 apple cider vinegar to water. I've also had success using pure raw coconut oil on a piece of cotton ball. The coconut oil melts when it comes into contact with the warm ear and does an excellent job of loosening stubborn, sticky wax deposits.) Avoid using a Q-tip; your dog's wiggling and attempts to escape might inadvertently cause you to insert the swab too far and damage his eardrum. Ouch!

6. While continuing to hold him firmly, gently massage the ear to allow the solution to work its way in. Let go of your dog and stand back. Your dog's going to shake his head, and out should sputter a relatively satisfying gob of waxy, yeasty gunk that you won't want to get on your clothes. Use some cotton balls or gauze to wipe out the rest, and then repeat with the second ear.

Note: It's worth avoiding any swimming trips until the condition has totally settled down, because getting any water in the ear canal can cause the yeast infection to flare up again. This is especially important for floppy-eared dogs, whose large pinnae tend to trap moisture, creating the environment that yeast absolutely loves.

Voilà! You did it. Just repeat this process every few days and stick with a grain-free diet, and you should results before you can say "Jack Russell Terrier." Ideally, this will allow you and your vet to slowly wean your pet off steroids and antibiotics. Of course, if you don't see an improvement or if the condition is very severe, a more heavy-duty prescription-drug approach will need to be considered.

If you have an extremely conventional vet who isn't comfortable with a more holistic approach to ear health and only wants to push prescription steroid and antibiotic usage, it may be time to seek an alternative doctor. There are many wonderful holistic and integrative veterinarians who are well aware of the links between food and health and whose aim is to treat the root cause of the problem, rather than just suppress symptoms and medicate for months on end.

KEEPING YOUR PUP'S PEARLY WHITES IN GREAT SHAPE

While Dog-Obsessed owners may find the inner resolve to endure the scent of their dog's bad breath, mere mortals tend to be less resilient. More importantly, bad dog breath can actually be a warning sign of existing or brewing dental and other health problems, so it shouldn't be ignored.

Many owners presume that if their dog eats a crunchy dry food, dental health will take care of itself. In fact, the surface of kibble isn't abrasive enough to scrape tartar from the teeth. Would you rely on munching pretzels to clean your own pearly whites? Moreover, while some small breeds do chew their food, many medium and large dogs don't crunch up their kibble at all; if you've ever had the misfortune of seeing your dog throw up dry food, you probably noticed that most of those round brown pellets come back up whole. That's a pretty good indicator that no chewing or crunching actually took place, and it pretty much eliminates the possibility that the pellets scraped off any tartar as they went down. Even if your dog were to chew her food, most kibble is so packed with processed simple carbohydrates that it runs the risk of forcing starches and sugars *into* the gum line, increasing the likelihood of periodontal disease over the long term. Long story short, your dog needs a good teeth brushing just as much as you do; daily cleaning is the best prevention against dental disease.

Hate the idea of taking a brush to your pooch's molars? Remember that dental problems can pose a serious threat to your dog's health if they aren't identified promptly and nipped in the bud. Getting up close and personal with your dog's mouth ensures that you stay ahead of developing issues. Your vet or local pet store will actually sell you chicken-flavored toothpaste, and there are numerous canine toothbrushes on the market, so experiment with finding the one your dog likes best. Even brushing with just plain water is better than nothing! Start when your dog is young, even though your puppy's teeth may be beautiful and gleaming white. You need to get him used to having a toothbrush in his mouth because, believe me, he won't like it if you try it when he's middle-aged.

Although dogs don't typically seem to suffer with true dental decay or cavities, any plaque that builds up for too long can turn into tartar (resulting in bad breath) and can cause bacteria to build up at the gumlines. These bacteria release toxins into the oral tissue, which can lead to gum disease, causing the gum tissue and the tooth to separate from one another. This creates "pockets" where yet more bacteria can congregate. This condition can cause your dog's teeth to loosen, and painful abscesses can form. Bacterial toxins can also enter his bloodstream, posing a risk to his kidneys, lungs, liver, and heart—and ultimately, his entire immune system.

Some breeds—small dogs in particular—are more prone to dental problems than others. As if small dogs didn't feel insecure enough! This may be a genetic issue, or perhaps it's because, as a general rule, small dogs are more finicky in nature, which can lead their owners to try to entice them with "sticky" canned foods and diets that contain higher amounts of sugar. Smaller dogs are also more likely to have crowded teeth, which can make brushing or cleaning more difficult and therefore less frequent.

> "Our bulldog, Daisy, sees a bulldog specialist and a 'regular' vet; has enough toys to fill up a good-size room; eats all organic, grain-free, locally sourced food; drinks from a fountain; and usually sits on the sofa while I sit on the floor! I could go on."
>
> —Honest Kitchen customer Gretchen Schweiss, who keeps on top of her dog's health (when she's not relegated to the floor)

In addition to death-breath, some other signs that your dog may have a dental problem include dropping food, slow eating, chewing on one side of the mouth, weight loss, and excessive face rubbing.

As I said earlier, regular brushing is essential for good dental health, but it's unfortunately not always a one-size-fits-all solution to keeping your dog's mouth healthy. Luckily, other at-home preventive measures may help. Let's start with the food you're giving him. Better food means better breath, so consider feeding your dog a "prey model" diet, which includes raw, whole foods (meat and organs alike) and other minimally processed ingredients that his ancestors would have eaten in a natural setting. Raw, whole food diets like this and most home-prepared diets don't contribute to the same levels of tartar buildup as kibble.

Not just because you love him, but also because you love fresh breath, give your dog a raw, meaty bone, such as a beef marrow bone, a few times a week. I am *certain* he won't complain about this, and it's a great way to provide both a natural diet and natural tooth care. There's a small risk of tooth fracture, so keep an eye on your dog to make sure he's not trying to actually destroy the bone or swallow it whole. Pure meat treats are also helpful. Try some chewy fish skin treats, such as The Honest Kitchen's Beams. Stay away from treats produced in China, where quality, contamination, and widespread concerns with the safety of the food supply are a problem.

Hard chew toys with knobby or abrasive surfaces can also be beneficial, but their effectiveness depends on how aggressively and for how long your dog chews on them. Some food-based chews can also be helpful—not necessarily by removing tartar, but by eliminating or reducing the risk of tartar buildup in the first place.

You should always keep your dog hydrated, but adding a little something to his water may help with his doggie breath. You can find a few specialty dental care products on the market, including oral drops and products that are administered directly through your dog's drinking water to help reduce plaque buildup.

Even with diligent at-home dental care, your pup may need to see a doggie dentist periodically. This might be your regular vet (who will usually do cleanings under a general anesthetic) or a doggie dental professional who specializes in anesthesia-free dental cleanings. Whom you choose will depend on the severity of your dog's tartar troubles, as well as on the types of providers that are available in your area and the age and general health of your pup. Some vets are opposed to anesthesia-free cleanings because it's more difficult to reach the nooks and crannies between every single tooth while the patient's wide awake, and they worry that a superficial "all you can see" cleaning might give a false sense of security. Personally, I prefer not to put my dogs under anesthetic unless it's absolutely necessary, and I've had great results with the anesthesia-free approach. (Although Willow had to go under a couple of years ago to remove some cracked teeth, which I think she sustained during some overzealous wrestling with Taro. See Chapter 3, in which I discuss how much of my free time I spend straightening area rugs because of this wrestling!)

Ultimately, the way you approach your dog's dental health will depend on what you're comfortable with as an owner and the time you're willing to spend on his teeth. Remember that preventing a problem is much better than treating one. So whether you invest in a specialty dental product or good old-fashioned meat and bones, reducing the risk of plaque buildup is much less unpleasant for your dog and your wallet than a visit to the vet to have your dog's teeth pulled.

DIABETES

Holistic vets recommend a low-glycemic diet for pets with diabetes. Some vets suggest feeding a food lower in carbohydrates to avoid spikes in blood sugar levels; others recommend diets higher in soluble fiber in the form of organic whole grains to help keep blood sugar levels more constant throughout the day. A higher-fiber diet can also be helpful for maintaining a healthy body weight. Finally, feeding your pup twice daily is better than serving him only one daily meal.

PANCREATITIS

A lower-fat diet is recommended for dogs who are actively suffering from, or prone to, pancreatitis. Supplementation with digestive enzymes, probiotics, pumpkin, bromelain, and papain can help support pancreatic function, especially if your dog has a chronic case. Lipase supplementation is especially important. But in more severe, acute cases, it's sometimes better not to introduce new supplements, as this can further aggravate the condition. Make any changes to your dog's diet very slowly, over a period of 5 to 7 days, because abrupt changes in diet can aggravate or induce bouts of pancreatitis. Consult your vet for guidance.

Don't forget water! Management of pancreatitis is dependent on maintaining a proper fluid balance in the body, and good hydration is also a great way to help prevent a recurrence of pancreatitis. This can be best achieved by feeding your dog a diet that's high in moisture. Avoid dry kibble, as the body depletes its water stores to moisten and digest dry food.

ITCHY, SCRATCHY, OR OILY: WHEN YOUR DOG HAS SKIN AND COAT PROBLEMS

The condition of your dog's skin and fur is one of the best *outward* signs of the state of his health *inside*.

Chronically itchy skin, hot spots, dandruff, and a smelly, oily coat afflict a worryingly high number of dogs, and they can become chronic problems that cause years of pain and discomfort if the underlying causes aren't pinpointed and addressed. While the conventional approach to treating skin problems is to medicate with antibiotics, steroid injections, and sometimes harsh topical products, the side effects can almost be more harmful than the original problem, and the conventional "treatment" doesn't usually bring about a true cure. Instead, it merely masks the symptoms. Some steroids, such as cortisone, can actually weaken the immune system, liver, and kidneys, which makes a dog more vulnerable to infections and metabolic problems. Many prescription creams and lotions can also be overly drying to the skin or ears, exacerbating the problem in the long term.

In contrast, a more integrative or holistic plan looks at what's causing the problem, helps the body to heal itself by boosting the immune system, and, as much as possible, reduces exposure to the substances that are causing the issue in the first place. And as an added bonus, most natural supplements don't have too many adverse side effects!

You may be thinking to yourself, *My dog looks like an ad for Head & Shoulders. How can I tackle this?* Or perhaps you've noticed that your dog's once-shiny coat is looking a little oily, leaving you worried that the neighbors will assume you forgot to give him his weekly bubble bath. As with anything, you can't find a cure without finding a cause, so let's look at the origins of skin problems in dogs.

Seasonal Allergies

In the summer, fleas or environmental allergies may be the culprit. Many pets are sensitive to certain types of grass and weeds, and pollen can play havoc with a sensitive pup, just as it does with humans. If you travel with your dog in the summer, he may be coming into contact with new environmental allergens, leaving him an itchy, scratchy mess.

Reactions to Home Environment

Any time a "nonseasonal" bout of itching crops up, it's worthwhile to look back at what might have changed in your dog's environment in recent days or weeks. Is your house dusty or musty? Dust mites and mold are the most common causes of environmental allergies. Did you switch to a new laundry detergent or fabric softener to wash his bedding, or did you get your carpets cleaned? Did you wax the floor with a new product or use pesticide on your grass?

Diet

In Chapter 5 we talked about how a poor diet can affect total health and result in food sensitivities, but let's recap and apply what we learned to see how it relates to skin problems. Grain is one of the most common causes of food sensitivity in pets. Lots of pets are sensitive to gluten, which can cause an inflammatory response that manifests itself as itchy skin or red, inflamed feet. A grain-free diet is a great first step toward helping your dog overcome this frustrating, upsetting problem.

If it's not possible to feed your dog a diet that's completely devoid of grain, the next best thing is to choose a food with only organic, whole grains rather than highly processed simple carbohydrates or grain fractions. Grain fractions (gluten, husks, or hulls) can be more problematic than the whole grain because the body may hyper-respond—via inflammation—to a food that's been broken apart from its natural state.

Besides being free of chemical pesticides and other compounds that may harm your dog, organic food, by definition, cannot be genetically modified. This is relevant because one school of thought, as I discussed in Chapter 4, is that GMO grains are more likely to cause an adverse reaction in a sensitive pet.

Some dogs are sensitive to ingredients other than grain, such as particular meats, vegetables, or even herbs. These problems are generally less common, and a pet who seems to be allergic to a certain meat (say, chicken) because she gets itchy every time she eats her chicken-flavored kibble may actually be just fine when eating real, home-prepared raw or lightly cooked chicken. The exception is lamb, which I never recommend for dogs with red, hot, itchy, and inflamed skin conditions.

If you're still not sure what's causing your dog's skin problems, but you suspect it has something to do with his diet, try the elimination diet I describe in Chapter 5. In just a few short weeks, you should be able to uncover which foods are the culprits.

TURKEY FRITTATA WITH BASIL AND PEACHES

Remember the last time *you* tried to cut out carbs and other sugars? For most people, it's not so easy to give up sweets, breads, and alcohol, and your dog may be no different when it comes to carbs. While he's on the mend, treat him to this delicious grain-free snack that's just a little bit sweet. Serve it as an occasional meal replacement. (It's not just a breakfast food!) *Makes 6 to 10 servings*

6 free-range eggs, beaten

¼ cup grated Parmesan cheese

1 teaspoon butter

2 slices nitrate-free cooked sliced turkey, torn or chopped

1 fresh peach, pitted and finely chopped

2 tablespoons chopped fresh basil

1 Preheat the broiler.

2 In a medium bowl, use a fork to combine the eggs and cheese. Set aside.

3 In a nonstick, ovenproof skillet over medium-high heat, melt the butter. Add the turkey and peach and cook, stirring frequently, for 2 minutes. Add the basil and stir to combine. Pour the reserved egg mixture into the pan and stir to combine. Cook for 4 minutes, or until the eggs begin to set.

4 Carefully place the pan under the broiler and cook for 3 to 4 minutes, or until the frittata is slightly browned and fluffy. Cool before serving.

Now that you've found the cause of your pup's skin problem, what do you do? I've found that a number of easy solutions—sometimes taken alone, sometimes together—can give any dog immediate relief.

- **Natural diet.** I've said it before and I'll say it again: A natural, minimally processed diet that's free of chemical preservatives and fillers can go a long way toward combating the problem of itchy skin—from the inside out. Depending on your specific dog's tolerances, a grain-free diet may also help.

- **Supplements.** Antioxidants such as Animal Essentials Green Alternative (my favorite) can help a pup out of his weakened, vulnerable state. Adding them to his diet a few weeks ahead of a planned trip may bolster his system's natural defenses against environmental pollutants, which can trigger an itch, and some antioxidants have natural anti-inflammatory properties.

- **Calendula.** It's my anti-itch herb of choice, providing relief and healing in record time. You can make a tea by steeping calendula flowers in hot water, letting it cool, and then applying it to problem areas. Many calendula gels, sprays, and lotions, which can be found in most good-quality health stores, are also excellent for soothing and calming skin irritation and hot spots. I especially like the one made by Boiron.

- **Zinc-based creams.** These can help promote hair regrowth in cases of excessive hair loss and hot spots. **Caution:** Dogs should not ingest these. If you have a dog who's prone to licking and the sore is within tongue's reach, consider applying coconut oil topically instead. Take him for a walk to let it soak in. If any oil is left and it gets licked off later, there will be no harm done to your dog.

- **Apple cider vinegar.** This can be diluted with an equal amount of warm water and used as a wash to calm hot spots and skin irritation. Dr. Alvarez recommends a 1:9 vinegar-to-water dilution.

- **Oatmeal baths.** A natural, homemade oatmeal bath can be incredibly helpful. Simply add a few large handfuls of rolled oats to a large pan of hot water, allow the water to cool, and then pour it over your dog in the tub. You can also place the oats in some muslin cloth, tie it off, and immerse the whole thing in the bathwater to create a milky soak. Squeeze the bag gently over irritated areas. Your dog will likely love it (and may lap up the water, thinking it's his breakfast!). Whether or not you let him drink the bathwater is up to you, but be sure to rinse him thoroughly, lest he smell like an oatmeal cookie for days.

- **Gentle shampoo.** Our line of all-natural, botanical Sparkle shampoo bars is kind to your pup—and to the Earth, too. They're handmade from a base of organic goat's milk produced on a family farm in the Deep South. The milk is blended with olive and coconut oil, plus precious, functional herbs and botanicals that gently nourish and address the different needs of the skin and coat. They're surprisingly easy to use and helpful for a variety of skin and coat woes.

- **Sulfur.** This homeopathic remedy—which is available in 30c "pellets" at most health food stores—can be used for eczema-like rashes and other skin complaints.

- **Diatomaceous earth.** When used in soap or shampoo, this soft, sedimentary rock provides the mineral silica, which has tremendous benefits for total skin health.

Taken together, foods, supplements, and natural topical products form part of an overarching, holistic plan to combat problem skin. Just remember to always consult with a veterinarian for guidance on a program that's right for your dog. If you find that a "traditional" vet is resistant to doing anything but treating the issue with steroids or other medications, you should seek out a holistic vet immediately. The Web site for the American Holistic Veterinary Medical Association (www.ahvma.org) is a great place to look for one.

THE F-WORD

What four-letter word is the foulest of all? Without a doubt: F-L-E-A.

No one wants a flea problem. Having one feels dirty, seems shameful, and above all, clouds your enjoyment of snuggles with your beloved pet. Flea problems can run the gamut from mild annoyance to full-blown insecticidal warfare, and while ridding your house of fleas may require a professional's help, there's no reason you can't treat the unpleasant side effects your dog will experience right at home.

Flea allergy dermatitis is one of the most common consequences of a flea problem, manifesting as redness, itching, and scratching. In severe flea infestations, a dog can even be bitten so much that he develops anemia due to blood loss.

Tapeworm infestations go hand in hand with flea attacks because fleas ingest tapeworm eggs, and then your dog inadvertently eats fleas while he nibbles at his coat in frustration. Luckily, anemia and tapeworm infestations don't typically happen to the Dog Obsessed because we spend *such* an inordinate amount of time fussing with and examining our companions that fleas rarely get a chance to settle in.

But even with a moderate amount of itching, what's an owner to do? Time will heal all flea wounds, but in the meantime, these natural solutions can help.

- **Diatomaceous earth.** This is a great product for killing fleas in yards and homes and can really help destroy fleas at all stages of their life cycle. It doesn't contain harsh chemicals and can be used freely on furnishings and carpets, as well as in outdoor areas. Vacuuming up the excess product (as well as fleas, eggs, and larvae) is a vital step in controlling fleas, too.

- **Pennyroyal.** A renowned flea repellent, this herb can be planted around yards, and particularly near doorways, to help keep fleas at bay. In addition, pennyroyal essential oil can be diluted in water and sprayed liberally in indoor and outdoor areas. **Note:** Pennyroyal in any form should not be used around pregnant animals or people.

- **Nematodes.** These microscopic worms found in soil are a highly effective option for controlling fleas in lawns and other outside areas. They feed on flea eggs and larvae and help to control flea populations naturally. Nematodes can usually be found at garden supply stores or online.

- **Electronic flea trap.** This is a handy and worthwhile investment to combat fleas in the home without the use of chemicals.

- **Essential oils.** Tea tree, citronella, lavender, lemon balm, rosemary, and other woodsy essential oils can be applied directly to the inside of a pet's collar to act as a natural flea repellant. Or simply add 2 or 3 drops of essential oil to ½ liter of water, then spray your pet carefully, as well as your pet's surroundings. Remember, dogs have very sensitive sniffers, so be sure to dilute essential oils well, and be careful not to apply them near your pet's face. These oils can also be toxic if ingested, so be extra careful when applying them.

- **Neem oil.** This vegetable oil, used as an ingredient in shampoos and sprays, can work wonders to kill and repel fleas. However, neem should be used with caution the first time because some pets can be very allergic to it.

- **Soothing herbal tea rinse.** To relieve your pet's itchy skin, steep a couple of chamomile tea bags in 1 gallon of water, then add a handful of rolled oats and some dried comfrey leaf and/or aloe vera leaf. Allow the tea to cool slightly, then strain it and soak your pet's skin and coat with it. Allow your pet's coat to dry naturally without rinsing it off.

- **Evening primrose oil.** This is excellent for helping to combat and soothe the adverse effects of flea bites and can be applied directly to irritated areas of the skin. Raw coconut oil is also incredibly soothing when applied to sore skin.

- **Other homeopathic remedies.** *Urtica urens* (a remedy made from nettle), sulfur, Rhus tox (prepared from poison ivy), and *Pulex irritans* (made from human flea) are all used to treat various flea bite reactions. The homeopathic remedy *Apis mellifica,* which is actually made from bee venom, is also helpful in some cases, especially when your dog has a more severe reaction, such as hives.

- **Supplements.** Vitamins C and E and essential fatty acids in the form of a good-quality fish oil, can increase your pet's immunity and reduce his inflammatory response.

- **Diet.** A good, natural diet is essential, and most pets who consume a healthy, whole food diet tend to suffer the ill effects of fleas much less than their counterparts who consume heavily processed food. It's thought that this is because a colorful, wholesome diet with plenty of natural antioxidants and phytonutrients provides much better support to the immune system.

HEARTWORMS AND TICKS

While we're on the subject of vermin, let's talk about two of the other common yet potentially life-threatening pests who want nothing more than to treat your dog like an all-inclusive resort: heartworms and ticks. I've asked my friend Dr. Patrick Mahaney to weigh in on the subject of these nasty creatures because he deals with them day in and day out.

Q: What exactly are heartworms?

A: Heartworms are parasitic worms spread by mosquito bites, and the disease they cause may be fatal. Fortunately, not all mosquitoes carry heartworms, as the parasite only enters mosquitoes after they feed on the blood of a heartworm-positive animal.

Q: Where and when can heartworms be found?

A: Heartworm disease is common in warm and humid climates; it's seen year-round in some parts of the United States and seasonally in others. Even in locations where heartworm disease is less prevalent, it can be spread when heartworm-positive dogs are brought to that area (as occurred in Southern California after Hurricane Katrina) or when there are plentiful disease carriers, such as coyotes and other wildlife.

Q: What are the signs and symptoms of heartworm disease?

A: Symptoms can be mild to severe and include lethargy, increased respiratory rate and effort, coughing, decreased appetite and water consumption, unkempt appearance, anemia, multisystem organ failure, collapse, coma, and death.

Q: How can I make sure my dog doesn't get heartworms?

A: Prevention is the best medicine. Preventive medications can be applied topically or given orally and are administered every 30 days or as directed, so consult with your veterinarian about the most appropriate course of action. Just to further emphasize the importance of prevention, the treatment for heartworm disease typically involves arsenic-based drugs, such as melarsomine dihydrochloride, which are toxic both to heartworms and the animal being treated. Hospitalization, diagnostic testing (blood tests, x-rays, etc.), and other treatments are often required in association with heartworm disease treatment, which creates a medical bill vastly exceeding the price of preventive medications.

Q: Is there anything else I need to do to prevent heartworms?

A: Pet owners should keep doors and windows closed or use screens to prevent mosquitoes from coming inside. Additionally, pets that live in or travel to heartworm-endemic areas should have blood testing for heartworm performed at least every 12 months as part of a wellness examination. Be aware of your pet's potential to become sickened by mosquito bites and heartworm disease, and take a commonsense approach by partnering with your veterinarian to protect your pet.

Q: What about ticks? Should I worry about them?

A: The primary concern pet owners should have regarding ticks is the potential for infectious organisms, including bacteria, viruses, and parasites, to be transmitted through tick bites. Lyme disease, Rocky Mountain spotted fever (RMSF), and ehrlichiosis are the most common tick-borne diseases veterinarians diagnose in dogs.

Q: What are the signs and symptoms of these diseases?

A: Clinical signs of tick-borne diseases include lethargy, fever, decreased appetite and water consumption, muscle and joint soreness, and reduced mobility. As the diseases progress, more severe signs, such as pale mucous membranes (gums), tachypnea (elevated respiratory rate), anemia, multisystem organ failure, collapse, seizures, coma, and death can occur.

Q: I just found a tick on my dog, but I don't think he'd had a chance to bite yet. Should I still be concerned?

A: Two or more hours of continuous feeding are required for infectious organisms to transfer from the tick into the host. If you remove a tick before a bite occurs, there's a near guarantee that infectious disease transmission won't occur. If the tick appears engorged, immediately remove it and consult with your veterinarian about testing the tick or your pet's blood for tick-borne diseases and to determine if prophylactic treatment is merited.

Q: Where and when are ticks usually found?

A: The tick life cycle depends on warm temperatures and moist environments. In some parts of the United States, spring and summer are the seasons when pets are more susceptible to tick bites, while other regions harbor year-round threats. Urban areas generally pose less risk for ticks than suburban and rural environments due to the overall reduced prevalence of green spaces. Unlike fleas, ticks don't jump onto your pet. Ticks crawl on the ground or wait on a leaf or blade of grass to opportunistically latch on to the animal's fur. Fields, parks, and woods can be high-risk locations, in part due to the presence of wildlife that also serve as blood sources for ticks.

Q: I just hate ticks. How can I prevent my dog from getting them?

A: If you can't avoid tick-endemic areas, then consult with your veterinarian about the topical, oral, or collar-based products that best suit your pet's needs. Some products prevent both flea and tick infestations, while others also deter heartworm and intestinal parasite infections, so it's crucial to seek your veterinarian's guidance.

PERFECT PAW HEALTH

Most dog owners won't experience problems with their dog's paw pads because they aren't a common site of injury. But pads can get torn on rough terrain or cut by foreign objects. Be sure to see a vet if the injury is a major one, but if not, you can provide relief right at home.

1. Wash your dog's paws with a diluted antiseptic bath. Betadine is a great choice.

2. Apply an antiseptic cream, such as Neosporin.

3. Your dog will want to lick the cream off, so you'll need to apply a small bandage to ensure that he doesn't. To do so, put a piece of gauze on the cut or scrape, then wrap your dog's paw with a pressure bandage, continuing up his leg and over the ankle joint. Leave his toes exposed, and above all, be sure to consult with him about what color bandage he likes best. If you don't have a bandage, an old sock will do the job, too. Just secure the top with some tape to help hold it in place. **Caution:** Don't leave the bandage (or taped sock) on longer than 2 hours. Check regularly to make sure there's no evidence of toe swelling, which indicates that the bandage is too tight.

The paw problems you're more likely to encounter are redness and irritation, which cause incessant (and rather annoying) licking as your pup tries in vain to relieve his paw pain. The cause may be topical—something he's walking on in the home or yard—but a widely overlooked culprit can be diet. In fact, chewing at the paws (causing the associated inflammation and redness) is a classic sign of food allergies. Refer to Chapter 5 for help finding the cause of a food allergy and battling it.

Even Dogs Need Pedicures

You may like them for yourself, but long nails are unhealthy for your dog. They can lead to changes in gait and foot structure, which can increase the risk of arthritis and other mobility disorders. Plus, the clip-clopping sound, accompanying scratches on hardwood floors, and snags in expensive cashmere blankets can prove quite irritating. I always stress that dogs' nails should be kept short, but trimming them can be a source of trepidation for many pets and may be equally intimidating for you.

While it might be tempting to drink a small drop of something to take the edge off before you begin the task of nail clipping, the false sense of security that alcohol gives might lead you to cut too close to the quick. Instead, consider a nice, calm walk before getting out the clippers so you're both more relaxed from the outset. An alternative strategy is to pop the clippers in your pocket before you sit down together to watch some evening television. Once your pup is safely snoozing, have a go at casually snipping off a nail or two before he's even realized what's happening. Hydrating his evening meal with a cup of strong chamomile tea might help to deepen his slumber. It can take about 20 minutes for the effects of chamomile to kick in, so plan ahead.

If you want a dog whose nails and paws you can handle with ease, just remember that good experiences during puppyhood are key. Gently holding and stroking a pup's feet when he's young will allow him to get used to the sensation and will make it easier to keep his nails in good shape and to treat any problems that may occur. An older dog who's petrified of having his feet touched can be challenging to work with, but with patience, he should gradually build up confidence. You can casually touch his paws while watching TV or relaxing at home (sometimes the back of your hand is less intimidating than the front), and offer lots of praise or a belly rub when he

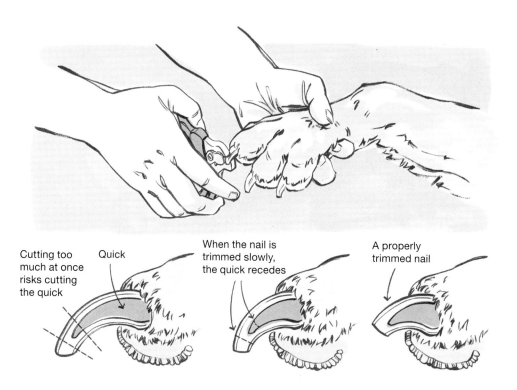

Cutting too much at once risks cutting the quick

Quick

When the nail is trimmed slowly, the quick recedes

A properly trimmed nail

doesn't flinch. Go very slowly and just do a couple of touches in one session to begin with. Offer treats to make it a really positive experience. Eventually you should be able to handle his paws for longer periods of time, and then you can start touching his nails with a clipper or other nail tool.

If your dog experiences nail trauma, don't panic. Injury to the nail from a door or mystery mishap (or even overzealous clipping) is more common than most people think, but in many cases the problem can be handled at home. Nail wounds are painful and sometimes bloody, but don't rush off to the vet immediately unless the bleeding is excessive. Soaking the affected foot in some warm salt water can provide soothing relief and help to prevent an infection from developing.

A homeopathic remedy called *Hypericum* is helpful for reducing inflammation and speeding up healing. If the worst happens and you cut a nail so close to the quick that it's hanging off, exposing raw tissue underneath, clip the nail off (avoiding the actual "raw" tissue) and apply a wrap of calendula ointment mixed with several drops of *Hypericum* tincture. You should change the wrap daily, soaking the injured area in a calendula tea bath beforehand. Healing usually occurs within 10 days, but if there is persistent pain, swelling, redness, or discharge, see your vet right away.

GENTLE CARE FOR OLDER DOGS

We all want our dogs to grow old with us, but unfortunately, a geriatric dog is prone to many chronic conditions, including arthritis, kidney failure, and more. The golden years don't have to be difficult, though. A variety of different foods and supplements—recommended by holistic vets, including my friend Dr. Leilani Alvarez, who has overseen and contributed much of the health advice in this book—can help manage your older pup's health and even steer him away from a never-ending cycle of pills and visits to the doctor.

I discussed food-as-medicine in Chapter 4, so please refer back to that chapter for details, but here's a brief overview of some of the nutritional components that are specifically helpful for elderly dogs.

WHAT IS HOMEOPATHY?

I asked my friend Dana Ullman, MPH, to give us a quick introduction to homeopathy. Dana has authored 10 books on homeopathic medicines, including the bestselling *Everybody's Guide to Homeopathic Medicines* (coauthored with Stephen Cummings, MD), and his Web site, www.homeopathic.com, provides more than 100 free articles on homeopathy, plus access to online courses, books, medicines, research, and veterinary products. Thank you, Dana!

Homeopathic medicine is a 200-year-old system that uses "nanodoses" of medicines made from various plants, minerals, animals, and even chemicals. Its primary premise is that the symptoms that humans and animals experience—like fevers, inflammations, discharges, and even growths—are part of their defenses. Instead of using medicine to counteract symptoms, homeopathic medicines are used for their ability to cause in healthy creatures similar symptoms to those that the sick person is experiencing. Using nanodoses of a substance makes it safe, and mimicking the body's own wisdom helps the body heal itself.

For example, homeopaths use nanodoses of bee venom (*Apis mellifica*) for people who have hives or a swollen throat who experience symptoms similar to those that bee venom causes: redness, burning pain, swelling, hypersensitivity to heat, and relief by cold applications.

While medicines may provide temporary relief from symptoms, homeopaths are concerned about the side effects that these drugs have and that the action of the drugs may suppress the disease process, thereby creating a more serious illness. Today, homeopathy is the leading alternative therapy used by physicians in Europe, where around 30 percent of Europeans are known to have used it. The Swiss government commissioned a review of research on homeopathy and found that clinical studies, laboratory research, epidemiological evidence, outcome studies, and historical evidence all provide evidence for the biological effects and clinical efficacy of homeopathic medicines.

- *Omega-3 fatty acids,* found in foods like salmon, are anti-inflammatory and help protect against many kinds of cancer. They also guard the brain, eyes, and heart against the effects of aging.

- *Antioxidants,* found naturally in many fruits and vegetables, shield cells against oxidative damage.

- *Probiotics* promote intestinal and whole body immunity as the body ages.

- *Turmeric,* which has natural anti-inflammatory and tremendous antioxidant properties, can help to offset aging and improve flexibility and joint mobility.

- A *glucosamine* and *chondroitin* supplement like Dasuquin, which is supported by excellent scientific research, may also support and maintain the natural structure of the joints.

- While not a food or supplement, *acupuncture* is incredibly helpful for chronic inflammatory conditions, including arthritis, and neurological conditions, such as disc disease. It can also provide terrific pain relief and is free from harmful side effects.

If your dog does come down with a chronic age-related illness like liver, kidney, or urinary disease, just what should you feed him? I consulted with Dr. Alvarez, and her recommendations are below.

LIVER HEALTH

First, make sure all appropriate tests have been run by your vet. The most common one is a bile acids test, which is a simple blood test that should be run after a 12-hour fast. One of the best natural therapies for combating liver problems includes eliminating toxins from the diet and the environment, in addition to feeding your dog some simple supplements. Milk thistle (silymarin) is an herb that has been used for centuries for its amazing healing properties. It works wonders for repairing liver damage and has anticancer properties. SAMe is a powerful antioxidant that also helps to improve liver health. In addition, excellent hydration and acupuncture can make a huge difference. Finally, parsley as a whole food additive could be beneficial for general liver support.

KIDNEY DISEASE

Any high-moisture diet will help to keep your pet hydrated, which is super important if he has kidney, liver, or urinary tract problems. But it's not just the moisture level you should look at: Talk to your vet about a lower-phosphorus, low-sodium diet with moderate levels of good-quality protein. Avoid feeding protein in the form of by-products to pets with kidney issues because this type of protein is really difficult for the kidneys to assimilate. Finally, extremely restricted levels of protein are not generally recommended for dogs with kidney disease, except in the late stages of kidney failure.

URINARY TRACT HEALTH

Because they may come on suddenly, with really ugly symptoms, bladder problems are some of the most upsetting issues dogs face. Luckily, they may be very treatable. Urinating blood, peeing too frequently, or straining or yelping while going to the bathroom can happen to any dog, but it's more likely to occur with older female dogs or dogs with diabetes. These symptoms may be signs of cancer, prostate disease, trauma, a urinary tract infection, or bladder stones or crystals, so it's always important to get a proper veterinary diagnosis before treatment begins. At the very least, a vet can prescribe pain pills to alleviate your pet's distress.

Infections

Urinary tract infections are often the result of bacterial growth and require antibiotics. In severe cases, the infection may go up the urethra to the kidneys and cause a kidney infection, which is a painful and life-threatening condition. Antibiotics destroy good bacteria in the gut, so when your dog's on them, it's a good idea to add a probiotic to his food. Be sure to take him outside for frequent potty breaks, too; holding it for too long can allow the bad bacteria to keep growing.

Crystals

On an ultrasound, urinary tract crystals look like snowflakes in a snow globe, but since they may cause your dog a lot of pain, they're anything but cute. Fortunately, because they may just be a way of eliminating the normal products of metabolism, they aren't necessarily a serious problem. However, some pets can experience more serious health concerns, such as blockages, from crystals, and they may also develop into stones. If your vet finds crystals in your dog's urine and decides they warrant treatment, he'll tackle them with a regime that's based on what type they are. When you're at home, I recommend using test strips to monitor your dog's pH so you can supplement his diet accordingly and tackle the problem before it becomes worse. Be sure the sample is fresh, as urine can test false positive for crystals if the sample is just a few hours old.

Crystals come in a few forms based on the pH level of your dog's urine. *Struvite crystals* flare up when the urine is either too alkaline or not acidic enough. The main cause is a bacterial infection, and making the urine more acidic will dissolve crystals and prevent new ones. There are many supplements, such as Berry Balance, made by Solid Gold Health Products for Pets, and Tinkle Tonic, made by Animal Essentials, that can help increase the acid level of your dog's urine, but be wary of pet foods that advertise that they promote urinary tract health, as they may contain substances that make the urine's pH *too* acidic. When that happens, *calcium oxalate crystals* may result. These are the opposite of struvite crystals; they form when the urine is too acidic or not alkaline enough. Unlike struvite, they cannot be dissolved and must be surgically removed. They can be prevented with potassium citrate (in pills or powder form), which alkalinizes the urine.

Incontinence

If your dog is having frequent accidents, he may also be having hormonal, behavioral, or physiological problems, which your vet can diagnose and treat.

No matter what the problem is, you should first feed him a healthy diet free of additives. Many "prescription" dog foods are full of by-products and chemical preservatives, so a homemade diet high in moisture is often best. Dry food robs your dog's body of moisture, so avoid that, and always give him plenty of water. If he's hesitant to drink it, add it to his food. Your dog must pee frequently so he can flush out whatever's causing his bladder problem.

Home remedies may also help your dog maintain bladder health between vet visits. These include:

- **Cantharis.** Also called Spanish fly, this is a great homeopathic remedy to consider for cystitis.

- **Cranberries.** These help prevent bacteria from adhering to the bladder wall and tissues of the urinary tract. A quality supplement is the best choice, but if you add juice to your dog's water, be sure it's pure and not sweetened. You can also add fresh or dried berries directly to your dog's food.

- **Echinacea.** As a tincture, this can provide soothing relief for an acute infection.

- **Horsetail.** This helps with UTIs, especially when there's blood in the urine.

- **Marshmallow.** I don't mean you should just give your dog marshmallows! Look for the actual herb, which reduces inflammation and irritation of the urinary tract.

You can make any or all of these last three herbs (echinacea, horsetail, and marshmallow) into a tea. Add ½ teaspoon of echinacea or horsetail to 2 cups of hot water and simmer for about 10 minutes. Add ½ teaspoon of marshmallow after removing the brew from the heat. Allow the tea to cool and then administer it with a dropper every couple of hours.

PET FIRST AID

There are a few essential items you need to have on hand for those times when your dog has a minor accident. It could be a one-on-one with a porcupine, a romp in the park that leaves him sore and limping, or a cut from broken glass left on the floor. Obviously, it's absolutely essential to seek medical attention if there's a serious health problem or you can't deal with something at home, but if not, stock up on the items below and call yourself Dr. Dolittle.

- **Muzzle.** If you're applying first aid to your dog, he might be so upset or in so much pain that he'll try to bite you out of fear or panic. A muzzle can prevent this.

- **Calendula.** This is ideal for stopping itching and promoting healing. Gels are preferable to creams to really soothe irritated areas.

- **Arnica.** This over-the-counter cream or gel is good for sore muscles as well as general aches and pains. The water-based gel tends to be easier to apply to larger areas, as it mats up the fur less. (As with any topical medication, watch out for lickers, as many medications contain alcohol, which is toxic to dogs.) Arnica homeopathic pellets in the 30c potency, given orally directly onto the tongue, are also worth a try.

- **Apis.** Use this homeopathic remedy for stings. Give your dog an oral dose of the 30c potency directly on his tongue right away and then at 20-minute intervals after a sting.

- **Benadryl.** If any signs of swelling are observed following spider bites or bee stings, a 1 mg/pound of bodyweight dose of Benadryl (use the children's kind for smaller dogs) can help to reduce the severity of the reaction. Do not combine it with other drugs. Extreme or immediate swelling calls for an urgent visit to the vet, as this reaction can be life-threatening.

(continued on page 125)

CHICKEN AND BANANA LOAF

Dealing with a bladder issue is no joke! Reward your dog for being a trouper with this treat. Just cut the loaf into slices that are sized appropriately for him. *Makes 1 loaf, 8 to 12 slices*

2 cups Thrive dehydrated dog food

1 cup warm water

½ cup cream cheese (at room temperature)

½ cup fresh ground chicken

1 ripe banana, mashed with a fork

2 free-range eggs

1 Preheat the oven to 350°F. Lightly coat a 1-pound (or 8" x 4½" x 2¾") loaf pan with olive oil.

2 In a large glass bowl, hydrate the Thrive with the warm water. Stir thoroughly. Add the cream cheese, chicken, banana, and eggs. Stir thoroughly to form a thick batter.

3 Transfer the batter to the loaf pan and bake for 40 minutes, or until it's slightly crispy on top. Cool completely and cut into slices that are appropriately sized for your dog. The loaf can be stored in an airtight container in the refrigerator for up to a week.

S&*# HAPPENS

Let's pause for a moment and talk about the thing we see every morning or night—the thing that we analyze and obsess over and that, when it fails to make an appearance, causes us to bite our nails with worry, wondering when it'll show up.

Dog poop can be our best friend or our worst enemy, depending on its appearance. I've again enlisted the help of Dr. Patrick Mahaney to talk about the types of poops your dog may experience throughout his life.

- **TOOTSIE ROLL:** Firm, moist, and in a few pieces. This is a healthy poop!

- **MORE POOP, MORE OFTEN:** If your dog is going more frequently than normal and in larger volumes, there's probably a problem. Most dogs need a diet with 5 to 6 percent fiber a day, but most kibble is 15 percent, which causes your dog to poop too much, too often. Cut down on the kibble, and the amount will shrink.

- **CHALK POOP:** If your dog has white poop, that may mean he's getting too much calcium in a raw food diet. Cut down on the cheese and yogurt, stat! It also could signal more significant problems, such as exocrine pancreatic insufficiency (EPI), in which the pancreas produces insufficient enzymes to properly digest foods and absorb nutrients. If that's the case, consult with your veterinarian; your dog may need digestive enzymes added to his food.

- **WATERY POOP:** The most alarming kind. This means diarrhea, probably due to colitis caused by an infectious organism such as a parasite, bacteria, or virus; a dietary problem; or a reaction to certain drugs. In addition to the liquid appearance of the poop, there may also be mucus or blood present, or your pup may be farting, straining to defecate, or going more often. Be sure to make an appointment with your vet to deal with colitis as quickly as possible.

- **GREASY POOP:** Your dog might be getting too much fat in his diet. Curb the fatty table scraps and stick to regular mealtimes. If this isn't enough, consider putting your dog on a lower-fat diet. Mucus in the stool can also make poop look oily, so you might want to consider giving your vet a stool sample for testing.

- **POOP WITH A PIECE OF A CHEW TOY IN IT:** It happens! Better that than one of your socks. . . .

- **Tweezers.** These are useful for removing everything from splinters to porcupine quills. A pair of tweezers is also handy for tick removal; I've had good success with applying a generous dose of nail polish remover or surgical spirit to ticks to disable them and then pulling them out with a firm grip at the base. Keep an eye on the area for a day or so afterward to make sure there's no excessive redness or swelling. (Either could be a sign that a mouthpart is still embedded in the skin, which puts your dog at risk of possible gangrene.)

- **Cotton balls.** Use these for everything from cleaning wounds to removing eye goop.

- **Betadine.** This is an all-around great antiseptic for cleaning minor grazes and small wounds. (Don't attempt to treat deep or puncture wounds at home, especially if they're caused by a bite; a drain and antibiotics will probably be required to prevent an infection.)

- **Bandages.** Human adhesive bandages don't stick to dogs, so you'll need a gauze or cloth bandage like you'd use if you had an ankle injury.

- **Rescue Remedy.** Available at most pet stores, this flower essence combination is a must-have for reducing a pet's stress. Just add 2 drops to your dog's drinking water.

- **Carbo Veg.** Another homeopathic remedy, Carbo Veg can work wonders for treating cases of gas. In his book *Homeopathic Care for Cats and Dogs,* the fabulous homeopathic veterinarian Dr. Don Hamilton recommends this, saying it's a "grab first," potentially life-saving remedy if it's administered for bloat while you're on the way to the vet. The pellets can be popped directly onto the tongue.

- **Arsenicum.** Another homeopathic remedy to keep on hand for general gastrointestinal upset, arsenicum is excellent for treating cases of diarrhea that arise from ingesting bad food, trash, dirty water, and such. Give 2 to 4 pellets directly onto the tongue.

Chapter 7

THE DOCTOR IS IN

FINDING AND KEEPING THE BEST
VETERINARIAN FOR YOUR DOG

ettling on a veterinarian is one of the most important decisions the Dog Obsessed will ever make. In an ideal world, a veterinarian will be with you through all of your dog's important milestones—from his first shots to the surfing party you might throw for his fifth birthday—so you want to find someone who'll care for him as well as you do. Look for someone who's experienced, professional, and communicative and whose beliefs about health care are aligned with your own. If you're holistically minded and prefer a moderate, herb-based, integrative approach, for example, you're not going to love a vet whose primary treatment plan is heavy-duty steroids and antibiotics for a minor hot spot. Additionally, you need someone who's not afraid to do the things you'd never dream of doing—such as removing your dog's testicles or extracting a stool sample from his bottom.

The Dog Obsessed may even have several vets or pet care professionals on hand. At one point, Raquel, who works in our marketing department, and her husband, Bailey, had a primary care vet, a holistic vet, a chiropractor, an acupuncturist, and a cardiologist for their brood of three dogs. That's not just Dog Obsession, that's good care and pure love!

To find a great vet, you could just rely on Yelp or Google, or you might ask a stranger in the dog park for a recommendation, but you'll probably want to do a little more digging. A moderate amount of obsessing about which vet to use is completely normal! A good vet won't mind if you ask a million questions about even the smallest things (though it might be best to keep it to a dozen, in the interest of getting your doctor-client relationship off to a positive start). Your attention to detail, late-night worrying, and diligence in caring for every aspect of your dog's health will resonate with most vets, who love dogs just as much as you do.

TYPES OF VETERINARIANS

Every year approximately 2,000 eager animal lovers graduate from one of the 28 US or 19 international veterinary colleges accredited by the American Veterinary Medical Association (AVMA). Most go into private practice for companion animals—what you think of as your friendly neighborhood veterinarian, whose office smells faintly of Betadine and dog shampoo and who has photos of happy dogs and cats on the wall—but some branch out into specialized areas. There are vets who treat only livestock, vets who specialize in only birds, and vets who work at zoos caring for exotic animals.

The likelihood is that you'll be seeing a companion or small animal veterinarian with your pup, and that person may have received additional training in a specialized area of medicine such as dentistry, radiology, or ophthalmology. Those concentrations require board certification and additional years of study beyond the 4 years of veterinary school, and you may be referred to one of these specialists if your pet requires testing or treatment your regular vet isn't trained to do or doesn't have the equipment for.

Choosing the right veterinarian often boils down to the kind of person *you* are. If you've had great experiences with conventional medicine, you might focus on finding a more traditional veterinarian who focuses on Western medicine. Prefer someone a little more unconventional, who chooses Eastern medicine and herbs over pills? A holistic vet may be for you. Here are the various kinds of vets I've encountered in my lifetime and whom you'll likely meet on your hunt.

The Traditionalist

You might think of this person as the elderly vet who wears a lab coat, treats your dog like a patient rather than a furry friend, and shuns "woo-woo" treatments like acupuncture. But the traditional veterinarian isn't as stuffy as you might have once imagined. Rather, he or she is someone whose expertise lies in conventional, Western medical therapies and tests rather than treatment with herbs, chiropractic care, nutrition, or supplements. The traditional vet will likely treat an illness with an FDA-approved prescription medicine first and foremost, recommend surgery or chemotherapy for a tumor, and, in general, deal with an ailment with an eye toward fixing its symptoms quickly.

Many, but not all, veterinary hospitals are accredited, which means that they've been evaluated and approved by the American Animal Hospital Association (AAHA). You can search for an accredited vet at the AAHA's Web site (www.aaha .org), but know that just because an office isn't accredited doesn't mean it's not good. You should simply do your research to determine if they meet the rigorous standards for quality and care the AAHA has set forth.

More and more, though, you'll find that many conventional veterinarians are *far* from conventional and will either replace or complement traditional treatments with Eastern medicine and alternative therapies, which brings me to the next category of vets.

The Holistic or Integrative Vet

Twenty years ago, you might have imagined a trip to a holistic vet as something like this: Her office smells of patchouli, she wears Birkenstocks, and the dulcet tones of Bob Marley can always be heard in her waiting room. That stereotype likely never held true, and today, integrative veterinary medicine isn't considered "out there." In fact, it's completely accepted and oftentimes expected.

Holistic means that you think about and therefore treat a disease with consideration for the whole animal—his mind, body, and environment—rather than just from a physical, symptoms-based standpoint. A holistic vet might look at a thyroid problem and want to do more than just treat the symptoms with drugs. She'll try to find the underlying causes for your dog's imbalance, prescribing nutritional therapies and recommending herbs that will nourish the thyroid in an attempt to address the condition. Few holistic veterinarians shun Western medicine entirely—after all, they've been trained in it at veterinary school—but if a condition is mild and not life-threatening, they'll choose prescription medication as a last resort. Medicine almost always has side effects that are sometimes worse than the actual condition itself, so a holistic vet will look for solutions that will cause the least harm to the dog.

The Web site for the American Holistic Veterinary Medical Association (www.ahvma.org) is a terrific resource for finding a vet with an integrative, holistic focus. However, just because a vet isn't in their database doesn't mean that he or she won't recommend alternative treatments; that particular vet simply may have not joined the AHVMA.

PROBIOTIC MINI CHICKEN MEATBALLS

Digestive upsets and imbalances cause far too many vet visits. This recipe can help. Pro Bloom instant goat's milk is jam-packed with more than 5 billion active culture probiotics and digestive enzymes to boost total health and immunity at the gut level.

Makes up to 36 mini meatballs

1 cup Force dehydrated dog food

¼ cup Pro Bloom instant goat's milk

1 cup warm water

1 pound cooked ground chicken, cooled

2 free-range eggs, beaten

3 tablespoons roughly chopped fresh basil

½ cup fresh blueberries

1 In a large glass bowl, combine the Force and Pro Bloom. Add the warm water and stir thoroughly. Add the chicken, eggs, basil, and blueberries. Stir thoroughly until combined. (The blueberries will break apart slightly.)

2 Using your hands, make marble-size balls of the mixture. Store them in an airtight container in the refrigerator (for up to 4 days) or freezer (for up to 3 months). If you're freezing the meatballs, place them in a single layer on a large baking sheet and freeze them solid to prevent them from sticking together. Then transfer the frozen meatballs to a resealable plastic freezer bag or other airtight container and return them to the freezer.

Traditional Chinese Veterinary Medicine (TCVM)

If you're thinking of seeing a TCVM vet, their offices must be in Chinatown, they're probably not "real doctors," and your pet will never be treated with conventional treatments, right? Wrong. Traditional Chinese veterinary medicine is really just a subset of holistic veterinary medicine focusing on food therapy, acupuncture, herbal treatments, and tui na, which is a hands-on body treatment (like massage and chiropractic care) that attempts to get energy flowing within and between the joints. In food therapy, each food is considered warming or cooling, and when a disease occurs, various food combinations are looked at to see what may be causing the symptoms. To call themselves TCVM practitioners, veterinarians must be certified and be licensed DVMs (doctors of veterinary medicine). So there's a slight chance that your regular old white-coated vet in the strip mall off the interstate may practice TCVM *in addition to* Western medicine.

To find a traditional Chinese veterinary medicine practitioner, you can consult with a nonprofit organization called the American Association of Traditional Chinese Veterinary Medicine (AATCVM). They have an online database of TCVM doctors (see their Web site at www.aatcvm.org), but bear in mind that there may be some vets who are not listed, as they may not have joined the organization. If that's the case, simply ask your vet about the TCVM training he or she has received. Other TCVM veterinarians may be a part of other organizations, too; for example, Dr. Mahaney, whom we've consulted with on a number of issues discussed in this book, received his certification in acupuncture through the International Veterinary Acupuncture Society (IVAS).

HOW TO FIND A VET

We Dog Obsessed may pick out our vet long before we pick up our dog. But if you're still puzzling over how to find the best vet possible, there are a few things you can do to settle on someone who'll treat your beloved pet as well as you do.

First, get a referral. And not just one; ask every like-minded dog owner you know whom they'd recommend. If you're seeking a holistic or integrative vet, it might be worth asking around at your acupuncturist's or chiropractor's office. Also consult with your pup's breeder or rescue group and see whom they recommend.

Once you've narrowed down your list to one or two people you like, visit their offices. And bring your dog! You want to see if the staff warms up to your dog in the

SAYING GOODBYE

Unfortunately, at some point, a trip to the vet may mean one thing: It's time to say goodbye to your beloved dog. Most veterinarians and their staff will help you during this difficult time—and more importantly, they'll make your pet as comfortable as possible. To make the transition a tiny bit easier and more peaceful, some vets are also able to come to your home.

There are several holistic remedies that are recommended for dealing with grief, both for the owner and for other pets left behind. Ignatia is a homeopathic remedy for loss, heartbreak, and pain, and it's recommended for periods of prolonged grief. The flower essences can also come into play during times of sadness after a loss: Honeysuckle is useful for general bereavement. Willow is indicated for feelings of self-pity. Sweet chestnut is the recommendation for pets and people displaying signs of sorrow and despair. Star of Bethlehem is helpful for the aftereffects of shock, trauma, or loss.

After you've had time to process your loss, you may find it helpful to memorialize your dog and your life together. Consider these options.

- **PLANT A TREE IN HIS HONOR.** Maybe you could choose his favorite spot in your backyard, or maybe you could donate a tree to his favorite local park. A memorial tree is not just a wonderful way to cultivate new life at a time when you're dealing with loss, but it also adds something beautiful and vibrant to the outdoor world your dog loved so much. When you walk past your dog's tree or watch it change colors while you're sitting on your back porch in the fall, you can reminisce about all the beautiful times you had with him.

- **DONATE TO A CHARITY.** There are hundreds, if not thousands, of worthwhile charities related to dogs and dog rescues, and all of them need your help. Almost all will take donations in your dog's honor, so you or the friends and family who knew and loved your dog can send in gifts in your dog's name. If you can't give money, many organizations and shelters need volunteers to foster dogs, work shifts at the shelter, or assist in rescue efforts.

- **DONATE FOOD.** Leftover food can be a sad reminder of your loss. Shelters desperately need food, so donating your dog's favorite uneaten meals can help a needy pup enjoy mealtime as much as he did.

- **ADOPT A NEW DOG.** It may take some time before you can even think of bringing home a new dog, but for some, it provides comfort. The marvelous thing about dogs is that they respond so instinctively to your needs. A pup won't be turned off by how much you've turned inward during this difficult time. Instead, he'll gravitate closer to you as he offers unconditional love.

appropriate way, if the atmosphere suits you and your pup, and if you find the doctors and technicians to be warm, smart, and caring. There's something to be said for a veterinarian who's located close to you, too. You need to be diligent about keeping appointments for illnesses and preventive care, so you may not want to choose a vet office that's an hour's drive away. Don't necessarily pick the closest vet, but don't pick one who's too far.

Be sure to ask whether a vet is accredited. Not being accredited through the American Animal Hospital Association isn't a deal breaker, but bear in mind that their standards of care are high, so if the veterinary hospital you're leaning toward isn't listed with them, it's extra important to visit the office to see if you're comfortable.

Remember to find an emergency vet, too. Most regular vets aren't open 24/7, so be sure to research emergency veterinary hospitals that are close to you in case your dog has a late-night accident or illness that just can't wait till the morning. Your vet's office may have recommendations, or, again, ask other dog owners where they go.

Above all, ask lots of questions. Dr. Patrick Mahaney and I have created a list (see opposite page) that may help you settle on a new vet, but don't feel shy about investigating even further! Talk with the vet directly and see if she is receptive to you, if she answers your questions quickly and clearly, and if she has the breadth of knowledge and experience that you need for your dog. If he or she looks at you quizzically, or worse, acts like there's something wrong with you for being Dog Obsessed, find another vet and move on.

PET INSURANCE: IS IT WORTH IT?

If you have more than one pet, the costs of pet health care can really add up; and if your dog has a major illness, surgery, or an accident, you may shell out thousands upon thousands of dollars. I know of one person whose Irish Wolfhound was so dismayed to see him leave the apartment one morning that he leapt out of their second-story window, broke his back, and underwent a $12,000 surgery! Thankfully, he lived to the ripe old age of 14, but his owner never again left the windows open.

Mounting policy costs may make you question whether it's worth it to have insurance. There are many reputable insurance companies out there, but before you decide to pay for a policy for your dog, there are a few issues to bear in mind.

First, costs can add up. As with health, homeowner's, or car insurance, you have to meet a certain deductible before insurance starts to cover costs, and there may be co-pays. For example, you may need to incur $200 in expenses before you're covered for 80 percent of qualified care. Rates may increase every year, and if you want more coverage, you'll pay more. Some policies don't cover routine wellness exams (only accidents and illnesses), and others won't pay for alternative treatments (supplements, herbs, etc.). In addition, you'll always need to pay your vet the full amount and then file for reimbursement from the insurance company.

If you own an older pet, you may have to shop around for coverage. Some companies won't cover elderly pets, and almost all charge significantly higher rates for them. Most companies won't cover preexisting conditions, either.

Despite these hurdles, many people report that the peace of mind that comes with insurance is a lifesaver. Instead of fretting about how much the vet bill is going to be when your sick dog gets a battery of tests, you know you're going to be covered (at least in part). Pet Plan (www.gopetplan.com) is a reputable, trustworthy pet insurance company and a favorite of staff at The Honest Kitchen. They offer a variety of different plan options and provide lifelong coverage for all chronic and hereditary conditions. Every company is different, so always ask about the specifics of each policy. Your veterinarian's office may also be able to offer a recommendation.

HOW TO CHOOSE A VET

There are so many things to think about when you're choosing a vet. Use this handy checklist to keep track of all of your questions.

- ☐ Are the hours convenient for me?
- ☐ Is the vet accredited?
- ☐ Are the offices clean and comfortable?
- ☐ My dog hates cats. Is there a separate waiting area for the enemy?
- ☐ Is the staff friendly?
- ☐ Will they review costs with me before I agree to a service and give me the option (without a guilt trip) to refuse certain treatments or tests?

- ☐ Do they have an integrative/holistic focus?
- ☐ Do they specialize in TCVM?
- ☐ Do they offer boarding and/or grooming?
- ☐ Do they make house calls?
- ☐ Do they answer questions via e-mail?
- ☐ What is the average wait time?
- ☐ Will the vet make follow-up calls to ask about my dog's progress?

REDUCING STRESS DURING TRIPS TO THE VET

The prospect of a vet visit can send many dogs running behind the couch. While some pets love visiting the vet because of the car ride there, the affection the staff showers on them, or the rough-and-tumble, impromptu playdates in the waiting room, most start shaking the moment they walk into the office.

How can you make your dog relax and realize that there's absolutely nothing to fear at the vet?

1. **Exercise.** Unless he's very sick, take your dog out for a brisk 30-minute walk before going to the vet. He should be sufficiently tired when you scoop him up and put him in the car that he may not even notice where he's going.

2. **Crate in the car.** Not only is putting your dog in a crate in the car the safest way to transport him, but it will also make him *feel* safe. Line his crate with his favorite blanket so he has positive associations with the car.

3. **Bring reinforcements.** Bring along treats, healthy snacks (unless he's fasting for a blood test or procedure), a favorite chew toy, or a beloved blanket so that your dog feels right at home in the vet's office. You may be surprised to discover that when some dogs sit on the ground and nibble a toy or a Kong, they get so distracted that they don't even notice where they are.

4. **Walk around and look ahead.** When you get to the vet's office, walk around the outside just a bit. Let your dog pee on a nearby tree so that he feels the grounds are his, then guide him into the waiting room. When you're in the waiting room, make sure he looks ahead, at you, at the wall, or anywhere else but at other dogs.

5. **Go straight to the room.** If your dog is such a nervous wreck that he can't sit for a minute in the waiting room without falling apart, call ahead and let your vet know that you'll sit in your car and wait until he's ready for you. When the vet calls, you can proceed straight to a room.

Above all, always be positive with your dog. Reassure him that the vet is nice and that visiting the vet regularly will help him lead a long, happy life. He'll pick up on your tone and your relentless positivity, and you may be surprised to catch his tail wagging when he sees the doctor walk into the room.

DUCK AND ORANGE CUPCAKES

After a trip to the vet, reward your brave pup with these colorful, tangy cupcakes. They're slightly on the decadent side, but a little extravagance is sometimes justified, especially if it's to help him recover from the stress of how vets tend to take one's temperature.

Makes 12 cupcakes

1 cup Halcyon dehydrated dog food

1 cup warm water

½ cup orange segments, chopped

6 ounces ground duck meat or ground chicken

2 free-range eggs, beaten

⅔ cup cottage cheese

1 Preheat the oven to 375°F. Place paper liners in a 12-cup muffin pan.

2 In a large glass bowl, hydrate the Halcyon with the warm water. Add the orange, duck or chicken, eggs, and cottage cheese. Gently stir until thoroughly combined.

3 Divide the mixture among the paper liners. Bake for 40 minutes, or until the cupcakes are just crispy on top and a knife can slide out clean. Cool before serving. These cupcakes can be frozen or stored in an airtight container in the refrigerator for up to 3 days.

Chapter 8

THE EMOTIONAL LIVES OF DOGS

ANXIETY, JEALOUSY, AND OTHER ISSUES

From jealousy over a new baby to the out-of-control rage that some small breeds show toward dogs 10 times their size, our pups often have feelings that seem more complex than ours. We may scratch our heads wondering why they dislike the Fourth of July—especially when we cook special cupcakes to ease them through the fireworks—but we nonetheless sympathize with them to the point of fussing. We're so worried about their health and happiness that we buy reverse osmosis water filtration systems so they don't have to endure the impurities in tap water, and we build them special forts out of blankets when the forecast calls for thunder. Yet their moods *still* flare up.

Despite our seemingly endless patience, dealing with a dog's emotions can prove dizzying as we navigate hundreds of products and recommendations, plus well-meaning advice from friends and family. All we want to do is make our dogs happy, and it's not always easy. Luckily, you don't have to spend a fortune to ensure that your dog gets all the help he needs to develop into a stable, well-balanced—and yes, possibly a tiny bit spoiled—creature.

INDEPENDENCE ITTY-BITS

If your Nervous Nellie is worried about fireworks, these tiny treats are great for luring him to a Fourth of July picnic. They can also be scattered on your lawn for a fun scavenger hunt that will keep your pup busy for a little while. *Makes up to 36 mini, bite-size treats*

1 cup Embark dehydrated dog food

1 cup warm water

1 small slice ripe watermelon

½ cup ground turkey

1 free-range egg, beaten

1   Preheat the oven to 350°F. Lightly coat a baking sheet with olive oil.

2   In a large glass bowl, hydrate the Embark with the warm water.

3   Cut the watermelon into small chunks, and place it in a medium bowl. Using a potato masher or fork, gently mash the melon to form a pulp. Stir the watermelon into the Embark mixture. Add the turkey and egg. Stir until the mixture is thoroughly combined.

4   Using your hands or 2 teaspoons, form the mixture into very small dollops and place them on the prepared baking sheet. Bake for 20 minutes. Turn off the oven but leave the treats inside for up to 1 hour to let them dry out and crisp up. These treats can be frozen or stored in an airtight container in the refrigerator for up to 4 days.

HOW TO LEAVE YOUR DOG ALONE WITHOUT LOSING YOUR FURNITURE (OR YOUR MIND)

It's best not to mention this to your dog, but most of us love a little bit of quality time alone. Quite the opposite, dogs are pack animals and, as a general rule, not fans of their own company. Yet there are times when we can't take them with us, and that may pose issues.

This is the case with my two Rhodesian Ridgebacks, Taro and Willow. They were practically born into a career at The Honest Kitchen, and they've never missed a day's work in their lives except when I, myself, am out of the office. They have practically no time home alone during the workweek and are in the habit of *always* being included. As a result, they're slightly incompetent when it comes to keeping their own company, and even though we always come home in the end, they get dreadfully offended when they're not invited to things like parent–teacher conferences at school, dinners at restaurants with friends, my barre classes, and visits to the children's orthodontist. Willow, in particular, is incredibly tuned in and usually figures out ahead of time that we're going somewhere she's not. She'll give me "the look," which is a delicate combination of hurt, disdain, and resentment, all rolled into one distinct facial expression.

Just what do you do if your dog can't stomach being without you? Much of your predicament depends on his age. If you've just come home with a puppy, you might be tempted to cuddle him even when you're in the bathroom, but it's best to get him accustomed to alone time right away. If you don't, he may suffer from separation anxiety for his lifetime, and the older he gets, the harder it will be to manage. Some older dogs have experienced a trauma that makes them hate being alone, and this may be tougher to unravel, but you can do it with diligence and care. There are very, very few dogs that can't be by themselves for at least short periods of time, and it's mainly a matter of management, bribery, and using a few tactics to outwit them.

You may have already experienced the destruction that a lonely, bored dog can unleash in your house. From scratched doors to throw pillows whose innards are strewn through every room, returning home and wondering what you're going to encounter can be unnerving. But of course your dog isn't a "bad dog." He's simply going through a rough patch, and getting him accustomed to downtime should reverse this.

How do you go about doing this? It's easy. To start, get your pup used to very short increments of time alone. To prevent him from obsessively following you, always close doors behind you when you move from one room to the next. Once you have brief moments of separation established, it's time to gradually extend the amount of time spent by himself. A perfect opportunity is crating your dog while you eat a family meal or run an errand.

You may need to employ props to prevent wanton furniture destruction, and that's fine. Distractions such as raw beef marrow bones or "interactive" toys like those from Planet Dog will keep your dog busy. Don't be offended, but while he's nose deep in a Kong that's been stuffed with something delicious, he may not even notice you've stepped out, let alone miss you.

When you have to leave, how you do it is up to you. Some people find it best to sneak out while their dog's head is turned, and others prefer to say goodbye. If you choose the latter, try to act cheerful when you leave, then be aloof and dismissive when you return, like going wasn't a big deal at all. I usually deploy a hybrid approach, whereby I give the pups a marrow bone or one of our Beams fish skin chews. They trot off to enjoy these, and I casually put on NPR, say, "Back in a minute," and slip out the door. We've come home to all sorts of scenes of devastation

over the years, including ransacked trash cans, chewed-up homework, an unraveled Boden cashmere sweater still in its bag with the tags on, nibbled stilettos (varying styles), chewed-up Ugg boots, children's toys (from teddy bears and dolls to train tracks and modeling clay, and everything in between), plantation shutters, two copies of the same (awesome) Karen Pryor book on dog training (see Recommended Reading on page 228), and a motor racing magazine with important articles my husband hadn't read yet. But the destruction of personal property doesn't happen every single time we go out, and I do still think this low-key approach is the best way to leave.

Bear in mind that confinement in a crate or designated "dog area" is the least stressful option for most dogs. They seem to be more comfortable in a smaller spot that feels like a den, rather than in an expansive area that can lead to an anxiety-induced stupor, pacing, and the possible chewing of items not meant to be chewed. There are exceptions, though, like Willow. She will not, under any circumstances, tolerate being locked in a crate. From the moment she began going into her crate specifically to do a wee as a young puppy, she's had a really odd relationship with crating. She'll scream, claw, rip bedding to shreds, and get in an absolute lather if closed in one, so I don't even try it anymore.

We Dog Obsessed typically know dozens of other dog owners just like us, so if your pup suffers from separation anxiety, by all means, give a friend or neighbor a call. Schedule a few play dates with dogs who might be willing to have a run around with yours to tire him out before alone time. If it's a workday and a playdate simply isn't an option, you can put your micromanaging skills to use by creating structure in your dog's day. A busy dog is often a happy dog! Your sample schedule might look something like this: A rigorous post-sunrise walk, coffee in hand; a Kong filled with peanut butter (or hydrated Honest Kitchen food, for added nutrition) before you leave (to distract him); a visit from the dog walker at noon; calming music (he prefers classical) left on after the dog walker leaves; hugs, kisses, and a treat when you arrive home. Some dogs thrive on a schedule, and just knowing that they'll soon be busy will calm them when they're alone.

If all of this doesn't do the trick, it may be time to employ a trainer. Or you might start thinking about getting another dog to keep your lonely pup company. With a new friend jogging circles around him, he may soon be *begging* for alone time.

Finally, there are a few management techniques that can also be utilized to help mitigate the adverse effects of your dog being left alone and not in a crate. Besides being destructive, some dogs turn into terrible thieves when they're home by themselves, either as a result of anxiety or because they're opportunistic criminals. Because of this, it's essential to make sure that any and all food has been safely stored out of reach. From direct personal experience, I know that it's especially important to put away any snacks that might have been left in children's backpacks, as well as loaves of bread, stashes of Halloween candy, the butter dish, chocolate Advent calendars, and any bags of raw potatoes and parsnips that may have been left out, ready to peel and cook for a Thanksgiving feast for 27 people. I say this in hopes that it might save you from having to endure some of the things we've returned home to after various appointments and lovely evenings out over the years.

WHEN YOUR DOG'S ANXIETY ISN'T ABOUT YOU

Sometimes anxiety stems from something much bigger than being alone. It could be a fear of the dark, fireworks, or the UPS man, or it could stem from some sort of trauma that happened long before you came into his life. Whatever the reason, when your dog begins panting, obsessively licking, or even vomiting when he has no underlying illness—and no amount of reassurance from you helps—it's quite possible that anxiety may be the problem.

The Dog Obsessed Aren't Surprised to Hear That . . .

You may begin to doubt this when your dog ignores your commands because he's too busy staring down a skunk at close range (and I sometimes blame the fact that my dogs might not be able to understand my British accent), but an average mature, adult dog is as intelligent as a human 2-year-old and can understand approximately 250 words and gestures.

While you can't go back in time and fix whatever issue caused your dog's fear, there are a number of natural solutions that may prevent your dog from going on medications like Xanax or Valium, which are frequently prescribed for nervous dogs and can be given before an event that might spark their anxiety. No one wants a dog who's a pillhead— prescription medications can have harsh side effects, and besides, you have other things to worry about (like baking him his birthday cake)—so I encourage you to try these natural solutions before rushing out for a prescription.

- Traditional Chinese veterinary medicine practitioners recommend adding cooked barley and oats to the diet to help relax an anxious pet.

- B-complex, B_{12}, and folic acid calm the nervous system.

- Phenylalanine, an amino acid, is also useful for easing anxiety, promoting a state of natural relaxation, and having a positive effect on mood and behavior. L-phenylalanine is found in such foods as beef, poultry, pork, fish, milk, yogurt, eggs, cheese, soy products, and certain nuts and seeds.

- Turkey, containing tryptophan, is reputed to have a calming effect on both animals and humans. You know how you long for a nap after Thanksgiving dinner? It's not just because you're stuffed as full as the turkey was. It's also the tryptophan.

- Traditional Chinese veterinary medicine says that beef can help relax thin animals, who may lack confidence, while lamb, mutton, and rabbit should be avoided because they increase insecurity due to the food animal's fearful nature.

- Flower essences, which are infusions or decoctions made from the flowering parts of plants, work on the emotional, mental, and energetic states of animals, helping to provide balance. Consider using honeysuckle, gorse, rockrose, mimulus, larch, walnut, and chestnut bud. See page 147 for tips on administering flower essences to your dog. The book *Bach Flower Remedies for Dogs* by Martin J. Scott and Gael Mariani is a great resource for more information on using flower essences for both people and pets.

- Rescue Remedy is a terrific combination of flower remedies. It's available as drops that can be added to water or food or dispensed directly onto the tongue. You can get it over the counter at health food stores and some drugstores.

- Homeopathy also balances energy and helps the body heal. Consider arsenicum album, Aconite, and Gelsemium. Herbs such as chamomile, oatstraw, passionflower, valerian, skullcap, and St. John's wort can all help, too.

- Hiring a professional behaviorist can be invaluable, especially when your dog has developed anxiety or fear about something specific.

- Many people swear by the ThunderShirt, which is a gentle compression vest for dogs. Like a swaddle or a big hug, the gentle pressure of the shirt makes a dog feel safe.

DEALING WITH JEALOUSY

Just as with humans, jealousy can stem from a variety of different causes in dogs. Your pup might be mourning for the attention he used to get before you got a cat (who now dares to sit in *his* spot on the couch), or he may be so possessive of you that seeing you snuggle with your new boyfriend feels like a personal affront. Whatever the cause, dogs can feel displaced and anxious as a result of insecurities. In extreme cases, envy can manifest as physical behavioral problems such as biting, growling, or jumping on you to an uncomfortable degree. Jealousy can resolve on its own, but more often than not you need to tackle it head-on, so it's important to look at the causes first.

If an animal newcomer is the culprit, give your dog time and space to adjust, combined with individual attention and lots of love so that he doesn't feel left out. If a new baby is the cause, it may help to try to include your pet as much as possible, rather than shutting him out. Your dog may like to come to the nursery and lie on a special blanket while you feed or change your newborn, for example. Some people even swear by giving their dogs a piece of clothing that smells like the baby so they'll start to feel bonded to and protective of the new child. When the baby goes to

bed, make that your special time with your dog. Snuggle with him on the couch or give him a special treat that will make him feel loved. Above all, remember that your pup was your first baby—and remind him of that!

Author and veterinarian Cheryl Schwartz says that dogs can feel our emotions and take them on, and I couldn't agree more. Think back on all the happy times you've had. If your dog was with you, he was likely happy, too. In her fabulous book *Natural Healing for Dogs and Cats A–Z,* Schwartz says that jealousy can stem from anger. If we "come from a place of compassion and understanding," recognizing the complex emotions our dogs are feeling, we might alter the negative bond the dog feels due to being pushed aside for another creature.

In combination with lots of love, flower essences can also be incredibly useful for turning a jealous or envious, emotional dog into the happy ball of fur and fun you used to know. Here are some of the best choices.

- **Chicory:** primarily for possessiveness
- **Holly:** combats jealous emotions that stem from anger
- **Mimulus:** helps with jealousy that arises out of fear
- **Vine:** assists with inflexibility in new situations
- **Walnut:** helps with the acceptance of new things

Flower essences typically come in small glass bottles. Never try to give your dog drops directly from the glass dropper in case the dropper breaks or gets bitten. Instead, add the drops directly to his meals, into his bowl of drinking water, or mixed with a little water in a spray bottle, which you can then use to mist either your dog or his environment. You can also use your fingers to apply flower essences directly to acupressure points on his body, such as on the top of his head, inside his ears, or on his gums.

DEALING WITH A SHY OR RECLUSIVE DOG

Those of us with dogs who'll jump with rambunctious joy on anyone who comes over—from the pizza delivery man to an aging great aunt—might long for a dog who's introverted at least *some* of the time. But others worry that their dog just isn't as friendly as he should be.

Some dogs just naturally have a rather shy temperament, while others become reclusive because of life events or insufficient socialization while they're young. My Rhodesian Ridgebacks are incredibly loyal to me, but characteristically for the breed, they're quite withdrawn when they meet new people and even have a "take it or leave it" attitude with many of our friends. I don't mind this too much, but some dogs take shyness to the extreme and end up being quite socially awkward.

Some pups are so aloof that they struggle to bond with their guardians. You might meet one of these people and understand immediately why his dog is second-guessing the attributes of his home life, but for situations where it's *really* the dog that's at issue, there are a few things that can be done to help his social life at the dog park.

First and foremost, take things slowly. Gradual desensitization to stressful situations is key; immersion isn't usually a successful strategy when it comes to dogs. Rather than marching straight to the local coffee shop with your nervous pup in tow, consider just walking by to begin with, so she can observe from a distance. Similarly, a few daily strolls past the dog park before venturing in might help to offset social anxiety and allow your dog to weigh up what's going on and get a read on the energy of the place.

Always choose your park time wisely. When you do enter the dog park, pick a quiet time when only one or two other pups are present. The fewer dogs that are there, the less nervous your shy dog will be. Better yet, try to find a puppy playmate that your dog can bond with at home, to help build up his confidence, and then see if your pup's friend can accompany you on your first few excursions.

Finally, making your own homemade dog treats is an *excellent* way to purchase your dog's affection and build up his trust in you. And don't feel guilty about it! As long as the treat is healthy, you're doing nothing wrong. Homemade treats tend to taste much nicer than the poor-quality commercial options that some brands put out, and they'll automatically be infused with your love and positive intention, so they can really help in your quest to command attention and woo even the most withdrawn and socially awkward animals.

EATING POOP (OR WHEN THINGS BECOME *REALLY* STRANGE)

The technical name is *coprophagia,* and it's a hideously disturbing thing to witness. But disgusting as it sounds to us humans, many animal species indulge in the questionable pastime of eating their own (or someone else's) poop. Strangely, the general consensus is that it isn't always something to fret about—at least as far as our animal companions' own health is concerned.

To our pets, feces consumption isn't too different from any other sort of scavenging that's part of their natural hardwired instinct, and it's no more problematic than grazing on a bit of fresh spring grass. Some experts contend that consumption of dung from herbivores such as cows, horses, and sheep may actually be beneficial for dogs, providing a rich source of good bacteria and other nutrients. The risk, of course, is that they'll consume medications or chemical dewormers with which these herbivores were treated, or that they'll contract intestinal parasites as a result of eating worm-laden dung. So if you're fine with your dog diving headfirst

OMEGA BARS

These delicious and incredibly healthy bars are so easy to make. Watch your shy dog come running when he smells them baking! *Makes 12 to 18 bars, depending on size*

1 cup Zeal dehydrated dog food

1 cup warm water

4 ounces salmon (cooked fillet or good-quality canned fish, such as Wild Planet brand)

4 ounces canned sardines

½ cup ground flaxseed

2 free-range eggs, beaten

1. Preheat the oven to 350°F. Using a paper towel, lightly coat the bottom and sides of a 9" x 9" baking dish with safflower oil.

2. In a large glass bowl, hydrate the Zeal with the warm water. Add the salmon, sardines, flaxseed, and eggs. Gently stir until thoroughly combined.

3. Transfer the mixture to the baking dish and flatten it using a large spoon or spatula. Bake for 30 minutes, or until it's slightly crispy on top. Cool completely. Use a sharp knife to slice into individual bars sized appropriately for your dog. These bars can be frozen or stored in an airtight container in the refrigerator for up to 3 days.

into a bit of horse poop, just know the risks—and watch for signs of any gastrointestinal distress afterward.

Of course, most of us don't want an animal to eat his own poop (or anyone else's, for that matter), and those of us with small children certainly don't want them to be kissed by a dog who's consumed feces of any kind. From a holistic perspective, there are some things that can be done to manage and prevent the problem, and I've described those below. First and foremost, though, you should rule out a medical condition such as exocrine pancreatic insufficiency (EPI), which might be causing the poop eating. If your dog's health checks out just fine, it's likely behavioral—for example, a learned habit from watching someone else do it—or the result of his diet.

The Nutritional Element

Nutritional factors may play a role in the incidence of coprophagia, and many experts agree that animals on a poor-quality diet may be more susceptible to picking up the poop-eating hobby. In many cases, transitioning to a fresh, whole-food diet with lots of raw or minimally processed ingredients will help to ameliorate the problem. Food sensitivities and malabsorption issues can also be factors, so if you suspect those, try the elimination diet I described in Chapter 5.

Supplementation with minerals in the form of kelp, spirulina, or other high-nutrient foods is recommended no matter what. To add digestive enzymes or probiotics, which improve the absorption and assimilation of nutrients, try Animal Essentials Plant Enzymes and Probiotics or our Pro Bloom instant goat's milk. Several

companies now make supplements specifically designed to discourage dogs from eating their own feces, too. A couple of notable examples are For-Bid and an aptly named supplement called Stop Eating Poop (S.E.P.) made by Solid Gold Health Products for Pets. These products cause the feces to take on a foul taste, which deters dogs from consuming it.

Finally, instead of giving your dog one or two larger meals, you could try giving him more frequent, smaller meals throughout the day. He'll be so happy he's eating so often that he might imagine he's full and won't be tempted to snack.

Behavioral Issues

You cringe remembering the day your child came home from kindergarten and proudly announced the four-letter word she'd just learned from a new friend. Dogs aren't much different. They may witness another hound at the dog park happily munching on a bit of poo and think, *If he can do it, why can't I?* Coprophagia also seems to be more common in dogs who live with cats. At first they can't resist the high-protein delicacies in the litter box, and when they grow tired of getting litter in their beards, they move on to other types of feces and broaden their poop-eating palates.

In other instances, stool eating can be an attempt to alleviate boredom, loneliness, or anxiety that results from being left alone or some other stressful situation. Some dogs might self-comfort by having a nibble on the leg of one of your chairs, but others, sadly, choose to eat poop. If you suspect that's the case with your dog, leave him with an interactive treat toy or a meaty bone while you're out, and see if that helps.

Management

Whatever the cause of your dog's nasty habit, a multipronged approach is more likely to yield success than focusing on one factor alone. Here's what I suggest.

- **Clean up your house and yard.** This is absolutely essential. When it comes to dogs, out of sight usually means out of mind, so remove any temptation in the form of stray poops from your lawn and flower borders. Try to be proactive and scoop the poop the moment it appears, putting it in a secured trash can or other receptacle right away. You should also hide your cat's litter box so your dog isn't tempted to dive in, but be sure to show the cat where you've put it so you don't end up with more ugly surprises.

- **Use a leash.** If you're not already using one, try using a leash to prevent access to or contact with feces while you're on a walk or out in the yard.

- **Teach "Leave it."** Teach your dog the command "Leave it!" To do this, start him on a leash and reward him with a well-timed click, a few treats, and lots of praise each time you successfully call him away from feces. Don't reward him for coming away *after* he eats poop; the treat should only come for successfully

OWNERS SPEAK!

10 Dogs Whose Personality Quirks Are Beyond the Pale

In some cases, there's no amount of management, training, or therapy that's going to fix an emotional issue. So just sit back, laugh, and learn to love these crazy dogs!

"We bought a new bed, and our 55-pound dog couldn't climb into it. She can jump onto the couch, into the car, and onto our *old* bed, but for some reason, not our new bed. So now she has a dog ramp."
—Kelsey Rae Thiessen

"Maya likes to sit, look outside, and lick the windows." —Dawniel Dudash Testa

"If you scold Colt, my 6-month-old King Shepherd X Bouvier, he throws himself on the floor and cries." —Hilda Wall

"I thought it would be fun to teach my dog, Lewdo, to 'drive.' Now he hops over into my seat, puts his paws on the wheel, and won't budge." —Julie Keelman

"My 15-year-old Italian Greyhound, Bells, hates rugs. The minute we put one in the bathroom or near the front door, she pees on it." —Brandi Lampman

"At 6:15 every morning, the pool pump turns on. When Tucker hears the sound of it, he goes completely insane until someone lets him out. He then runs laps around the pool while growling at the bubbles that the pump puts out."
—Christine Drews

"My 6-month-old dog, Chase, surprised me this morning by unzipping himself out of his pen, jumping on the sofa with his Kong, and turning on the TV to watch the news." —Jeff Tathwell

"Ritz is cold all the time, and he won't lie down unless you cover him up or tuck him in. Yet when you open the freezer, he runs to get an ice cube every time."
—Fred Jlynnn Denny

"My 14-year-old dog, Tommy, likes to steal dollar bills and hide them in his cage. The last time I cleaned it out, I found $11!"
—Tricia S.

"My sweet Pug boy, Buddy D, is a major pain in the neck when it comes to TV watching. Like any normal dog, our other Pug, Elvis, will bark if a dog barks on TV. But Buddy D is different. He really and truly watches TV, and he attacks when any animal appears on screen. He dislikes blonde women on TV, and we cannot watch *Wheel of Fortune* at all. Everything about the Wheel causes him to go berserk—the sounds and, of course, Vanna." —Christine Ashley Page avoiding the undesirable behavior. Other commands, such as "Stop!" or "Look at me!" can also be taught and used to interrupt the activity, hopefully before it actually begins.

- **Try additives.** Some pet owners say they've had success after they applied hot sauce or chili powder to stools out on the lawn, but I've found that given the time it takes to apply these seasonings (not to mention the slightly odd glances you might receive from neighbors), it's more efficient to actually pick up and remove the poop instead.

AGGRESSION (OR WHEN YOUR 10-POUND DOG HAS A NAPOLEON COMPLEX)

All too often, we see dogs who more closely resemble powder puffs than canines lunging at dogs large enough to crush them with one paw. You may wonder, *Who does this tiny terror think he is?* While it may seem funny or cute to think of a Chihuahua nipping at the heels of a Husky, in general, dog aggression is a red flag, and it has to be dealt with quickly.

Aggressive dog behavior can take many forms: growling, snapping, barking, lunging, or, at its most extreme, biting. A dog who's exhibiting these behaviors is trying to tell you that he's deeply uncomfortable with the situation he's in, and it could stem from any number of causes or be influenced by a variety of factors. Let's look at some.

Fear

I don't mean the slightly neurotic alarm he feels when he hears his collar clang against his food bowl. I'm talking about a fear of being harmed. The dog who lunges at a cat often genuinely believes that the cat is about to scratch him (unless, of course, said cat bears an uncanny resemblance to a squirrel, in which case there may be other motives at play).

Possessiveness

When your dog growls as you approach his bed, he may be trying to guard the chew toy he has nestled in his paws. Or a dog may bristle and snarl when someone gets close to you on a walk, trying to tell the other person that *you* belong to *him*.

Territorial Aggression

Most of us know that dogs are territorial. They love their beds; they love their couches (mind you, I said "their" couches, not yours); and they love their backyards, where they spend many sunny afternoons. But a dog may believe that every tree he pees on is his, and he may mark the entire perimeter of your house with urine to delineate his personal kingdom. If another dog crosses the line, it's viewed as an invasion, and aggression ensues.

Redirected Aggression

Because it often involves two dogs who are best friends suddenly turning on each other, this kind of behavior is frequently met with head scratching by dog owners. For example, your dogs may hear the mailman come to the door, and unable to reach him from their crates, they may begin to fight with each other in frustration.

I always advise seeking out a professional trainer to help unravel the root cause of the aggression and find a long-term solution. In addition, consider the following:

- **See a vet.** He or she will make sure there are no underlying medical conditions contributing to the situation. If your dog's not feeling well, he might act aggressively, even if it's completely involuntary.

- **Buy a muzzle.** If your dog is lunging or biting at dogs or people, yet you have to take him out in public, use a muzzle to signal to others that you have him under control.

- **Spay or neuter your dog.** Studies show that dogs who haven't been spayed or neutered are more aggressive.

- **Remove the temptation.** If your dog is possessive of a chew toy to the point of lunacy, take away the toy. Feel free to replace it with something that makes him a little less bonkers, like a healthy treat.

- **Crate him.** Often crating or confining your dog to a "safe" space will distract him from whatever is enraging him. As a bonus, you'll be ensuring others' protection.

TURKEY CHERRY KEEN BUNS

When your aggressive dog is finally cool, calm, and collected again, how can you reward him? Try these tasty treats, which contain calming turkey in case he still has a little spunk left in him. *Makes 12 buns*

1½ cups Keen dog food

1½ cups warm water

1 free-range egg, beaten

4 slices cooked turkey meat, torn up into small pieces

¼ cup grated Cheddar cheese

¼ cup dried pitted cherries, plus 12 extra for decorating

½ cup mascarpone or cream cheese

1. Preheat the oven to 350°F. Place paper liners in a 12-cup muffin pan.

2. In a large glass bowl, hydrate the Keen with the warm water. Add the egg and stir to combine. Add the turkey, cheese, and cherries, and mix together.

3. Divide the mixture among the muffin cups and bake for 35 to 40 minutes, or until the tops of the buns are slightly crispy.

4. While the buns are still warm, spread on the mascarpone or cream cheese as frosting. Place a dried cherry on top of each bun. Cool before serving. The buns will keep in the refrigerator for up to 3 days.

Chapter 9

HOLIDAYS, PLANE TRIPS, AND MORE

THE JET-SETTING LIFE OF THE DOG OBSESSED

Many people dream of a social life full of exotic vacations; lavish dinner parties at friends' houses; and carefree, happy times spent in the great outdoors. The Dog Obsessed are no exception—save for the fact that we really only want to do these things if we can do them with our dogs. It's not that we don't love human company—we just can't imagine how *anything* could be fun if our canine companions are left home alone.

We take our dogs camping and have probably invested in at least one extra man's worth of tent space to accommodate our pups; we can't stand the idea of going to a family reunion without our dogs at our sides (who else are we going to snuggle up and chat with when the going gets tough?); and we even trek thousands of miles across the country—and sometimes even around the world—with them in tow. But how do we explain ourselves to those who might look at us quizzically when we talk about teaching our pups campfire etiquette? And just how does one pick a hotel that's good enough for her pup? Being Dog Obsessed doesn't mean you're forced to stay at home, and this chapter will help you navigate the many social opportunities you may seek out with your pup.

THE RULES OF BEING A GOOD HOUSEGUEST

Most of us love taking our pups to visit friends and family. We adore our dogs, and we adore our friends, so in an ideal world, having them all together should feel like we're one big, happy family. But sometimes you'll find yourself in a house that's not quite as pet friendly as your own. Just what do you do? If you're me, you try your best to make sure your pet doesn't make a nuisance of himself—unless your goal is actually *not* to be invited back, which might be the case if you're visiting certain relatives.

There are a few rules I always follow when I visit others with my dogs. These mandates are easy and sensible, and they won't inconvenience your dog in the slightest. Your host will likely thank you for being so considerate, and as an added bonus, he may just thank your dog, too—and even make the effort to furnish him with a nice treat or special meal while he's there.

Rule #1: Respect the Couch

While some of us think it's amusing (and quite justified) to make houseguests sit on the floor while a dog stretches out on the sofa, many people don't appreciate being prohibited from sitting on their *own* furniture, especially when the reason they can't sit there is your dog. Even if there's room for everyone, try to respect the fact that some hosts may find dogs on the couch uncivilized. Unlike you, they may not possess a special vacuum for removing pet hair, and they may find that using rolls of tape to remove fluff and dander is too much of a chore. I highly recommend bringing along your dog's own bed and situating it close by, so your dog doesn't feel left out. If being relegated to his dog bed is going to be too upsetting, and your host is open-minded, a clean blanket laid on the sofa, with the dog placed directly on top of that, might be the perfect compromise.

Rule #2: Honor the Kitchen

It's also important not to take up too much space in the kitchen. Many of us feed our pups raw or home-prepared meals, and while this is a great way to make sure your dog is getting the best kind of nutrition, it can be cumbersome to lug an entire cooler full of meat to someone's apartment and presumptuous to expect them to make room in their fridge. Be considerate by buying small quantities of ingredients a day or so ahead of time, or consider packing a dehydrated or freeze-dried food that's more compact, but still made from minimally processed whole food ingredients.

Rule #3: Bring Appropriate Gifts

If your host has an allergy to pet dander, a nicely wrapped box of Benadryl can make a thoughtful and functional hostess gift. The gel cap format seems to work more rapidly than the conventional caplets. Just don't wrap them in a Tiffany Blue Box and tie it up with a lovely white bow because if you do, opening this gift can be slightly anticlimactic for the recipient.

Rule #4: Watch Out for Accidents

Set up pee pads in discreet, tucked-away areas—somewhere your pet can find but that's relatively free of foot traffic. If an accident does happen, be sure to clean it up promptly and thoroughly, even if you've had a late night. Trust me, there's no ruder awakening for a host than cleaning poop from between her toes before she's even put the coffee on.

Rule #5: Go with the Flow

Being a good houseguest requires flexibility. While your dog will likely need a routine—exercise and trips to the bathroom—refrain from dictating the schedules of others to suit your dog. Some people can become resentful if some of their plans have to be abandoned, especially if you cancel dinner reservations because your dog needs a snack or a cuddle at 9:00 p.m.

Rule #6: Tire Out Your Dog

A good romp in the woods, run on the beach, or other vigorous exercise can really tucker out your dog, helping him feel calm in otherwise strange surroundings or during disrupted routines. A happy, tired dog is more relaxed, so he's less likely to cause stress-related destruction of your host's possessions or furnishings. A good whizz around in the fresh air (especially if there's a blustery wind blowing, which allows you to do a bit of yelling at no one in particular) can also help *you* to unwind from houseguest-related stressors.

Rule #7: Crate If You Can

If your dog's crate trained and your host has the space, consider taking a crate with you to make sure your dog stays out of trouble when you aren't able to supervise. A juicy, raw marrow bone or an interactive treat toy like a Kong can keep him occupied while he's confined, too. A flexible canvas travel crate is an excellent investment if you travel frequently or only need the crate on occasion. These are easy to store because they can fold away under a bed when you're not using them. They're much better suited to dogs who aren't destructive chewers, though; without proper supervision, enthusiastic chewers can quite easily nibble their way out through the canvas and run riot in your guest accommodations.

Rule #8: Survey the Perimeter

If it's your first time visiting a new house with your dog and you're planning to let him go leash-free outside, make sure there aren't any holes in the fenced-in backyard. Not only is chasing after a runaway dog terribly stressful, but few things are worse than breaking up a family reunion so you can all canvas the neighborhood.

Rule #9: Make Time to Rest

Exercise is excellent, of course, but overstimulation while you're at someone else's house can be a real bother, especially for younger pets who are easily jazzed up. If your pup tends to get "wired tired" and excessively amped up due to all the comings and goings of traveling, try to spend some quiet time together to get some much-needed R & R. A gentle walk in the fresh air followed by a snooze on the couch might

The Dog Obsessed Aren't Surprised to Hear That . . .

As if we need further proof that our dogs love to be with us at all times, a recent neuroimaging study conducted by scientists at Emory University showed that, when presented with a variety of smells, a dog favors his owner's scent above all others. And not only that, but his brain lights up, with neurons firing like lights on a pinball machine, when he smells it. What does that tell you? If you want a happy dog, take him everywhere!

MEATLESS HOLIDAY CUPCAKES

My friend Megan and I try to make sure we always have enough raw beef marrow bones for everyone to have one (plus a couple of spares) when we bring our multiple dogs to one another's houses for Thanksgiving, Christmas, or summertime barbecues. You might also consider bringing along these delicious cupcakes, which will make the holidays extra special for your pup and his friends. *Makes 12 cupcakes*

¼ cup Pro Bloom instant goat's milk

1 cup instant quinoa flakes

½ cup ground flaxseed meal

2 tablespoons dried cranberries, plus additional for decorating

1 can (15 ounces) unsweetened pumpkin (not pie mix)

2 free-range eggs

3 tablespoons honey

½ cup cream cheese (optional)

1. Preheat the oven to 350°F. Place paper liners in a 12-cup muffin pan.

2. In a medium bowl, combine the Pro Bloom, quinoa flakes, flaxseed meal, and cranberries.

3. In a separate bowl, combine the pumpkin, eggs, and honey. Stir thoroughly to combine. One cupful at a time, add the quinoa mixture to the pumpkin mixture, stirring after each addition.

4. Divide the mixture among the paper liners. Bake for 25 to 35 minutes, or until a wooden pick inserted into the center of a cupcake comes out clean. Allow to cool for 10 minutes before removing the cupcakes from the pan.

5. Use a knife to spread a small amount of cream cheese (if using) on the top of each cupcake, and decorate each with a couple of cranberries.

be just what's needed to get his behavior back on track—and avoid disrupting your host's routine.

With a little forethought and planning, it can be a pleasure to visit others with your animal companion. But if for some reason staying with them just won't work out, check out pet-friendly hotels at www.fidofriendly.com/travel-map, invite friends and family to come and stay with you, or invest in a pet sitter or stay at a boarding facility.

BON VOYAGE! TAKING A ROAD TRIP WITH YOUR DOG

Going on a road trip with your dog can be pure pleasure if you plan everything well. Dogs are terrific companions and can encourage you to go places and see things you wouldn't normally (a brisk hike off the beaten path to get a little exercise, perhaps?), and being in the car with them helps to alleviate some of the boredom that comes with too many miles spent on the road. So if you're going on a trip by car and want to take your pup with you, start by securing the must-have items listed on page 29. After that, there are a few things you can do to make sure that everything runs smoothly

and everyone has a fun, safe time.

Before you set off, avoid dehydration and urinary tract problems by making sure your dog gets a good run and a chance to relieve himself and then taking plenty of fresh, clean drinking water with you. Don't forget a bowl! If you're a careful driver, you can set up a bowl near your dog, or you can fill it up when you stop for regular potty breaks.

Head off travel sickness by being strategic about what you feed your dog both before you leave and during your trip. Smaller, more frequent meals can lessen the risk of travel sickness, and some pets even do better by fasting entirely. Adding a small amount of dried ginger or ginger tea to a light meal before you depart can also be beneficial for pets who are prone to car sickness.

Once you're on the road, be sure your pet wears his identity tags at all times. If the tags are printed with your home phone number, consider taping over that with your cell number or a number for the hotel or home where you'll be staying. Being in a strange place can make pets anxious and more apt to bolt—and less likely to find their way back to you—so it's essential that you can be reached at all times, anywhere.

Keeping a dog safe in the car is a huge concern for many owners—and with good reason. Far too many dogs are injured or killed every year in car accidents, even minor ones. While there's quite a bit of contradictory data concerning the adequacy of canine car restraints and seat belts, it's probably better to err on the side of safety and use one. New sights and sounds can make a dog extra excited and thus more likely to leap around in the car, which can be a distraction for the driver. Worse, if a big dog isn't properly restrained within a vehicle, he can fly through the windshield on impact or kill a person in the car if the force of a crash throws him at them.

Along the same lines, while it might be fun to see a dog's big grin or windswept face as he hangs out of an open car window, it's simply unintelligent and downright dangerous to allow dogs to ride this way. Dogs who lean out of car windows or ride uncrated in pickup trucks are at a dramatically increased risk of eye injuries from flying debris and can also actually fall out of moving vehicles, with horrific consequences. Unfortunately, I know this because I've seen it happen. A few years ago, I was walking with my dog for an evening play in the park. Another driver, who happened to be heading there herself, was allowing her dog to hang out of the window. As they passed us on a bend in the road, the forces of physics caused the large Labrador to literally fly out of the open window. He was wearing his leash, the handle

Top Five Reasons Why Traveling with a Dog May Be More Fun Than Traveling with a Human

1. A dog will never ask, "Are we there yet?"

2. He stops to pee when you stop to pee.

3. You never fight over what music to listen to.

4. In theory, he *should* require less luggage.

5. You can confuse other drivers by holding animated conversations with your dog.

of which became hooked around the seat belt buckle. The result? The 80-pound dog was left dangling by his neck from the window of a moving car. The driver slammed on the brakes, and after sprinting toward the car, I lifted her dog to create some slack in the leash, allowing her to untangle it from the seat belt. After I lowered the grateful dog to the ground, he got back in the car and off they went—unharmed, thankfully, but things could have been much worse.

While it's up for debate whether or not a leash was a good thing for this Labrador and his owner, I always have my dogs wear their leashes in the car. Why? Because if I were to have an accident, I'd like rescue crews to be able to safely remove my dogs from the car, which would be more difficult if they were trapped or cowering inside a crumpled vehicle in only their collars. Wearing a leash reduces a dog's likelihood of running away because he can more easily be grabbed while he's still inside the vehicle, and that improves his chances of being taken to safety.

Finally, a word about pickup trucks. While flatbeds aren't ideally suited to dogs at all, a crate is really the only way to make the journey remotely safe, as it prevents a dog from being thrown around the back of the truck, or worse, jumping or being tossed out. Ideally, a dog should always ride in the backseat of a car, as it prevents him from distracting the driver, but that's not an option in most pickups. If it isn't, consider crating him or letting him ride restrained in the front seat.

FLYING WITH FIDO

Flying with your dog is a bit trickier than taking a road trip. Think you don't like the lack of legroom and the stale air on most airplanes? Just think how your dog feels! Seriously, we all wish that air travel with our beloved pets was a bit easier, but the truth is that, especially if you have a larger pup, it's not. Flying with a dog involves checking into numerous rules and regulations, paying fees, hoping that your dog doesn't bark on the flight, and, above all, making sure he's happy and well taken care of from taxi and takeoff to landing. Many of us who are Dog Obsessed decide that it's just too much trouble to fly and opt to drive instead—or we leave our beloved pets at home. But if that's not an option or you're *determined* to get on a plane, it's certainly far from impossible. And, assuming he's riding with you in the cabin, you may be pleasantly surprised to find that your dog actually enjoys the flight!

First, check with the airline *far* in advance to learn what their pet policy is. Each airline is different, so never assume that one trip will be the same as the last you took. Most of them charge fees ranging from next to nothing to $500, so you'll have to decide what you're willing to pay, and then compare airlines from there. In addition, most airlines limit the number of pets on a flight, so you'll need to book in advance to guarantee that you can get your dog on board.

One huge consideration is just where your pet will sit. You may assume that you can just pay for an extra seat, but unfortunately, every passenger needs to be strapped in with a seat belt—and airlines won't allow you to use a canine seat belt, no matter how much you beg. Some airlines only allow pets to fly in cargo in a crate (that's where your bags are, under you, in the dark), while others permit a pet to be your carry-on if and only if they're in a soft travel carrier.

On a side note, in order to take their pups with them in the cabin, some people have been known to slightly bend or otherwise leverage existing service dog or emotional support animal rules with paperwork obtained online and faux service vests. It's not my place to judge, and their motivations for doing this are clear, but I do wish at least one airline would step out from the crowd and find a way to accommodate bigger dogs in the cabin so people didn't have to resort to this.

How you want to transport your dog is up to you, but I personally would *never* advocate letting a dog fly with the cargo, unless the need to get them from point A to point B in a hurry is a life-or-death emergency or there's simply no other option (for example, if you've been posted abroad with your job). It's dark, cold, and lonely down there, and I can't imagine any pet who'd want to spend hours in such an isolated place. Unfortunately, that means that most large dogs—who can't fit under the seat in front of you—will have to stay home. But if you're like me, you have a wonderful support network who'll love and care for him while you're away.

If you've decided to fly with your dog, make sure his vaccinations are up to date, and then obtain a health certificate from your veterinarian dated at most 10 days before you're traveling. Not all airlines require this, but some do, and it's almost guaranteed to be needed if you're flying internationally. Speaking of which, if you're flying outside of the United States, you must check your destination country's laws regarding incoming pets.

Some countries require dogs to be quarantined for weeks, and that's the last thing you want to discover when you land.

Let's assume you have a travel-size/carry-on dog, you've made it through all the paperwork and other paraphernalia, and you're finally on the plane, with him comfortably positioned under the seat in front of you for the next 3 hours. Just how can you keep him entertained? Unfortunately, most airlines won't let you take out your dog during your flight, so don't expect to have him on your lap watching movies. However, I've witnessed several passengers completely ignore this rule during my many miles of business travel over the years. One included an absolutely adorable older lady who let her even more adorable Lhasa Apso sit on *my* lap for the flight once we'd got to chatting and he took a shine to me! The three of us managed to remain undiscovered all the way to San Diego.

I generally advise against giving your dog a sedative for the flight—sedatives can cause respiratory problems during the pressure and altitude changes that occur in the air. Just do what you always do in boring or stressful situations: Give your dog chew toys, healthy snacks, and comforting reminders of home (blankets or toys) so the flight will pass quickly. Also, be sure your dog visits the bathroom and has plenty of exercise before boarding so that he'll be as comfortable as possible. The last thing you want is a pup who has to fly with his legs crossed, or worse, a dog who has an accident at 20,000 feet. (There's almost no air circulation in a plane, so any unsavory smell will travel as many miles as you do.) If you're still worried about his ability to hold it in and fear he may pee his pants in midair, there are doggie diapers available in most pet stores or online.

Bone voyage!

HOW TO SETTLE ON AND INTO A PET-FRIENDLY HOTEL

You've arrived at that beachfront hotel you've been dreaming of for the past 500 miles. With visions of sitting in a lounge chair, rum punch in hand, while your dog reclines on the sand under the shade of a parasol next to you, you're shocked when the hotel tries to turn you away, citing your dog as the reason. You *thought* you'd checked everything out weeks in advance, but clearly, something got lost in translation. What went wrong?

The pet policies of some hotels are confusing at best, baffling at worst. But you can prevent any misunderstandings or last-minute vacation catastrophes by making sure you follow the checklist below, which covers all the odds and ends of staying in a pet-friendly hotel.

☐ **Call ahead to remind them.** Check all of the hotel's regulations (such as the size of dog permitted and their requirements for kennels) online *and* over the phone. It might sound unnecessary, but many establishments that promote themselves as "pet friendly" have pretty stringent size restrictions, surcharges for larger pets, pet cleaning fees, and regulations about whether or not you can leave your pet unattended in your room. Some hotels have only a few rooms reserved for people with pets, so when those are full, there won't be space for your pup. If you reserve online, a glitch in the system or human error may lead to your dog's reservation being lost, so it's always best to follow up and talk to a human being to remind them that you're coming with your dog.

☐ **Understand the leash laws.** Most pet-friendly hotels have areas where you can exercise your dog, but to avoid getting told off or kicked out, it's important to make sure you only go leash free in designated areas. Many pets are fine with leashes, but others can become quite frantic when they encounter all the wonderful sights and sounds of the great outdoors, but aren't allowed to have a good run wherever they please.

☐ **Check IDs.** As with road trips, make sure your dog's identification tag is securely attached and that all contact information is up to date. If your home phone number is listed on the tag, consider getting a travel tag that lists your cell number. If your pet goes missing and is located by a passerby or another hotel guest, he could still end up in the shelter if no one can get you on the phone.

☐ **Be sure to pack his bowls and bed.** For your dog's comfort, bring his food and water bowls, blanket or bedding, and any favorite toy that will comfort him and make him feel at home. Rescue Remedy is great to take along, too. A few drops in his drinking water or even behind his ears can help to calm nerves that are frazzled after traveling.

☐ **Think of your neighbors.** Bring a large rug or blanket and some beef marrow bones or other long-lasting chew treats to help keep your pup occupied if you have to leave him unattended in the room. Even pets who don't usually suffer from separation anxiety can become unnerved in unfamiliar surroundings, and a treat that will last a while will prevent him from howling until you return.

A couple of pet-friendly hotel chains of note are Kimpton (www.kimptonhotels.com), which proudly advertises that if your pet fits through the door, they'll welcome him in with a no-fuss check-in, and Provenance Hotels (www.provenancehotels.com), a smaller upscale boutique chain with properties in several states offering pet-friendly accommodations, a pet amenity kit, pet beds, and bowls in the room.

CAMPING WITH YOUR PUP

There are hundreds of great dog-friendly vacations to choose from. From New York City, which recently mandated that dogs are always allowed to dine at outdoor restaurants with their owners, to wineries and craft breweries, many of which love to have dogs in their tasting rooms, more and more people are finding that dog-unfriendly vacation spots aren't necessarily the norm. But many Dog-Obsessed travelers like me just love camping! Hiking with your dog is terrific exercise, and many campgrounds welcome pets with open arms. And if you choose to rough it by sleeping off the trail, having your dog in the tent can really ease your fears about unwanted visitors, such as bears or raccoons. In Chapter 2, I provided a full list of the odds and ends you might want to bring on a camping trip, but the following 10 tips should also help you plan before you pack your backpack.

1. **Call ahead to be sure you won't be turned away when you arrive.** You'll also want to check all regulations, such as any size limits on permitted dogs and requirements for containment or leash restraints. It might sound unnecessary, but many campgrounds that are listed as pet-friendly actually have pretty stringent restrictions about where your dog can go within the campground and on the surrounding trails. Some campgrounds actually go above and beyond to make sure your pup has a fabulous time on the trip—but regulations still apply.

2. **Obey the rangers.** Most national parks allow dogs at campgrounds but require that they are tethered or on a leash at all times. Some pets are fine with this, and the squirrels certainly appreciate it, but many dogs can become quite frantic at all the wonderful sights and sounds of the great outdoors. It can create a stressful situation for everyone if your dog struggles to settle down and can't have a good run to blow away the excess energy. Keep in mind that in many areas, dogs are not allowed on hiking trails at all—even if they're leashed!

3. **Decide ahead of time where your dog is going to sleep.** Most of us love to snuggle with our pups inside a cozy tent, but some dogs are bed hogs and ruin a good night's sleep by gradually pushing you out of your own sleeping spot. It's quite uncomfortable to wake up with your face pressed against the side of a tent. Other dogs are happier sleeping under the stars and get a bit panicky when zipped inside a rustling cocoon of canvas. It's worth having a practice run at home to see what sleeping arrangements are going to work best and to get your dog used to the idea if he hasn't been camping before.

4. **Set up your campsite to be as pet friendly as possible.** A shady spot for your dog's bed (consider a specially designed camping dog bed that's resistant to wear and tear) that's far enough away from food supplies and dangerous camp stoves is a must. A long-line leash with convenient attachments such as carabiner clips is great for giving your dog a little freedom while he's secured, if your chosen campsite is strict about dogs being leashed at all times (which many are). For a little extra security, consider attaching it to a harness rather than a collar, especially if your pup is prone to the

Travel First Aid

I keep a homeopathic first aid kit on hand for travel. It contains just three simple remedies that all conveniently begin with the letter A, but cover all the basics! Apis (taken as dissolvable pellets) is fantastic for bites and stings; arnica (available as a cream) is ideal for bumps and bruises, as well as any muscle soreness from overexertion; and arsenicum (taken as pellets) is my go-to for gastrointestinal upset.

pursuit of squirrels. For more skittish dogs or those who feel that being tied up is beneath them, consider bringing a crate to safely confine them in the camp. Make sure you're comfortable, too; a great chair and comfy bed can make a world of difference to your own camping experience!

5. **Be sure to observe proper outdoors etiquette when meeting other dogs.** Your dog may or may not be accustomed to meeting new dogs; even if he is friendly and calm, be aware that not all dogs are created equal, and others may be less comfortable in new situations. Don't let your dog bound up to others, especially if they're leashed, and don't allow nose-to-nose greetings unless you're certain that your dog has impeccable manners and you've checked with the other owner to make sure it's okay for the pups to say hello.

6. **Consider the weight of your dog's food when deciding what to pack.** Kibble can be very bulky to travel with, and cans are extremely heavy because you're hauling around a lot of water weight. Consider a more travel-friendly food option, such as freeze-dried or dehydrated foods, both of which are compact and lightweight but provide healthy, high-moisture meals when prepared with warm water. Our Proper Toppers are the perfect meal in the great outdoors; they're complete and balanced, with the added bonus of superfoods for an extra health boost. Dehydrated food can expand to four times its original size and weight when hydrated, so it makes a very satisfying meal for hungry pups who've been busy in the fresh air all day. Some dogs have sensitive tummies, so if you do plan to carry a new kind of food on a camping trip, be sure you've acclimated your dog to it before you leave.

7. **For your dog's comfort, bring along some of his things from home.** It's a good idea to pack his own blanket or bedding and any favorite toy that will comfort him and make him feel at home. Take along an interactive toy or some beef marrow bones (if you have the space and a cold place to store them) to keep him busy during quiet times.

8. **Make sure your dog's identification tag is securely attached and that all contact information is up to date.** If your home phone number is listed on the tag, consider getting a travel tag that lists your cell phone number, or add some securely attached tape with the number of the campground itself if your cell phone will be out of range.

9. **Don't forget supplies to help repel unwanted insects and to soothe any bites or sore paws.** In addition to all the fun and games, being out in the fresh air can make your pooch (and you) more susceptible to some of nature's less pleasant factors, such as rough, hot terrain and mosquitoes.

10. **Take along some pet waste bags, too.** You want to make sure that paw prints are all you leave behind. Poopbags.com makes a great, biodegradable bag that will decompose along with your dog's waste.

HOLIDAY TURKEY AND CRANBERRY MINI MUFFINS

This recipe is fun to make and tastes delicious. It's a real departure from boring old dog treats, and it's perfect for the holidays because it makes use of some delicious seasonal ingredients, such as pumpkin, cranberries, and turkey. As a bonus, it's laden with antioxidants and other important nutrients that support the immune system during times of stress (like the holidays). You'll need a miniature muffin pan for this recipe. Makes 24 mini muffins

½ cup flaxseed meal

½ cup dried or fresh cranberries

¼ cup wheat germ

1 tablespoon kelp powder

1 teaspoon vitamin C powder (optional)

¼ cup canned unsweetened or cooked fresh pumpkin (not pie mix)

2 free-range eggs

¼ cup ground turkey

1 tablespoon olive oil

1 Preheat the oven to 350°F. Generously coat a 24-cup miniature muffin pan with olive oil.

2 In a large bowl, combine the flaxseed meal, cranberries, wheat germ, kelp powder, and vitamin C powder (if using). Stir to thoroughly combine. Add the pumpkin, eggs, turkey, and oil. Stir to form a thick batter.

3 Divide the batter among the cups of the muffin pan. Bake for 25 minutes, or until the muffins are firm to the touch. Cool thoroughly before serving. The muffins can be frozen or stored in an airtight container in the refrigerator for up to a week.

SURVIVING THE HOLIDAYS

For some people, the holidays can be a stress-filled nightmare even under the simplest circumstances, but when you add a pet to the mix, the opportunity for mishaps shoots up tenfold. Suddenly, you're not just worried about whether your Aunt Mary will like the scarf you gave her; you're also terrified that your dog's going to choke on tinsel or that some naughty nephew is going to get in his grill or slip him a piece of dark chocolate. Luckily, there are many ways to prevent the holidays from turning into a disaster.

To start with, if you're planning to have a holiday party at home, make sure your pup is secure and safe when people are coming in or going out. Ask your visitors to respect your dog's likes and dislikes regarding being petted or held, too; this is especially important with children who may not yet have developed good "pet manners."

Be sure that holiday guests understand what foods you do and don't want your pet to be fed by revelers. If he's hanging out with everyone, a "no scraps" rule might be simpler to enforce than trying to train guests on which individual foods are pet-safe.

Danger doesn't just lurk on the table, though. Tinsel and other holiday

decorations, such as glass baubles and dreidels, can be potentially fatal if your dog swallows them. Watch out for candles, greenery, and paper, too. Battery-operated candles (which still need to be kept out of a dog's reach because they, too, can be harmful if chewed) can help to reduce the fire risk. Holiday plants like holly, ivy, mistletoe, and poinsettia are hazardous—and potentially fatal—if consumed, so keep them up high and out of reach. Holiday stress—with all its visitors, disrupted routines, and travel—can sometimes cause a pet to nibble on foliage in an attempt to ease anxiety-related tummy aches. Wrapping paper and ribbons can also be safety concerns. Many dogs love to tear up discarded wrapping paper and leave a shredded mess behind. While this can be fun to watch, be sure that any ribbons or other adornments are removed before he begins, and just keep a close eye on him to make sure he doesn't swallow any paper. If puppies and inquisitive older pets are likely to go wild, make sure they don't have free access to decorations on the tree or around the house.

Speaking of the tree, it's best to slowly introduce your dog to it, and then always watch him like a hawk when he's around it. A dog has no idea that the outdoors can come indoors, and he might feel there's no reason not to use your tree as a urinal. After all, this is what he does in the backyard! I have a friend whose Bernese Mountain Dog—upon seeing the tree for the first time—relieved himself not just on it, but also on all the presents that sat underneath it. Christmas trees are also surprisingly easy to pull right over if they aren't well secured, and if you have electric tree lights, this can end in a terrible tangle for an unsuspecting pet who was just looking for a little fun with the baubles. You might consider using an x-pen to block access to the tree entirely.

Lest I sound like the holidays are an accident waiting to happen, there are also so many fun things you can do with your dog! From getting holiday photos (be sure to make him wear a Santa hat or a pair of reindeer antlers, if he's up for it) to long walks through the snow, don't forget to take the time to reflect on how thankful you are for your pup. His very presence may be the greatest gift you receive this year.

What to Do with Holiday Leftovers

Need you even ask? Feed them to your dog, of course! Just do so in moderation—up to 10 percent of his daily ration is a good guide. These holiday foods are sure to make him feel included in every aspect of your family's celebration. If your dog does overindulge, the homeopathic remedy nux vomica can be helpful, but if you notice any sign of bloating, vomiting, or other digestive problems, including diarrhea or constipation, visit your vet immediately. And on a side note, if you find the holidays to be just entirely too stressful and end up hitting the wine in order to cope, nux vomica is an excellent remedy for hangovers, too.

- **Thanksgiving turkey, holiday ham, or Sunday roast.** He can eat these alone or with his food just as long as you don't give him so much that he'll get a tummy ache. Remember to avoid giving him cooked bones (as they can splinter), and beware of too much fat or gristle, as it can lead to pancreatitis. Try to avoid prepared meats that have added nitrites and preservatives, and whenever you can, choose free-range, natural, and grass-fed meats.

- **Green bean casserole.** Your dog will love the natural sweetness of the beans and creamy sauce, but scrape off the onion topping. Onions are toxic to dogs.

- **Sweet potatoes.** Yummy! These are an excellent source of beta-carotene; just be sure to steam or bake them because it's difficult for dogs to digest them raw. Your dog doesn't need the extra calories from marshmallows, brown sugar, or maple syrup, so avoid casseroles containing these ingredients.

- **Cranberries.** Stay away from canned or homemade cranberry sauces that are full of sugar (you don't want to cause ear infections or some other yeast-related disorder), but fresh or dried cranberries are terrific for dogs who are prone to urinary tract infections.

- **Pumpkin and squash.** These are excellent for a dog's health, and most dogs just love them. Just be sure to serve them unadorned—additives like wine, cream, and onions aren't healthy for dogs.

- **Winter greens.** Chard and kale are great sources of vitamins and antioxidants. Brussels sprouts and cabbage are also loaded with nutrients, but they tend to cause gas. Add them to your dog's food if they're raw, lightly steamed, or sautéed, and avoid additives like salt, wine, soy sauce, and butter.

- **White potatoes.** These contain fiber and are a great source of vitamins B_3, B_6, and C, as well as potassium, iron, and copper. Just cut off the shoots and green parts of potatoes, which can be toxic.

AVOID!

- **Stuffing and corn pudding.** These usually contain onion and sometimes raisins (both toxic to dogs), as well as ingredients like bread and cornmeal, which aren't very nutritious.

- **Desserts and cheeses.** They can cause a sore tummy.

- **Relishes, pickles, and sauces.** They typically contain heavy spices, sugar, onion, and other ingredients than can unsettle a dog's gastrointestinal tract.

- **Onions, chocolate, macadamia nuts, grapes, raisins, and candies containing the sweetener xylitol.** Never forget that these foods are toxic to dogs and cats and should not be offered in the form of leftovers or people-food additions to your dog's usual meals.

HALLOWEEN CHICKEN, PUMPKIN, AND APPLE LOAF

Your dog didn't complain when you dressed him up, and then he faithfully followed you and your kids around the neighborhood while they trick-or-treated. Yet now he's not allowed to eat *any* candy! Make him feel included in the gluttony with this tempting treat.

Makes 1 loaf, 8 to 12 slices

2 cups Force dehydrated dog food

2 cups warm water

½ cup canned unsweetened pumpkin (not pie mix)

1 apple, cored and finely chopped

2 free-range eggs, beaten

½ cup cooked chopped chicken

¼ cup grated Parmesan cheese, plus additional for topping (optional)

1. Preheat the oven to 350°F. Lightly coat a 9" x 9" loaf pan with olive oil.

2. In a large glass bowl, hydrate the Force with the warm water. Add the pumpkin, apple, eggs, chicken, and cheese. Stir until thoroughly combined.

3. Pour the mixture into the loaf pan. Grate a little extra cheese on top (if using). Bake for 50 minutes, or until the top is firm to the touch and slightly crispy. Cool thoroughly before cutting into slices sized appropriately for your dog. You can also dice the slices into tiny cubes to use for training. The slices or cubes can be stored in an airtight container in the refrigerator for up to 3 days or frozen in an airtight container or individually portioned resealable plastic freezer bags.

Chapter 10

RUN, PLAY, AND FETCH

EASY, ESSENTIAL EXERCISES FOR A HAPPY, HEALTHY PUP

Whether it's watching TV, snuggling, or sleeping in on a Saturday morning, almost all of us love sitting around and doing next to nothing with our dogs. But just like humans, dogs need exercise—both for good health and the emotional release it provides.

Getting out and about and raising your heart rate just a bit can be a wonderful way to bond with your dog, too. Your pup may puff up with pride while he's jogging beside you, or you might experience the exquisite joy—and possibly the deep sense of relief—that comes when he *finally* catches the Frisbee you've been tossing to him every morning for the past 2 months.

Whatever you choose to do, exercise should be a fun part of your daily routine with your dog; it's a great way to improve overall health and longevity while also making everyone happy. And when he comes running inside with a big, toothy grin on his face, you'll know he's thanking you for it!

HOW MUCH EXERCISE IS ENOUGH?

Most dogs who aren't thick around the middle don't need a tremendous amount of exercise. We touched on this subject in Chapter 6, but I'll sum it up again: Most dogs really only need the equivalent of about two brisk 30-minute walks a day. Depending on his age, breed, and metabolism, though, your dog's exercise requirement may be slightly more or less.

My Pug, Johnson, who was completely blind (the rescue we got him from when he was 8 told me he could see a little bit, but when we took him home and he walked right into my dishwasher, I started to question that information), exercised very little. He was a slow mover and enjoyed just sniffing his way along for a block or so. But he was equally content spending the entire day snoozing and then getting up for a wander in the garden and a nice warm meal. We bought him a dog stroller so my children could take him for a push and get him a bit of fresh air, but he didn't seem to love it; he would have rather been down at street level having a good snort of all the wonderful aromas our sidewalk had to offer. Despite his minimal exercise (and rather like Jane Lynch's dog, Olivia, who has only the one eye but still knows how to party), he always kept a positive attitude and made it a point to enjoy life. A lesson for us all.

For other dogs, exercise in general should be fairly intensive but not exhausting. Your dog's heart rate should go up, but not to the point where he's panting excessively and his oversize, bright pink tongue is lolling out of his mouth (a warning that heat exhaustion could be setting in). Struggling, stopping every 2 feet, and staring daggers at you are also signs that the workout's just a little too hard.

Herding and sporting dogs are hardwired for more exercise, so in an ideal world, they should get a 60- to 90-minute workout once or twice a day. If you own one of these dogs, you understand how active they need to be, so I'm not telling you anything you don't already know. If you don't let them outside for a good run, they'll tear your house to bits, so exercise is, in many ways, a self-preservation technique—for you and your belongings, that is.

Terriers are high-energy dogs, but not as dynamic as sporting or herding breeds. They need to get their heart rate up for about 60 minutes a day, but they're such busy little creatures that just running around the house (typically under your heels) may satisfy a lot of their exercise requirement. When they're not at risk of getting stepped on, just taking them outside for errands may allow them to work out as much as they need.

Many hounds can take their daily workouts in short bursts, so letting them loose in the dog park a few times a week may satisfy them. As a bonus, you might enjoy watching them sprint from one side of the park to the other, completely oblivious to the fact that what they perceive as fun is actually really good for them. Finally, toy dogs don't need much exercise—and like terriers, their short legs mean that they get winded faster than other dogs—but since they're prone to obesity, be sure to get them outside and on the move as often as possible.

While some of us may outfit our dogs with activity trackers—and yes, there are many very good ones on the market that are specific to dogs—if you don't have the means to buy one, just use your best judgment to see if your dog's getting enough exercise. If he isn't putting on weight, you're probably meeting his needs, though don't use that as an excuse to slack off and skip his daily walk (or feed him extra treats). Keep up with what you're doing or follow the plan I outline below. Again, just make sure your dog isn't panting or struggling when he's getting his workout. If he is, you need to slow him down, take shorter walks, and gradually work up to a longer exercise routine. But if he comes inside looking happy, drinks a good amount of water, then goes straight to his dog bed for a nap—and wakes up frisky and happy— you'll know he's staying fit.

Finally, Dr. Alvarez recommends having your pet checked out by a vet before beginning any exercise plan. There may be health risks, especially for pets with heart and lung conditions or a history of orthopedic or soft tissue injuries.

2 WEEKS TO GREAT HEALTH: A FUN AND EASY EXERCISE PLAN FOR YOUR PUP

Getting an unhealthy, lazy, overfed, or just plain plump pup in shape doesn't have to be boring. If you're sick of plodding along the same sidewalk on the same street day after day, it's definitely time to come up with some new, fun exercises that you and your dog can do together. Luckily, there are hundreds of options, and I've created a plan that combines heart rate–raising activities with creative games that will trick your dog into thinking he's just *playing*—not actually *exercising*.

I developed this program for the average dog, who needs about two 30-minute workouts a day, so you should adjust it based on your dog's breed and age. If you own a Maltese, he needs less exercise, so you can skip one activity a day if you choose. If you live with a Pointer, you'll need to lengthen each 20-minute session or combine them into one 60-minute training period, plus take a walk later in the day. Dr. Alvarez recommends a quick warm-up leash walk (10 to 15 minutes or less) to prevent injury before really rigorous activities like fetch or other sprinting or jumping activities. Feel free to substitute one activity for another, or if you discover that your dog hates something I've suggested, skip it altogether and repeat another workout. Above all, have fun—and enjoy the side benefits of bonding with your dog and getting in better shape yourself.

Week 1

Sunday morning: It's the weekend, so have your coffee and read the paper with your pup. Then head outside for a brisk 20-minute stroll.

Sunday late afternoon: After you've watched your favorite cooking show or woken up from a nap, go out to your backyard or the park and play fetch with your dog. Use a tennis ball, a stick, or whatever your dog fancies. If, like my Rhodesian Ridgebacks, he gazes at you in disbelief when you throw something off into the distance and then stands there wondering how long you're going to wait before you set off to fetch it yourself, you could try to initiate a racing game with him. Or see if you can put him in a sit-stay while you back away slowly, and then call him to you so he can get in a bit of a run. (Repeat this several times or until one of you gets bored.)

Monday morning: Start the week off right by heading to the nearest dog park for a half hour or so. See if your dog can make friends with a pup who's willing to indulge him in a bit of a run-around so that you can relax, drink your coffee, and chat up your fellow park-goers. If you're a dog park newbie, see page 187 on dog park etiquette before you set off.

Monday early evening: You come home in the rain—what to do? Buy an inexpensive laser pointer and let your dog chase the red dot around the living room for 20 minutes. Just be sure to clear some space; you don't want him to get so excited that he knocks over the coffee table.

Tuesday morning: After sending your dog outside for a quick sprint in the backyard, why not spoil him with some treats by playing Hide a Wish? (See page 208 in Chapter 11 for full instructions.) Although he'll be taking in some calories during

NOURISHING CHICKEN LIVER SMOOTHIE

What's more enjoyable after a hard workout than a delicious, nutritious smoothie? For dogs, it's a cold and refreshing *chicken liver* smoothie! This iron- and protein-rich meal takes nerves of steel to make because pureeing the livers in the blender is quite an unpleasant task, but this smoothie gives your dog incredible nutrition at a time when he needs it most. Plus, he'll lap up every last drop. Unfortunately, he probably won't offer to clean your blender afterward. *Makes 6 to 10 snack-size servings*

8 ounces raw chicken livers*

½ cup chopped melon (such as cantaloupe)

1 cup sliced fresh kale, tough stalks removed

½ cup live culture plain yogurt or kefir

1 In a blender, combine the chicken livers, melon, kale, and yogurt or kefir. Blend until smooth.

2 Use small quantities as a topping on your pet's usual meals, or pour a good quantity into his food bowl as a healthy snack between meals. Store any leftovers in an airtight container in the refrigerator for 2 to 3 days, or freeze in ice cube trays.

*Note: *The chicken livers can be roasted in the oven for about 15 minutes at 350°F, if you prefer. Try to use organic livers if possible, and always purchase them from a reputable butcher or natural food store.*

this game, you can limit them by using a low-fat treat. For a slightly higher calories-burned-to-calories-consumed ratio, just throw one treat at a time and make him run to get it.

Tuesday early evening: Take a long sunset walk around your neighborhood. Be sure to get your dog's heart rate up by encouraging him to jog or walk quickly. You can do this in intervals interspersed with periods of slower walking.

Wednesday morning: Return to the dog park, coffee in hand. Your dog will love seeing the new friends he made earlier in the week. A nice alternative here could be to head to a local hiking trail if you have one close by. One with a bit of an incline will increase his heart rate and the number of calories burned.

Wednesday evening: Too tired to go outside? No worries! Why not let your dog try the treadmill? Lure him onto it with a treat, then turn it on at its lowest speed, gradually increasing the pace to whatever makes your dog comfortable and doesn't tire him too much. Some dogs feel more assured if their owners stand in front of them and offer treats as an incentive to stay on. Whatever you do, never tie your dog to the treadmill—it's too dangerous if he stumbles or tries to run off.

Thursday morning: Head into your backyard for a game of Goin' Fishin'! (See page 207 in Chapter 11 for full instructions.)

Thursday early evening: Unwinding at the dog park after work can be a blast. Take an extra 10 minutes there just for fun. If you're lucky enough to live close to a dog-friendly beach, you could swap the dog park for a jog on the sand.

Friday morning: Get your dog's heart rate pumping by allowing him to trot up and down the stairs. Stand at the bottom with him, throw a toy up the stairs, and send him to fetch it. Call him back down, using a treat to lure him, if necessary, but don't encourage him to rush too fast. Repeat this process over and over again. Just start this exercise slowly and, to avoid tumbles, make sure he's comfortable using the stairs. If your dog is likely to slide

across the landing and into a wall (or something equally dreadful), it goes without saying that you should find another form of exercise that morning.

Friday afternoon: The work week is over! Celebrate by hopping in the car and taking a nice long walk or jog outside of your neighborhood. Or perhaps walk to dinner at a pet-friendly restaurant or get takeout at a friend's house, with your dog in tow.

Saturday morning: It's okay to sleep in! Take it easy—exercising can wait. Why not start the morning with some delicious pancakes (see page 186), then head outside for a game of fetch? This time, don't use that same old tennis ball. Try a Frisbee, instead. It's a bit more challenging to catch, but at this point, your dog may just be up for it.

Saturday afternoon: Cap off your first week of exercise with a celebratory trip to the dog park, but take a different route so that your dog will think you're going somewhere else. He'll be thrilled when he discovers that he's back at his favorite spot! You could also take him with you to do errands on foot. My first dog, Mosi, adored running errands and taught himself to carry the mail from The Honest Kitchen's first post office box back to the house. He felt ever so important, and he got in his daily activity at the same time.

Week 2

You're 1 week in, and your former couch potato dog might be starting to show some signs of increased energy. Perhaps he's even looking a little bit trim. You might be surprised that he's looking forward to his morning walk, and in fact, he wants to try jogging!

Week 2 of this program is really about just stepping up what you did in Week 1. Add another 5 to 10 minutes to each exercise session, or add in a third workout. (But don't feel pressured to make it as long as the others.) Substitute in new exercises from the list below, or if you find something you like, just stick with that. Whatever you do, be sure to get out and about so that you continue on this path to good health.

New exercise ideas include:

Hide-and-seek. While your dog is gated off or in his crate (so that he won't sense what you're up to), scatter a few treats in discreet places around your house. Give him a treat to entice him (not too many—remember, he's trying to stay fit!) and then let him loose. He'll dart around the house until he's found them all.

Swimming. If the weather's nice and your dog is comfortable in the water, consider taking him for a quick swim. If you're not sure if your dog's a natural

POWER PANCAKES

The name says it all. These delicious pancakes will power up your pup and get him ready for his Saturday morning workout. *Makes 8 to 10 pup-size pancakes*

1 cup Force dehydrated dog food

1½ cups warm water

2 free-range eggs, beaten

½ cup oat flour

¼ cup fresh blueberries

Butter or safflower oil for cooking

1. In a large glass bowl, hydrate the Force with the warm water. Add the eggs, oat flour, and blueberries. Stir to combine.

2. In a skillet over medium heat, heat a small quantity of butter or safflower oil. Pour spoonfuls of the batter into the pan and cook until just golden brown on the bottom. Turn and cook until the underside is golden brown. Transfer to a plate to cool.

3. Repeat with the remaining batter. Serve in place of, or as an accompaniment to, your dog's usual meal. The pancakes can be stored in an airtight container in the refrigerator for up to 3 days.

swimmer, I've outlined a plan for getting his feet wet (see page 189).

Blowing bubbles. Perhaps it's because dogs have no clue what they are, or maybe it's because they're absolutely baffled when bubbles land on their noses, but most dogs just *love* bubbles. Invest in a bubble blower that will send dozens of bubbles into the air, then sit back and watch your dog chase after them. For a little extra fun, you can try out the Bubbletastic Dog Bubble Machine, which has—wait for it—*bacon-scented bubbles.*

Doggie day care. Give yourself a break and send your dog to day care for the day. He'll run around so much that he'll be absolutely pooped when he gets home. You'll meet all of his exercise requirements in one fell swoop.

Tag. Some dogs just don't like to fetch. If yours is one of them, you can help him get his exercise in by playing tag. Teach your dog to touch the palm of your hand with his nose (this is called tagging). Once he has the hang of it, you can then walk or run away. Call him and watch him sprint toward you and have him nose your palm again. Continue this for as long as your dog is interested or until you feel his workout is complete.

DOG PARK ETIQUETTE

A trip to the dog park can be the best thing that ever happened to a dog owner. Not only is it an easy way to ensure that your pup's getting enough exercise, but it's also a great way to tire out a dog who's prone to getting restless—and then chasing your cat, chewing your rugs, or doing other inappropriate things indoors. The dog park's also a regular gathering place for city dwellers, and many a bachelor has decided to get a dog just so he can flirt with the single ladies who might be there. As long as your dog's enjoying himself and making new friends, there's absolutely nothing wrong with this!

But do you know the etiquette for dog parks? If you plan to spend your early mornings or summer evenings in one, follow these 10 rules to avoid dustups, angry looks from fellow owners, and even injuries.

1. **Mind the leash.** Keep your dog on-leash until you get to the off-leash area. This is not just respectful to other park users, it's also much safer for your dog. Fights are more likely to happen when a leashed dog is approached by one that's off-leash because the dogs can sense that there's a power imbalance.

2. **Keep 'em separated.** Unless you have a tough, self-confident smaller dog who can roll with the big guys, it's usually better to have your pooch play with dog friends of the same size. Luckily, most parks have a big dog section and a small dog section—and for good reason. Too much of a size difference between playmates can increase the risk of accidental injury, even if the roughhousing is all in good humor.

3. **Never leave your dog unattended.** While the dogs are free to roam (it's their territory!), you never know when your dog may encounter a fellow park-goer who's having a bad day. Hone your dog whispering skills and be ready to step in if the energy of play starts to change. Growling can be a normal part of rough-and-tumble play, but if your dog glares, turns his head away, or stares out of the corner of his eye, it might be a sign of a looming problem. Unfortunately, keeping a close eye on your dog also means you shouldn't use the hour at the dog park to catch up on e-mails.

4. **Always clean up.** Most parks have poop bags or scoopers, but it's best to bring one or two of your own. You can find some great eco-friendly options at www.poopbags.com.

5. **Ssshhh!** Try to prevent excessive barking; it can spoil other park-goers' quiet enjoyment and also raise the stress level among the pups who just want to play.

6. **Sorry, puppies.** Dogs younger than 4 months old should stay at home or be held to ensure that they remain out of contact with other dogs. Puppies won't yet have full immunity to all the possible diseases that can lurk at the dog park. Plus, while socialization is important, their "puppy manners" might offend some of the golden oldies.

7. **No food.** Don't serve your dog food or treats at the park; it's one of the biggest causes of scuffles and full-blown dogfights. Instead, keep some tasty dog biscuits handy to give as a treat when you leave. My dogs love The Honest Kitchen's Nuzzles treats!

8. **No shagging!** Intact males are not welcome at many dog parks. There's usually some leniency for adolescent males up to a year or so in age, but keep an eye out for any displays of interest in females and for dominant behavior either by or toward him, and intervene quickly if necessary. Females in heat should also stay at home until their cycle has ended. Nobody likes an unwanted pregnancy, and it's even worse if the father is a Nobody she only met once on a playdate.

9. **Keep hydrated.** If it's a warm day, a post-play bowl of cool water is essential. There are some great options—such as the travel bowl that Planet Dog sells—for serving your own bottled water on the go. Plus, having your own supply of water reduces the risk of your pup picking up an infection by slurping from the communal fountain.

10. **Exit gracefully.** Be sure to close all gates to the dog park or dog run after entering or exiting, and if your dog becomes unruly or plays too roughly (to the extent that he's bothering other attendees), leash him and leave immediately.

Above all, always observe the rules posted at your local dog park; each town has its own set of regulations. If you go to the wrong park at the wrong time or take off the leash when you shouldn't, the fines can be quite stinging!

TEACHING YOUR DOG TO SWIM

If you've spent even 5 minutes on social media, you've probably seen one of the million or so YouTube videos featuring swimming dogs. There are videos of bulldogs surfing the perfect wave, dogs sliding down waterslides, and adorable puppies encountering water for the first time. The squirmy little puppies hesitate before a pool, then jump in gleefully one after the other and paddle together with their little noses just above the water. While these unbelievably cute images melt even the hardest hearts, they also might lead you to believe that every dog is born with the innate ability to swim—or that every dog just *loves* the water.

Unfortunately, that's not the case. Some dogs will stand next to a pool or a lake and bark and whine; others go to the beach and run in the other direction when they see waves rolling toward them. While a small fear of water is normal—no dog wants to drown, of course—it becomes a problem if you dream of taking your dog surfing, but all he wants to do is lie in the sand with his head between his paws, looking glum.

When your visions of a beach vacation with your pup are ruined, what do you do? Before you try to force your dog into the water, know that there are some breeds that just aren't suited for it. We all know that Irish Setters, Golden Retrievers, and breeds with "water" in their names naturally take to swimming—they've been bred for it—but dogs with short faces (Pekingese and Shih Tzus, for example) become exhausted easily, which sends them into a panic in the water.

Dogs with short legs, such as Bulldogs, Pugs, Frenchies, and Dachshunds, just don't have the capacity to swim; they're either too top-heavy, or their legs are too stumpy to make them effective paddlers. In fact, Bulldogs and Pugs will sink like stones in the water, so if you own one, he should only go near the water when he's wearing a life jacket, just in case he falls in accidentally or fancies a quick, carefully supervised paddle. (See page 193 for information on choosing a canine life jacket.)

Finally, dogs with very short hair, such as Chihuahuas, just get too cold too quickly in the water, leading them to shy away from it even if they might be perfectly good swimmers.

But what if your dog falls somewhere in the middle? That is, you *know* he can swim, but getting his feet wet sends him into a tizzy. You're about to take a vacation near a lake, and your kids are fantasizing about paddling to the dock with him. You can either let them down easy, or you can ease your reluctant pup into the water in just a few easy steps.

First, a word of caution: If your dog absolutely won't go into the water no matter how hard you try, or if he absolutely panics when submerged, it's best to abandon your plans of swimming with him without some kind of flotation device. A dog who freaks out is at risk of drowning. He'll claw at you while trying to use you to stay afloat, and that compromises your ability to swim, which may then sink you both. Choose a hiking vacation instead, or if you're determined to get in a few laps with him, invest in a good-quality life jacket.

If you decide to brave the water, choose the spot for swim lessons carefully. Your best bet is the shallow end of a pool, but if you pick a lake, be sure there aren't too many weeds on the bottom, as you don't want your dog's feet to get tangled up. If you live near the ocean, aim for a calm day or choose a beach without too many strong waves.

Start slowly, and then proceed slowly. Your dog may be very scared at the prospect of getting in the water, so take all the time he needs and don't pile on too much pressure. Speak to him sweetly and provide lots of positive reinforcement, praising him with "Good boy!" when he gets his feet wet and doesn't try to bolt. Remember when you learned to swim? You took lessons, wore water wings, and were always supervised by your mom or dad. It took months for you to feel truly comfortable, so don't expect that your dog will become an expert in mere minutes.

Props and treats can also help. I always recommend leaving your dog's leash on (preferably attached to a harness rather than a collar) when he's first learning to swim. First, a leash prevents him from running away from you, as you can quickly step on it if he tries to hotfoot it in the opposite direction, and second, it's familiar to him, so it may help him feel more comfortable. Never shy away from using a life jacket or some other form of flotation device, either—it may just make those first shaky moments in the water more bearable. If your dog loves tennis balls, they can also be a great way to lure him into the water. Toss one just a few strokes

ICED RASPBERRY LATTE FOR PUPS

After an exhausting day in the water, reward your dog with this tall iced raspberry latte. He can lap it up slowly to keep cool while he's relaxing in the sun. Makes 1 cup

2 tablespoons Pro Bloom instant goat's milk

1 cup warm water

6 ice cubes

Handful of frozen raspberries

1   In a cup or small bowl, hydrate the Pro Bloom with the warm water. Pour into a blender. Add the ice cubes and raspberries and blend until smooth.

2   Serve ¼ cup to small dogs, ½ cup to medium dogs, and a full cup to big dogs.

BONE BROTH PUMPKIN SURPRISE

For postswim recovery on a chilly day, there's nothing quite like a nice warm bowl of bone broth with turmeric. The active curcuminoids in turmeric have terrific natural antioxidant and anti-inflammatory properties for an added health boost. Makes 1 cup

1 heaping teaspoon Instant Bone Broth with Turmeric

1 cup hot (not boiling) water

2 tablespoons unsweetened canned pumpkin

1   Add the broth mix to the warm water, and stir briskly with a whisk or fork so that the powder dissolves. Mix in the pumpkin and stir again.

2   Allow to cool sufficiently before serving.

out and encourage him to swim after it. Don't be shy about giving him treats, either; they can help coax him deeper into the water.

When you do dip toes—and paws—in, here's how to proceed. Keep walking with your dog further into the water until he begins to paddle with all four legs. You may need to support him by putting your arms under his belly, and that's fine. What you don't want is for him to paddle using only his front legs, since that will wear him out. Stay with your dog until he's back on dry land, praising him every step of the way. If your pup has to climb onto a dock or into a boat, he may be a little wobbly, so be sure to support him so he doesn't struggle and fall back into the water.

Learning to swim may take time, but you might be surprised to discover that you have a canine Michael Phelps on your hands in no time flat!

What to Look for When Choosing a Pet Flotation Device

You've dreamed of floating next to your dog in the pool—you reclining on a raft with a drink in your hand, your dog lying proudly on his own raft—but he's just not ready for that. Your pup needs a sturdy flotation device. (Perhaps he'll soon feel confident enough for the raft you've dreamed of.) What should you look for?

- Be sure that a canine life jacket fits him snugly. You should be able to insert two fingers between it and your dog's body, and under no circumstances should the jacket be able to go over your dog's head.

- The safest jackets have easy-release buckles. Your dog could get snagged on something when he's out of the water but still wearing his life vest, so you want something you can get off him quickly.

- Look for a jacket with a harness that allows you to lift him out of the water. Your dog might be having so much fun that he doesn't want to come out, so this may be a necessity!

My favorite is the K-9 Float Coat by Ruffwear. Besides being a great safety device for swimming at the beach or in the pool, it's also useful for dogs who love to raft, kayak, boat, surf, and paddleboard. The K-9 Float Coat is designed for dogs of all shapes and sizes and includes thoughtful details, such as a strong handle that's optimally positioned for lifting dogs out of the water and reflective trim for enhanced visibility.

Rest assured, your dog will still look cool wearing a life vest while he's reclining on a floating dog bed, surrounded by all the waterproof dog toys you rushed to the store to buy for him. He'll just be *much* safer than he would be without one.

Chapter 11

FUN, GAMES, PICNICS, AND PARTIES

PERFECT BIRTHDAYS, EXCURSIONS, AND MAKE-AT-HOME TOYS

Running around the backyard, digging holes, and rolling in the dirt is fun for most dogs, but it's not exactly the high level of spoiling that many of us aspire to give our pups. When time and money allow, we want picnics, parties, and celebrations fit for a king. And what's wrong with baking puppy cupcakes and making bags of party favors for your dog's day care pals?

Coming up with new toys and treats may be simple, but the fun your dog will have with them is priceless, so never feel shame if you don't spend a fortune on dog massages or a Louis XV Pet Pavilion. (Yes, it exists, and it costs $23,990.) There's nothing you can't do at home that won't be loved and appreciated by your dog, so enjoy every second that you put into making his social life special.

THE PUP-FRIENDLY PICNIC

Before we dive into the specifics of throwing an amazing party that your dog's friends will be talking about for years, let's start small and simple. What's easier than throwing a picnic, and what better way to enjoy a warm summer day in a local park? Most of us love to get together with other Dog-Obsessed friends and the pups they dote on, and throwing a casual picnic can be a real joy. As with the dog park, though, there are certain rules to remember to avoid jealousy and aggression, and because food is involved, this is especially important.

To start, it may seem cumbersome, but every dog needs his own blanket, so you should remind your guests to bring something for their dogs to sit on. If they protest, bring extras yourself, and soon they'll see the wisdom of it. Why? Most pups really want to feel included and do everything you do. Having them share your blanket can be too much for some dogs, though, because it puts food that's already on the ground directly in their line of sight. It risks setting your dog up for failure; he may snag your snacks before the fun has even begun. Bringing your dog's favorite, familiar blanket from home will help to calm his anxiety and make him feel part of the action, but he'll be less likely to get himself into trouble, as you can position him slightly apart from the feast, removing the temptation from his reach. If his self-control is a bit questionable, you can seat him on his blanket, then use a leash to tether him to a tree or another solid object. Just be sure not to attach it to any type of choke collar; a harness or martingale collar is much safer.

You could even make your dog feel really responsible if you let him carry his own gear to the picnic. A backpack from Ruffwear is roomy enough to hold a small blanket, travel bowls, and water. Its assistance handle and top-loading stash pockets are super handy, and its lightweight construction and good padding in all the right places will keep your canine sidekick comfortable all the way to the picnic site. Ruffwear recommends that dogs carry no more than 25 percent of their body weight in their dog packs. If your dog's new to the idea of having something on his back, take a few practice walks before picnic day, starting with a light load (like a water bottle) and working up to a heavier load as he gets accustomed to wearing his pack.

Speaking of water, don't forget to bring plenty. Most of us can survive a standard-length picnic with a few glasses of wine in plastic cups, but that won't work for your dog. Especially on a hot day, bring plenty of water for your pup and for others whose owners may have forgotten. I recommend carrying a gallon jug full—you can always drink some yourself.

To keep all the pups safe, watch the napkins and other picnic implements. You might find a bored or nervous dog chewing away on a paper napkin while you're busy talking to your friends. The last thing you want is for your dog to spend the next day digesting paper rather than the delicious treats you've prepared.

Along the same lines, keep unsafe people foods and drinks out of reach. Some popular picnic foods can be problematic for pups, including grapes, raisins, chocolate, macadamia nuts, alcohol, and cooked bones (for example, bones from a chilled roast chicken), so be sure to keep these foods in closed containers.

Don't forget the entertainment! A Frisbee or tennis ball can make for a wonderful prepicnic game for everyone. An interactive puzzle toy loaded with small treats like Proper Toppers can help to keep your pup occupied for a prolonged amount of time while the humans enjoy a leisurely lunch.

And now for the fun part! There are dozens of excellent treats and snacks you can make at home and that your pup and your guests can share at a picnic. Just be sure to make enough of these treats for every dog in attendance; they're so delicious that no one will want to be left out.

DUCK AND HAM DUMPLINGS

These savory dumplings are the perfect appetizer for a gang of hungry pups. The addition of pumpkin means they're gentle on sensitive tummies, too. *Makes about 18 small dumplings*

1 cup Halcyon dehydrated dog food

1 cup warm water

¼ cup canned unsweetened pumpkin (not pie mix)

2 slices nitrate-free ham, torn into small pieces

½ teaspoon ground cinnamon

3 tablespoons shredded sharp Cheddar cheese

1 free-range egg, lightly beaten

1 Set a large pan of water over medium-high heat and bring to a boil. Reduce the heat to a simmer.

2 In a large glass bowl, hydrate the Halcyon with the warm water. Add the pumpkin, ham, cinnamon, cheese, and egg. Stir thoroughly to form a thick batter.

3 Using your hands, roll the mixture into small balls or dumplings. Using a spoon, carefully lower the dumplings into the simmering water and cook for 12 minutes, or until the dumplings float to the surface. Cool completely before serving.

TURKEY AND RASPBERRY SUMMER MEATBALLS

Just the slightest bit sweet, these meatballs are so fancy and colorful that your guests will think you spent hours slaving away in the kitchen. Little do they know! *Makes about 24 small meatballs*

1 pound ground turkey

2 free-range eggs, beaten

3 tablespoons roughly chopped fresh basil

½ cup fresh raspberries

1   Preheat the oven to 350°F. Lightly coat a large baking sheet with olive oil.

2   In a large bowl, combine the turkey, eggs, basil, and raspberries. Stir until thoroughly combined. (The raspberries will break apart and spread throughout the mixture.)

3   Using your hands, make marble-size balls of the mixture and transfer them to the prepared baking sheet. Bake for 20 minutes, or until the meatballs are firm to the touch. Cool before serving. Store in an airtight container in the refrigerator for up to 4 days or freeze for up to 3 months.

PICNIC BARS

These bars are perfect for any kind of picnic. Dogs love the rich taste of cream cheese, and while the small amount of carrots won't significantly improve your dog's vision, the beta-carotene they contain is a terrific antioxidant for overall health. *Makes 12 to 18 bars, depending on size*

2 cups Keen dehydrated dog food

2 cups warm water

½ cup cream cheese (at room temperature)

½ cup fresh ground turkey

¼ cup grated carrots

2 free-range eggs

1 Preheat the oven to 350°F. Lightly coat a 9" x 9" baking dish with olive oil.

2 In a large glass mixing bowl, hydrate the Keen with the warm water and stir thoroughly. Add the cream cheese, turkey, carrots, and eggs. Stir to form a thick batter.

3 Transfer the batter to the baking dish. Bake for 25 minutes, or until slightly crispy on top. Cool thoroughly before slicing into individual bars and serving. These bars will keep in an airtight container in the refrigerator for up to a week.

AUTUMN CUPCAKES

Who says picnics are just for summer? Cap off an early fall picnic with this delicious dessert. Your dogs will lap up the apple and pumpkin after they finish frolicking in leaf piles and enjoying the crisp air. Makes 12 cupcakes

1 cup Halcyon dehydrated dog food

¼ cup canned unsweetened pumpkin (not pie mix)

2 free-range eggs, beaten

½ cup unsweetened applesauce

¼ cup cream cheese, for decorating (optional)

1 Preheat the oven to 350°F. Place paper liners in a 12-cup muffin pan.

2 In a glass bowl, combine the Halcyon and pumpkin. Add the eggs and applesauce. Stir thoroughly to combine.

3 Divide the mixture among the paper liners. Bake for 25 to 35 minutes, or until a wooden pick inserted in the center of a cupcake comes out clean. Allow the cupcakes to cool for 10 minutes before carefully removing them from the pan.

4 If desired, use a knife to spread a small amount of cream cheese on the top of each cupcake.

THROWING THE PERFECT PUPPY BIRTHDAY PARTY

The rules for throwing a puppy party aren't much different from the rules for picnics, but since you might have your party inside and the guest list might be slightly longer, you'll need to be extra careful about making your home safe for all dogs in attendance. A better bet might be throwing the party outside or renting out a dog-friendly space (perhaps the doggy day care?), but if that's not an option, follow these easy guidelines to make sure everyone has a safe and happy time.

- **Choose a closed-off spot.** Few of us mind having our dogs on the couch, but a party full of them romping on the sofa is a bit much even for the most devoted dog lover. Plus, there are all kinds of hazards, such as houseplants and vases, that can be knocked over, and you want to keep all of your guests safe. If you're throwing a puppy party indoors, consider clearing the furniture and breakables out of the room and closing it off with a gate so everyone remains in the secure area. Or better yet, take it outside and set up the party in your yard.

> **"I rented the doggy day care place for her birthday party!"**
>
> —Honest Kitchen customer Stormy Newman, who knows how to throw a one-of-a-kind birthday party for the dog she loves

- **Compile a carefully curated guest list.** While it's tempting to invite everyone from your pup's training class or doggy day care, it's important to think about the amount of space you have. Too many pooches in close confines can increase the risk of stress levels getting too high, which could lead to squabbles, and some dogs will simply feel overwhelmed and anxious. If some of your pup's friends are particularly rambunctious, un-neutered, or prone to aggression, it might be better to omit them from the guest list altogether, to help ensure that everyone can party safely (and that no one goes home pregnant).

- **Put down paper.** There's nothing worse than when a party guest has an accident right in the middle of all the fun. It's a chore for you to clean, and if a guest—dog *or* human—accidentally steps in it and then walks through the house, you might as well just call off the party immediately. Put newspaper on your floors to keep them clean.

- **Don't scrimp on food and drink.** It's unlikely that you'll want to supervise a party full of dogs alone, so encourage your human friends to stay by feeding them well and providing plenty of liquid refreshments. You'll need a few people on hand to help keep pups separated at cake time (or at the very least, to ensure that everyone gets a piece at more or less the same time, to help cut down on any jealousy). It's tempting to pass out great big slices of cake, but it's much better to offer smaller, bite-size pieces that can be enjoyed in a mouthful, again to reduce the risk of squabbles over who has the bigger bit. Do keep several bowls of clean water around; if the guests are playing party games, they'll need to stay hydrated.

- **Make sure the cake is a good one.** You'll want to be sure your dog knows that this is indeed a very special day. The way to his heart is probably through his tummy, so a delicious cake is the perfect way to earn his love. Be very careful with candles, though—don't have the cake at dog height while they're lit in case your pup tries diving in for a taste. If you're lucky enough to have a doggie bakery in your neighborhood, you can have lots of fun collaborating with them on a theme for the decorations. Otherwise, what better way to show your love for your pup than with a cake that you made with your very own hands?

WILLOW'S DECADE DELIGHT CAKE

I created this decadent recipe to celebrate my Rhodesian Ridgeback Willow's 10th birthday, and she shared it with her co-woofers at the office. It makes a good-size cake that's perfect to slice up and share with several dog friends. Children will love helping to make it, too, and while some people may frown on them licking the spatula you used to scrape the last bits of batter out of the bowl, mine were about to give it a go until they realized there wasn't one sugary component in the whole recipe.

Makes 1 cake, about 12 slices

3 cups The Honest Kitchen dog food (Willow likes Brave)

1 cup warm water

1 cup chicken broth or warm water

2 free-range eggs, beaten

½ cup cottage cheese

1 can (5 ounces) low-sodium salmon, sardines, or tuna

½ cup cream cheese

1   Preheat the oven to 375°F. Lightly coat 2 round 9" cake pans with olive oil.

2   In a large glass bowl, hydrate the dog food with the water and broth (or additional water). Add the eggs, cottage cheese, and fish. Stir to thoroughly combine.

3   Divide the mixture equally between the cake pans. Bake for 50 minutes, or until firm to the touch. Allow the cakes to cool completely in the pans. (Be sure they're sufficiently out of reach if your dog has a penchant for thievery, like Willow.)

4   Turn out one of the cakes onto a plate. (It might be slightly crumbly.) Using a knife, spread a thin layer of cream cheese on top of the cake. Turn out the second cake and place it on top of the first. Transfer about ¼ cup of the cream cheese to a piping bag* and decorate the top of the cake with your dog's name or some fancy decorations. Cut the cake into slices appropriately sized for your pup and his friends, and then serve.

Note: If you don't have a piping bag, you can frost the top of the cake with a layer of cream cheese just like you did the bottom section.

- **Consider goodie bags.** While they're certainly not mandatory, what party guest wouldn't like his own chew toy or bag of treats to take home?

- **Open presents when everyone's gone home.** Most dogs, even in their more senior years, still only have the IQ of a small child. They can become quite jealous of one another and are easily overwhelmed in new situations. Rather than risk a fight breaking out when another pup tries to steal the birthday boy's new plush octopus, open presents when things have quieted down a bit and the last guests have left.

EASY-TO-MAKE GAMES FOR MENTAL SANITY AND PHYSICAL ACTIVITY

All your guests—furry and human alike—have left your puppy party, and your dog's looking a little glum. He was having so much fun, but now that the party's over, he just doesn't seem ready to end the festivities. To prevent your dog from heading into a post-party slump, why not treat him to an easy-to-make game? I guarantee you he'll be so pooped after playing that you may not see him leave his dog bed for the rest of the afternoon.

Fun with Paper Bags (shhh, don't tell your dog, but this is actually a modified cat toy)

1. Find a paper bag. Any size is fine, but your large dog will likely prefer a bigger, sturdier one, like you'd get from the grocery store.

2. Scrunch up the bag and tie a thick, long piece of yarn or string around it.

3. Tie the other end of the yarn around a stick.

4. Hold the stick firmly and allow the yarn and paper bag to trail along enticingly behind you.

5. If possible, sprint back and forth in a fairly open area, encouraging your dog to follow along. Be sure to run as fast as possible, keeping your eyes up and planning each change of direction well in advance. This is the same sort of contraption people use to introduce their hounds to lure coursing, which is brilliant fun! Just be sure to hold on tight to the stick in case your dog outruns you and catches hold of the paper.

Duck Hunting

If you have a demanding dog, this game is great to play when you have company over and need a few moments to enjoy your own friends.

1. Place treats into the folds of an old shirt.

2. Roll and fold the shirt, adding treats, until you have a ball filled with well-hidden snacks.

3. If the sleeves are long enough, loosely tie them around the ball.

4. Place multiple treat-stuffed shirt balls around the room and let your pup discover them all!

It's so much fun to watch your dog unravel, paw, and nose the thing until all the treats are gone. Some dogs really are as thick as two short planks and will take forever to retrieve all the cookies, so this could go on for much, much longer than you might think!

Let's go duck hunting!

GIFTS FOR THE DOG OBSESSED

We all like to buy gifts for our dogs, but what about our Dog-Obsessed friends? Make sure they feel included by presenting them with one of these (perhaps, yes, slightly ludicrous) gifts.

1. You can have your dog's face made into pop art and printed on a custom T-shirt. Just visit popyourpup.com.

2. Does your friend own a Scottie? The Vermont Country Store sells shortbread cookies and licorice shaped like these adorable dogs.

3. Have a family member who's always on the road? PetChatz can be a great gift. This two-way audio/video system mounts on the wall—perhaps above the dog's food bowl—and allows a pet owner to speak to his dog remotely.

4. Real Dogs Wine is perfect for the dog lover who's also a wine lover. You can customize the label with a picture of your dog's face, and as a bonus, 10 percent of the proceeds go to rescue groups. Available at www.adogslife.net.

5. If you have loads of time on your hands and are a little crafty, why not knit a sweater out of dog hair? *Knitting with Dog Hair* by Kendall Crolius and Anne Montgomery will show you how.

Smoochie Poochie Race

This game requires at least two dogs and two people. Find an unoccupied hallway and have a friend hold back the dogs with a well-executed body block, a piece of lightweight furniture, or by simply holding their collars. Have the person at the other end of the hall yell "Treats!" and shake a box of hard treats, making an inviting sound. Simultaneously, unleash the hounds! The first one to the other side wins the most treats, but be sure everybody gets at least one to ensure there's no jealousy.

Be sure to give lots of love to pups who get confused by the commotion, freeze under pressure, or can't keep the pace. For added entertainment, ask the owner of the slowest or most confused dog to buy everyone else a drink.

Goin' Fishin'

Tie one end of a sturdy piece of string to an empty paper towel roll, and then tie a small treat to the other end. Skip around a private area of your backyard while holding the paper towel roll firmly in one hand. Whatever you do, don't let your neighbors see you, lest they think you've lost your marbles. Let your dog try to catch you and grab the snack. You may need to start sprinting if your dog is a fast runner; otherwise, the game will be over before it's even begun.

Unless you have a very small or slow-moving dog, I only recommend this activity for the outdoors because, believe me, you and your dog are going to bump into something if you pick up speed and try navigating lots of furniture. And take care to completely untie the string before your dog devours the treat.

Hide a Wish

Ask a friend to distract your dog so he doesn't see what you're up to. Break off little chunks of dog treats and hide them around the house in concealed but easily accessible places—say, under a chair or desk or behind the sofa. Stand aside and unleash your pup! Have your friend help you remember exactly where you hid the treats, as it's not terribly pleasant to find old food under the furniture weeks after the fact. If multiple dogs are participating, put a few pieces aside to pass to those who can't figure out what's going on or who simply take too long to find the goodies and end up losing out to the faster, brighter (and probably better-looking) pups in the group.

A note of caution: Many dogs are delighted by flying or dangling treats, but if you have a food-aggressive pup, we suggest letting him sit out these games. Take him for a walk so he isn't consumed with jealousy and resentment, or he may end up getting talked about in hushed, sarcastic tones after the party's over.

PUPPY STAR SIGNS

Ever wonder what your dog's star sign says about him? Knowing your dog's horoscope can help you unlock his mysterious personality.

AQUARIUS (JANUARY 20–FEBRUARY 18) Affectionate and compassionate, dogs born under Aquarius can often be found trying to leap into their owners' beds late at night.

PISCES (FEBRUARY 19–MARCH 20) Sensitive and selfless, the Pisces dog has the intrinsic ability to sense when his owner is in danger. (Less importantly but no less significantly, he can also smell dinner from a mile away.)

ARIES (MARCH 21–APRIL 19) A high-energy leader, the Aries dog can often be found trying to take advantage of his owner by feigning hunger even after he's eaten. This fire sign, however, has a deep desire to protect and makes an excellent watchdog.

TAURUS (APRIL 20–MAY 20) Taurus is the most practical of all the star signs, and dogs born under it can be stubborn. Need to take your Taurus dog to the vet? Good luck getting him into the car!

GEMINI (MAY 21–JUNE 20) Extremely sociable and fun, Gemini dogs can quickly become the opposite: serious and brooding.

CANCER (JUNE 21–JULY 22) So deeply emotional that they're often considered moody, this class of dog can be exceedingly loyal. Think of a long-eared hound howling for hours, waiting for his owner to come home.

LEO (JULY 23–AUGUST 22) With a deep need to be admired, Leo dogs are performers. Take your Leo to agility training so he can really show off his stuff.

VIRGO (AUGUST 23–SEPTEMBER 22) Intelligent and reliable, Virgo dogs are also a bit fussy. Your Virgo may take what feels like hours to find the perfect pooping spot, or he may insist on sitting in the exact same place on the couch every day.

LIBRA (SEPTEMBER 23–OCTOBER 22) Kind and peaceful, Libra dogs are sometimes *overly* affectionate. They hate being alone, so prepare to be followed everywhere, including out to the mailbox and into the bathroom.

SCORPIO (OCTOBER 23–NOVEMBER 21) Determined, forceful, and powerful, the Scorpio dog can be expected to chase cats, other dogs, and even deer. This unstoppable dog is the strongest of all the star signs.

SAGITTARIUS (NOVEMBER 22–DECEMBER 21) Extroverted and a lover of travel, this type of dog adores road trips, dog park play dates, and even just walking down the street.

CAPRICORN (DECEMBER 22–JANUARY 19) The most ambitious of the star signs, he wants nothing more than to succeed. Consider grooming him to become a show dog.

MEALS FOR YOU AND YOUR DOG— WITH WINE!

As we discussed in Chapter 4, the best way to ensure that your dog is getting optimal nutrition from his food is either to choose fresh, colorful, minimally processed ingredients (if you're cooking from scratch) or to pick a dog food that's similarly free of unnecessary additives and preservatives. You can always combine store-bought dog food with "human food," as well. Meals should be varied, chock-full of vitamins and minerals, and, of course, supremely delicious. We all want our dogs to dine as well as we do.

We've scattered recipes for some easy-to-make treats and meals throughout the book, but the recipes that follow will provide your dog with a full menu of breakfast, lunch, dinner, afternoon tea, snack, and dessert options for every day, special occasions, or any time you fancy giving him something delectable that's also good for him. Because none of these recipes contain dog food, there's no reason to feel squeamish about sharing everything with him. That's what this chapter is for! Finally, most of the produce and other ingredients can be swapped out as desired (for example, you can exchange green beans for zucchini or use oregano instead of sage), so feel free to adjust the recipes according to what you have on hand. There are no strict or stuffy rules here.

For those of us who like a drop of wine with dinner (or lunch—one must never judge!), I've enlisted the services of Ken Chalmers, wine connoisseur extraordinaire and owner of my local boutique wine shop, Bird Rock Fine Wine, which is a veritable treasure trove of incredible bottles from all over the world. Ken has kindly contributed some suggested wine pairings for the recipes in this section. Just be sure to keep the alcohol all to yourself, as it's toxic to dogs. If you'd like to check out Ken's selection of wines online, the address is www.birdrockfinewine.com, and yes, they ship!

DUCK WITH BASIL AND PLUMS

This is a delectable dish to surprise your pup with on a really special occasion, such as his birthday, or as a bribe or peace offering if you have to leave him with a sitter for a few days due to work travel or vacation plans. *Serves 2 people plus a small dog*

3 cups baby potatoes, sliced into quarters

8 ounces chilled boneless duck breast (available at specialty food stores)

1 cup low-sodium free-range chicken broth

2 plums, pitted and cubed

1 handful fresh basil leaves, chopped

1 clove garlic, minced

2 teaspoons raw honey (optional)

FOR THE PEOPLE
Salt and ground black pepper

Note: Although duck has a reputation for being quite fatty, the meat itself is actually exceedingly lean. The fat tends to accumulate right under the skin and can be fairly easily removed with your hands or a sharp knife. If you do remove the fat, it's worth freezing it for later use. Simmer it with some sliced potatoes to make scrumptious duck fat fries for yourself!

1   Bring a large pot of water to a boil. Add the potatoes, reduce the heat, and simmer for about 10 minutes. or until tender. Set aside.

2   Meanwhile, using a sharp knife, cut the duck breast into bite-size pieces. If your pup is overweight, has a sensitive stomach, or has had previous episodes of pancreatitis, remove any large areas of fat, which will be right under the skin. Place the duck in a large saucepan and pour in the chicken broth so the meat is completely covered. Place the saucepan over medium heat and bring the broth to a simmer. Add the plums, basil, garlic, and honey (if using). Simmer for 7 minutes, or until the duck is cooked through.

3   Spoon your dog's portion of duck and potatoes into his bowl and allow it to cool before serving. Spoon the human portions onto plates, season with salt and pepper to taste, and serve. Don't forget to lap up the love and adoration you'll receive from your pup for the rest of the day!

SUGGESTED WINE PAIRING
Try an Oregon Pinot Noir from the Willamette Valley, such as Evening Land. Both 2012 and 2013 are particularly good vintages.

SALMON, CHARD, AND SQUASH BAKE

Salmon is a good choice for pets with skin sensitivities that flare up when they eat more common meats, such as chicken or lamb. Salmon is also loaded with valuable omega-3 essential fatty acids, which support the eyes, heart, joints, and overall immunity.

Serves 2 people plus 2 large dogs

1 delicata or small peeled butternut squash, cut into ¼" cubes

4 deboned salmon fillets

1 bunch rainbow or green chard, shredded

½ cup extra-virgin olive oil (safflower or other oil may be substituted)

2 cloves garlic, crushed or minced (optional)

1. Preheat the oven to 350°F.

2. Place the squash in a saucepan with enough water to cover it. Place over medium-high heat and boil gently for 12 minutes, or until tender. Drain.

3. Place the salmon fillets in a 1"-deep baking pan. Arrange the squash around the fish. Scatter the chard evenly around the squash and fish. Drizzle the oil over the top and sprinkle with the garlic, if using. Cover the pan with foil and bake for 35 minutes, or until the salmon is opaque.

4. Transfer 2 portions to your dogs' bowls and allow them to cool sufficiently before serving. Leave the rest in the baking dish and serve at the table for the people.

SUGGESTED WINE PAIRING

Chardonnay is ideal with salmon. If you like a rich, oaky style, try the Mer Soleil Reserve from the Santa Lucia Highlands in Monterey County, California. If you prefer something a little subtler, try a good white Burgundy like Thierry and Pascal Matrot's Bourgogne Blanc.

SORT-OF-JAMIE-OLIVER'S SUMMERTIME SOUP

This is adapted from a fabulous recipe by Jamie Oliver, one of my favorite British chefs. If you don't own any of his cookbooks yet, I highly recommend all of them!

Serves 6 people plus 2 large dogs

6 cups low-sodium chicken broth

3 cups water

1 package (about 14 ounces) skinless chicken breast fillets, cut into ½" pieces

6 baby potatoes, quartered

2 carrots, finely chopped

2 large handfuls baby spinach

2 tablespoons chopped fresh basil

FOR THE PEOPLE

½ cup sour cream

2 tablespoons pesto

Salt and ground black pepper

1 In a large pot over high heat, bring the broth and water to a boil. Reduce the heat to a simmer, add the chicken and potatoes, and simmer for 12 minutes. Add the carrots and simmer for 10 minutes. Reduce the heat to low and add the spinach and basil. Stir so that the spinach is submerged and begins to wilt.

2 In a small bowl, combine the sour cream, pesto, and salt and pepper to taste.

3 Use a ladle to transfer portions to human and dog bowls. Make sure the dogs' portions are sufficiently cooled before serving. Add a spoonful of the pesto sour cream to the human portions and serve. Leftovers can be stored in the refrigerator for a couple of days. Store the pesto sour cream in a separate bowl.

SUGGESTED WINE PAIRING

New Zealand sauvignon blancs are normally a little too "zesty" to be good food accompaniments, but the pesto and sour cream in this soup would match perfectly. Try the Greywacke from Marlborough, made by Kevin Judd, the first winemaker at Cloudy Bay.

BEEF, CARROT, AND KALE STEW

Serves 4 people plus 1 dog, with some leftovers for the next day

3 tablespoons olive oil

5 cups cubed beef stew meat

2 carrots, cut into bite-size pieces

2 large tomatoes, quartered

1 small bunch celery, coarsely chopped

2 tablespoons tomato paste

1 cup shredded kale

FOR THE PEOPLE

4 large baking potatoes, baked

Butter, salt, and ground black pepper

1. In a Dutch oven over medium-high heat, heat the oil. Cook the beef, stirring frequently, until lightly browned. Add the carrots, tomatoes, celery, and tomato paste and cook until the celery is soft and translucent. Add enough water to cover all of the ingredients. Bring the mixture to a boil, reduce the heat to low, and simmer for at least 2 hours. (The longer you simmer it, the more tender the meat will be.)

2. Stir in the kale about 10 minutes before turning off the heat.

3. Ladle your dog's portion into his bowl and allow it to cool before serving. If your Dutch oven is pretty, you can serve directly from it at the table. If it's not, ladle portions onto plates and serve with the baked potatoes topped with butter and seasoned with salt and pepper. This recipe can function as an occasional meal replacement or as a topping for your dog's regular meals.

SUGGESTED WINE PAIRING

On a cool evening, a full-bodied California Cabernet like the Clos du Val 2013 from Napa Valley would be the perfect accompaniment to this warming, rich stew. Both the 2012 and 2013 are recent vintages to look out for.

AUTUMN BEEF STEW

Serves 4 to 6 people plus 1 or 2 dogs

3 tablespoons olive oil

4 cups cubed beef stew meat

1 butternut or other seasonal squash, cut into 1" cubes

2 carrots, cut into bite-size pieces

1 cup chopped green beans

2 large tomatoes, quartered

1 small bunch celery, coarsely chopped

Note: *Some buttery mashed white or sweet potatoes would make a nice accompaniment—for you and your pup. This recipe can be served as an occasional meal replacement or as a topping for your dog's regular food.*

1 In a Dutch oven over medium-high heat, heat the oil. Cook the beef, stirring frequently, until lightly browned. Add the squash, carrots, green beans, tomatoes, and celery, and cook until the celery is soft and translucent. Add enough water to cover all of the ingredients.

2 At this point, you can continue cooking the stew either on the stovetop or in the oven. If you're cooking on the stovetop, bring the mixture to a boil, then reduce the heat and simmer for at least 2 hours. To cook in the oven, preheat it to 350°F, transfer the stew to the oven, and cook it for at least 2 hours. (The longer you simmer it, the more tender the meat will be.)

3 Ladle your dog's portion into his bowl and allow it to cool before serving. Ladle portions into dishes for the people.

SUGGESTED WINE PAIRING

Squash, green beans, and tomatoes make me think of Italy. Why not try a Nebbiolo from Piemonte? You could splurge on a Barolo, or Ettore Germano's Langhe Nebbiolo for half the price. Seek out 2010 and 2011 vintages from Piemonte.

BAKED CHICKEN AND KALE

Serves 2 people plus 2 smaller dogs

1 pound free-range boneless, skinless chicken breasts or fillets, cut into bite-size pieces

1 bunch kale, chopped (tough stalks removed)

1 handful fresh basil, torn into strips

1 drizzle runny honey (optional)

2 cloves garlic, minced (optional)

1. Preheat the oven to 375°F. Liberally coat a baking dish with safflower oil.

2. Place the chicken in the baking dish and shake it gently to coat it with the oil. Scatter the kale and basil over the chicken. Drizzle the honey (if using) over the greens. Sprinkle the garlic (if using) over the top. Drizzle with a bit more safflower oil and stir to combine.

3. Bake for 20 minutes, or until the chicken is no longer pink, stirring halfway through the cooking time to prevent the greens from burning. Transfer your dogs' portions to their bowls and allow them to cool thoroughly before serving. Serve the people's portions on dishes.

Note: *Some boiled new potatoes or crusty French bread would make a nice accompaniment for the people. You can use this recipe as an occasional replacement for your dog's usual meals or as a whole-food topping for his regular food.*

SUGGESTED WINE PAIRING

Vermentino and baked chicken are a match made in heaven. Try a Vermentino from Corsica, such as Domaine Maestracci's E Prove. Rich and quite high in acidity, Vermentino is a very food-friendly grape.

CHICKEN STEW WITH TOMATOES AND GREENS

Serves 2 people plus 2 medium dogs

3 tablespoons olive oil

1 pound free-range boneless, skinless chicken breasts or fillets, cut into bite-size pieces

2 cloves garlic, minced or crushed

2 small potatoes, cut into about 8 pieces each

1 can (14.5 ounces) diced tomatoes

2 cups free-range chicken broth

2 teaspoons dried Italian seasoning

1 cup finely chopped greens, such as spinach, kale, or chard (tough stalks removed)

FOR THE PEOPLE

Salt and ground black pepper

2 tablespoons finely chopped fresh parsley for garnish

French bread and butter

1 In a Dutch oven over medium-high heat, heat the oil. Cook the chicken, stirring frequently, until browned. Reduce the heat and add the garlic and potatoes. Cook, stirring frequently, until the potatoes begin to soften slightly. Add the tomatoes, broth, and Italian seasoning. Simmer gently for 1 hour, stirring occasionally to prevent sticking.

2 Add the chopped greens, stir thoroughly, and turn off the heat. Allow the greens to wilt.

3 Ladle portions into your dogs' bowls and allow them to cool before serving. For the people, season the remaining stew with salt and pepper to taste and ladle portions into bowls. Garnish each portion with the fresh parsley and serve with the bread and butter.

Note: *This stew can be served on top of your pup's regular meals or as a meal replacement on special occasions. Store completely cooled leftovers in an airtight container in the refrigerator for up to 3 days.*

SUGGESTED WINE PAIRING

A dry white Bordeaux wine, particularly one with a small amount of Muscadelle, would be perfect. Try the Graville-Lacoste from Graves, which contains sauvignon blanc, Semillon blanc, and Muscadelle.

PUMPKIN POWWOW WITH CHICKEN AND SNAP PEAS

Serves 4 people plus 2 medium dogs

4 tablespoons butter, divided

3 cups fresh pumpkin or other seasonal squash cut into ½" pieces

1 pound skinless, boneless chicken breast fillets

1 clove garlic, crushed (optional)

1 cup snap peas, trimmed

2 sprigs fresh sage

FOR THE PEOPLE

1 cup morel, oyster, or other mushrooms

Garlic salt

Ground black pepper

¼ cup white wine

1 Preheat the oven to 375°F. Pour a few tablespoons of olive oil in a roasting dish and tilt to coat the bottom.

2 In a large saucepan over medium-high heat, melt 2 tablespoons of the butter. Cook the pumpkin or squash, chicken, and garlic (if using), stirring occasionally, until browned. Transfer to the roasting dish, along with the melted butter and any juices. Stir gently to ensure that everything is well coated with the oil.

3 Roast for 15 minutes. Remove the dish from the oven and add the snap peas. Tear the leaves from the sage sprigs and add them to the dish. Stir gently to combine. Roast for 10 minutes, or until the chicken is no longer pink and the pumpkin and snap peas are tender.

4 Spoon portions into your dogs' bowls and allow them to cool. Meanwhile, in a small skillet over medium-high heat, melt the remaining 2 tablespoons of butter. Add the mushrooms, garlic salt, and pepper to taste. Cook until the mushrooms are crisp and slightly browned. Remove from the heat and add the wine. Return to the heat and cook for 2 minutes. Transfer to the roasting dish, and stir to combine with the rest of the ingredients.

SUGGESTED WINE PAIRING
Arneis is a little-known white wine varietal from Piemonte in Italy. It is rich and relatively low in acidity, and it would pair excellently with the pumpkin in this dish. Vietti is a superb producer in Piemonte.

TURKEY SOUP

Serves 4 people plus a medium dog

2 cups cooked boneless roasted turkey leftovers

3 cups turkey broth

2 medium potatoes, cut up very small

2 ribs celery (including leaves), finely chopped

1 large carrot, finely chopped

2 cloves garlic (optional)

1. In a large pot, combine the turkey, broth, potatoes, celery, carrot, and garlic (if using). Place the pot over medium-high heat and bring to a boil. Reduce the heat and simmer for 1½ hours, or until the potatoes and carrots are tender.

2. Cool slightly and serve as a topping for your pet's regular meal. For the people, divide the remaining soup among 4 bowls. This soup can be stored in the refrigerator for up to 3 days. Serve chilled leftovers to your dog, or warm each portion slightly in a small saucepan on the stove. (Check the heat before serving.)

SUGGESTED WINE PAIRING
A California sauvignon blanc could pair very well with this turkey soup. Ones from Napa, though a little more expensive, are definitely worth seeking out. Round Pond Estate makes a great one.

POACHED SALMON ON A BED OF GREENS

Serves 6 people plus 2 medium dogs

2 pounds fresh boneless, skinless salmon, divided into 4 or more portions

3 tablespoons olive oil

4 large handfuls chopped baby greens, such as spinach, chard, or kale

FOR THE PEOPLE

4 tablespoons butter

6 ounces cremini mushrooms, sliced

Garlic salt

Ground black pepper

¼ cup white wine

½ cup heavy cream

1   Place the salmon pieces in a large pot and add enough water to cover them completely. Bring to a boil, then reduce the heat and simmer for 15 minutes, or until the fish is opaque. Turn off the heat under the salmon and leave it in the water to keep warm.

2   In a skillet over medium heat, heat the oil. Cook the baby greens, along with a splash of water, stirring occasionally, until the greens have wilted. Set aside.

3   In another skillet over medium-high heat, melt the butter. Add the mushrooms and garlic salt and pepper to taste. When the mushrooms have browned, splash in the wine—it should sizzle. Reduce the heat and stir in the cream.

4   Place some salmon and spinach in your dogs' bowls and the remainder on plates. Serve the dogs when their portions are sufficiently cooled. Spoon the mushroom cream sauce over the plated portions and serve.

SUGGESTED WINE PAIRING

I am a big fan of pairing salmon with a light Pinot Noir. Pinots from Mendocino County or Anderson Valley, California, tend to be a little lighter. Try the light but juicy Fel from Anderson Valley.

WHITEFISH WITH SUMMER VEGETABLES

This recipe can be made with any kind of whitefish, such as haddock, cod, or sole. Fish of almost any kind makes a wonderful, healthy addition to your dog's regular food once in a while, and this recipe is unbelievably simple to make! Some boiled baby potatoes would go well as a side dish. Serves 4 people plus 1 or 2 medium dogs

Olive oil

5 whitefish fillets, deboned

1 zucchini, sliced

½ cup cherry tomatoes

¼ cup string beans

2 tablespoons chopped fresh basil

2 cloves garlic, minced (optional)

FOR THE PEOPLE
Garlic salt

Ground black pepper

1 Preheat the oven to 400°F.

2 Coat a baking dish with a few tablespoons of olive oil and arrange the fillets in the dish. Scatter the zucchini, tomatoes, string beans, basil, and garlic (if using) over the top. Drizzle with additional olive oil.

3 Bake for 20 minutes or until the fish flakes easily, stirring halfway through.

4 Place a portion in your dog's bowl and allow it to cool before serving. Sprinkle some garlic salt and pepper onto the remaining portions in the baking dish, and serve the people's portions from that dish at the table.

SUGGESTED WINE PAIRING
Sancerre is made in the Loire Valley from the sauvignon blanc grape. It is exceptionally versatile as a food wine, and I love it with light, white fish. Try one from Lucien Crochet.

BOLOGNESE

Serves 4 people plus 1 larger dog

¼ cup olive oil

2 cloves garlic, crushed

1½ pounds ground beef (preferably grass-fed)

1 can (14 ounces) diced tomatoes

2 tablespoons tomato paste

Dash of soy sauce (optional)

Dash of Worcestershire sauce

2 teaspoons dried Italian seasoning

Handful fresh basil leaves, chopped

FOR THE PEOPLE

1 tablespoon olive oil

½ onion, finely chopped

1 pound spaghetti or other pasta, cooked

Parmesan cheese

Salt and ground black pepper

1. In a large skillet over medium heat, heat the ¼ cup of oil. Cook the garlic for 30 seconds. Add the beef, stirring to break up any large chunks, and cook until no longer pink. Add the tomatoes, tomato paste, soy sauce (if using), Worcestershire sauce, and Italian seasoning. Reduce the heat and simmer gently for 10 to 15 minutes, or until the sauce thickens and the flavors combine. Add the basil and stir.

2. In a small skillet over medium heat, heat the 1 tablespoon of oil. Cook the onion, stirring frequently, until translucent.

3. Spoon a portion of the Bolognese into your dog's bowl, and let it cool before serving. Mix the onion with the remainder of the Bolognese and stir to thoroughly combine. Serve the people's portions with the cooked pasta, sprinkle each portion with some cheese, and season to taste with salt and pepper.

SUGGESTED WINE PAIRING

Chianti goes beautifully with Bolognese sauce. Look for a riserva, preferably from 2010. The Marchesi de Frescobaldi Nipozzano Riserva is particularly good.

GRILLED TILAPIA WITH COUSCOUS, LEMON, AND CAPERS

Serves 4 people plus 1 larger dog

1 box (5.8 ounces) couscous

8 tablespoons butter

6 tablespoons fresh lemon juice (from 2 large lemons)

5 tilapia fillets

FOR THE PEOPLE

½ cup white wine

5 shallots, sliced

3 tablespoons flat-leaf parsley, chopped

¼ cup capers

Salt and ground black pepper

Note: *Serve the people's portion with a crisp green salad.*

1. Set the broiler to medium-high. Cover a baking sheet with foil.

2. Cook the couscous according to package directions.

3. Meanwhile, in a small saucepan over medium heat, melt the butter. Add the lemon juice and stir to combine. Reduce the heat to low and simmer gently.

4. Place the fish on the baking sheet and broil for 12 to 16 minutes, turning once.

5. In a small skillet over medium heat, combine the wine and shallots and bring to a boil. Add the parsley and capers, reduce the heat, and simmer for 5 minutes.

6. Place a portion of fish and couscous in your dog's bowl, and spoon on a small amount of the lemon butter sauce. Combine the shallot mixture with the lemon butter sauce. Divide the remaining couscous among 4 plates, top with the fish, and spoon a generous portion of the sauce over the top, allowing it to soak into the couscous. Season with salt and pepper to taste.

SUGGESTED WINE PAIRING

The Greek island of Santorini produces some very interesting white wines made from Assyrtiko and Athiri grapes. Track one down from Domaine Sigalas.

RECOMMENDED READING

Allegretti, Jan, and Katy Sommers. *The Complete Holistic Dog Book*. New York: Celestial Arts, 2013.

Flaim, Denise. *The Holistic Dog Book*. New York: Howell Book House, 2003.

Goldstein, Martin. *The Nature of Animal Healing*. New York: Ballantine Books, 1999.

Hamilton, Don. *Homeopathic Care for Dogs and Cats*. Berkeley: North Atlantic Books, 1999.

Hotchner, Tracie. *The Dog Bible*. New York: Avery, 2005.

Messonnier, Shawn. *Natural Health Bible for Dogs and Cats*. New York: Prima Publishing, 2001.

Palika, Liz. *The Ultimate Dog Treat Cookbook*. New York: Howell Book House, 2005.

Pitcairn, Richard H., and Susan H. Pitcairn. *Dr. Pitcairn's Complete Guide to Natural Health for Dogs and Cats*. New York: Rodale, 2005.

Postins, Lucy. *Made out of Love*. San Diego: The Honest Kitchen, 2013.

Pryor, Karen. *Don't Shoot the Dog!* Gloucestershire: Ringpress Books, 2002.

Puotinen, C. J. *The Encyclopedia of Natural Pet Care*. Los Angeles: Keats Publishing, 2000.

Puotinen, C. J. *Natural Remedies for Dogs and Cats*. New York: Gramercy Books, 1999.

Schwartz, Cheryl. *Natural Healing for Dogs and Cats A–Z*. Carlsbad: Hay House, 2002.

Scott, Martin J., and Gael Mariani. *Bach Flower Remedies for Dogs*. Forres: Findhorn Press, 2007.

Solisti-Mattelon, Kate, and Patrice Mattelon. *The Holistic Animal Handbook*. San Francisco: Council Oaks Books, 2000.

Stilwell, Victoria. *It's Me or the Dog*. New York: Hachette Books, 2007.

Tilford, Gregory L., and Mary L. Wulff. *Herbs for Pets*. Los Angeles: BowTie Press, 1999.

Volhard, Wendy, and Kerry Brown. *Holistic Guide for a Healthy Dog*. New York: Howell Book House, 2000.

ACKNOWLEDGMENTS

I'm incredibly grateful to my cowriter, Sarah Durand, for doing such a brilliant job of corralling all the rambling ideas in my head at the start of this project and for capturing the necessary, slightly British, quirky tone of voice as the ideas made it onto paper. Not an easy feat for a native New Yorker!

My deepest gratitude to Jane Lynch for writing the foreword. Jane is the epitome of the Dog-Obsessed, pup-loving owner this book is for, and I truly appreciate her support and willingness to help with this project.

Huge thanks to Natalya Zahn, whose warm, charming illustrations have truly helped to bring this book to life. I'm very grateful indeed to my friends Dr. Patrick Mahaney and Dr. Leilani Alvarez, two highly respected integrative veterinarians, for reviewing the health-care content in this book and making sure the advice given to readers is accurate and appropriate. Your input was invaluable.

Many thanks to my fabulous, supportive, and eternally witty team at The Honest Kitchen; for contributing so much fodder for this book and for enabling me to devote my time to working on it. It's been a labor of love, and it wouldn't have turned out the way it did if my coworkers hadn't let me miss a few meetings and covered for me while I slaved over the words on these pages!

Special gratitude, also, to the many Honest Kitchen customers who contributed photos, confessions, and beautiful anecdotes of Dog Obsession. Your stories inspired a huge part of this book and gave us a few laugh-out-loud moments, to boot!

A big thank-you to my agent, Yfat Reiss Gendell, and her tireless assistant, Jessica Fellerman, at Foundry Literary Media. Another big thanks to my editors, Jennifer Levesque and Ursula Cary; my designer, Rae Ann Spitzenberger; and the rest of the team at Rodale Inc.

Last but not least, a huge thank-you to my family: my lovely husband, Charlie; and our daughters, Thalia and Asha. Thank you for your patience, interest, and support while I worked on this project. Taro and Willow, thank you for always sitting close by (and sometimes right in my own personal space) as the words flowed. And a special thank-you, of course, to my beloved Mosi, who lives on in my heart and who really caused my Dog Obsession all those years ago.

INDEX

Boldface page references indicate illustrations or photographs. <u>Underscored</u> references indicate boxed text.

A

Abscess, tooth, 103
Accidents, 159, 163
Aconite, 145
Activity trackers, 181
Acupuncture, 119, 128, 132
Additives
    in foods, xii, 6, 54, 71, 121,
        176, 211
    to lawns, 153
Adenovirus, 39
Adopting a dog, <u>133</u>. *See also*
        Finding a dog
Afghan Hound, <u>26</u>
Aggression, 153–54
    dealing with, 154
    fear, 153
    possessiveness, 153
    redirected, 154
    territorial, 154
Airlines, 164–65
Alcohol, 211
Alfalfa, 87
Allergy
    flea, 110
    food, 57, 59, 84–87,
        90–91
    home environment, 107
    seasonal, 106–7
Aloe vera, 112
Alone time, 141–44
American Hairless Terrier, <u>26</u>
Amylase, 55, 90
Anal glands, 97
Anesthesia, 104–5
Anger, 35, 146
Animal Essentials, 121,
        150
Anthocyanins, 62
Anthoxanthins, 63
Antioxidants
    in foods, 59, 61–62, 81
    for older dogs, 119
    recipes with
        Bone Broth Pumpkin
            Surprise, <u>192</u>

Holiday Turkey and
    Cranberry Mini
    Muffins, <u>172</u>, **173**
Picnic Bars, <u>200</u>
Summer No-Cook Probiotic
    Cupcakes, <u>88</u>, **89**
Superfood Cupcakes, **8,** <u>9</u>
Turkey and Zucchini Loaf,
    <u>65</u>
    for skin problems, 109
Anxiety
    coprophagia and, 151
    natural solutions for, 145
    separation, 141, 143, 168
    signs of, 144
    social, 147–48
Apartments, dogs in, 49–50
Apis mellifica, 112, <u>118</u>, 122, <u>169</u>
Apple cider vinegar, 80, 100, 109
Applesauce, 63
Arnica, 122, <u>169</u>
Arsenicum, 122, 125, 145, <u>169</u>
Arthritis, 59, 91
Ash, 72

B

Baby (dog personality), 20, 22
Baby, dog's reaction to, 146
Backpack, 30, 196
Backyard breeders, 28
Ball and rope toys, <u>41</u>
Bandage, 125
Barking, 7, 10, 25, 50, 188
Barley, 145
Beams (The Honest Kitchen), 30,
        104, 142
Bed
    dog, 29, 45, 158, 167, 169–70
    sharing with dog(s), 45–48
Bedlington Terrier, <u>26</u>
Beef, 85, 86
Beet pulp, 57, 85
Bee venom, 112, <u>118</u>, 122, <u>169</u>
Benadryl, 122, 159
Berry Balance, 120

Beta-carotene, 62, 81
Betadine, 115, 125
Bichon Frise, <u>26</u>
Birthday party, 202–4
Bison, 86
Bladder problems, 120–22
    Chicken and Banana Loaf, <u>123</u>
Blanket
    at picnics, 196
    preparing for a new dog, 30
    for trips to vet, 136
    when dealing with new baby,
        146
    when traveling, 31, 33, 158,
        166–68, 171
Blowing bubbles, 187
Board certification, 128
Body condition score, **93**
Bones, 55–56, 66, 168, 171
Booties, 30
Boots, rubber, 30
Borage, 57
Boredom, 82
Boss, owners as, <u>21</u>
Bossy Britches (dog personality
        type), 20
Botulism, 80
Boundaries, 34, 44
Bowls, 29, 31
    cause of reluctance to eat
        and, 83
    small, 92
    travel, 162, 167
Brave (The Honest Kitchen)
    Duck and Orange Cupcakes,
        <u>137</u>
    Summer Seafood Nibblers, <u>18</u>
    Willow's Decade Delight
        Cake, <u>204</u>
Breath, dog, 102, 103, 104
Breeders, 24, 27, 28
Bringing new dog home, 33
Brushes and combs, 30
Brushing teeth, 102–3
Bubbletastic Dog Bubble
        Machine, 187
By-products, 55, 72

C

Cake, birthday, 203, <u>204</u>
Calcium, 42, <u>124</u>
Calcium oxalate crystals, 121
Calcium phosphate, 40
Calendula, 99, 109, 117, 122
Cameras, 5
Camping, 168–71
Canine distemper virus, 39
Canine parainfluenza virus, 39
Canine parvovirus, 39
Cantharis, 121
Carbohydrates
    in diet, 57, 59
    pet food ingredients, 72
    refined, 57
Carbo Veg, 125
Carotenoids, 59, 61
Carrier, pet, 31
Car travel, 162–64
Cats, 11, 48–49
Chamomile, 40, 80–81, 112, 116,
    145
Charity, donation to, <u>133</u>
Chestnut bud, 145
Chew treats, 104, 168
Chicory, 147
Chondroitin, 119
Christmas tree, 174–75
Chymotrypsin, 90
Citronella, 111
City pets, 49–50
Clothing, dog, 30
Coconut oil, 109, 110, 112
Colitis, <u>124</u>
Color of foods, 61–63
Comfrey, 112
Communication, 44
Companion animal, 16
Compression vest, 145
Conditioner, 30
Copper, 42
Coprophagia, 148, 150–51, 153
    behavioral issues, 151
    management of, 151, 153
    nutritional factors, 150–51
Corn, 57, 85
Cortisone, 106
Coton de Tulear, <u>26</u>
Cottage cheese, 60, 66, 78
Cotton balls, 125
Cranberries, 62, 121, 176
Crate
    aggression and, 154
    air travel, 165
    car travel, 164

house training, 36
transporting dog in, 136
visiting others, 160
when leaving dog alone, 143
wooden, 50
Crystals, urinary, 120–21

D

Dairy products, 59–60
Dandruff, 106
DAPP vaccination, 39
Dasuquin, 119
Day care, doggie, 187
Dehydrated foods, xiii, 67, **67,**
    69, 171
Dehydration, <u>90</u>
Dental health, 102–5
Dentist, dog, 104
Desensitization, 148
Destruction, 141–44
Diabetes, 62, 91, 105, 120
Diapers, doggie, 166
Diarrhea, 77, 81, 86–87, <u>124</u>, 175
Diatomaceous earth, 110, 111
Diet. *See also* Food(s)
    changing, 42–43, 76–78, 105
    elimination, 86–87, 107, 150
    grain-free, 57, 99, 107, 109
    health issues
        fleas, 112
        pancreatitis, 105
        skin problems, 107, 109
    high-moisture, 106, 119
    hypoallergenic, 85
    low-fat, 105
    minimalist, limited-
        ingredient, <u>98</u>
    prey model, 103
    raw, whole food, 103–4
    variety in, 54, 56, 82
Digestion, recipes for
    Bacon Berry Pancakes, <u>3</u>
    Duck and Ham Dumplings,
        <u>198</u>
    Halloween Pumpkin Ginger
        Nibbles, <u>15</u>
    Probiotic Mini Chicken
        Meatballs, **130, <u>131</u>**
    Summer No-Cook Probiotic
        Cupcakes, <u>88</u>, **89**
Digestion aids, herbal, 43
Digestive enzymes
    benefits of, 90–91
    Probiotic Mini Chicken
        Meatballs, **130, <u>131</u>**

in Pro Bloom (The Honest
    Kitchen), 59
Summer No-Cook Probiotic
    Cupcakes, <u>88</u>, **89**
use for
    coprophagia, 150
    exocrine pancreatic
        insufficiency, <u>124</u>
    pancreatitis, 105
Divorce, 5
Dog-human bond, 10
Dog park
    etiquette, 187–89
    exercising at, 181–82, 184–85
    lack of comfort at, 49
    learning coprophagia, 151
    shy or reclusive dog, 147–48
Dog show, 2
Donations, memorial, <u>133</u>
Duck Hunting (game), 206, **206**
Dust mites, 87, 107

E

Ear-cleaning solution, 100
Ears
    cleaning, 80, 99–101, **100**
    examination of, 96
    infections, xiii, 97, 99
Eating disorders, 81–83
Echinacea, 121–22
Eggs, 56, 63, 87
Ehrlichiosis, 114
Elimination diet, 86–87, 107, 150
Embark (The Honest Kitchen)
    Independence Itty-Bits, <u>140</u>
    Superfood Cupcakes, **8,** <u>9</u>
Emo (dog personality type), 17
Emotional cues, 10
Emotions, 138–54
    aggression, 153–54
    anxiety, 144–45
    coprophagia, 148, 150–51,
        153
    jealousy, 146–47
    leaving dog alone, 141–44
    personality quirks, <u>152</u>
    shy/reclusive dogs, 147–48
Essential oils, 111
Evening primrose oil, 57, 112
Exercise, 178–93
    blowing bubbles, 187
    doggie day care, 187
    dog parks, 181–82, 184–85,
        187–89
    hide-and-seek, 185

intensity of, 180
recipes for pre-and
     post-exercise
     Bone Broth Pumpkin
          Surprise, 192
     Iced Raspberry Latte for
          Pups, 192
     Nourishing Chicken Liver
          Smoothie, 183
     Power Pancakes, 186
reducing stress with, 136
requirements, 180–81
swimming, 185, 187, 189–91,
     193
tag, 187
tiring dog out with, 159
two-week program, 182–87
     week 1, 182, 184–85
     week 2, 185, 187
warm-up, 182
for weight loss, 92
Exhaustion, 90
Exocrine pancreatic
     insufficiency, 124, 150
Eyes
     chamomile tea for sore,
          80–81
     injuries, 163

F

Facetime, 4
Family, pets as, 4–5
Fats, dietary, 56–57
     greasy poop and, 124
     pet food ingredients, 72
Fatty acids
     essential, 56, 112
     omega-3, 57, 119, 213
Fear
     aggression and, 153
     barks as indicator of, 7
     of the outside, 50–51
Fiber
     in diet, 57, 59
     in kibble, 124
     pet food ingredient, 72
     sources of, 60, 81
Finding a dog, 24–29
     breeders, 25, 27–28
     pet stores, 24–25
     shelters, 25, 28–29
Fireworks, 50–51, 139, 140, 144
First aid, 122, 125, 169
Fish
     in elimination diet, 86

oily, 57
     sources, 55, 66
Fish oil, 57, 112
Flavonoids, 62, 68
Flax, 57
Flaxseed, 87
Fleas, 106, 110–12
Floors, 31
Flotation device, pet
Flower essences, 133
     for anxiety, 145
     in first aid kit, 125
     for grief, 83
     for jealousy, 147
Flying with your dog, 164–66
Folic acid/folate, 62, 145
Food(s), 52–72
     additives in, xii, 6, 71, 121,
          176, 211
     allergies, 84–87, 90–91
     amount, 92
     avoiding at dog parks, 189
     for camping, 171
     changing, 42–43, 76–78, 105
     color, 61–63
          dark green, 62
          orange, yellow, and green,
               62
          purple, reddish, and black,
               62
          red and pink, 61
          white, 63
     donation, 133
     essential for health and
          healing, 80–81
     finicky eater, signs of, 76
     GMO, 55, 57, 59, 107
     hydration of, 40
     ingredients
          allergic reactions, 85
          dehydration of, xiii
          human-grade, xiv
          minimally processed,
               85–86, 103
          on pet food label, 69–72
          quality, 69
          source of, 6
          to stock up on, 63, 66
     label, pet food, 69–72
     mealtime misgivings, 74–92
     organic, 107
     pet food types, 66–67, 69
          dehydrated and
               freeze-dried, 67, 69, 171
          frozen, raw, 67
          kibble, 66–67
          wet, 67

prescription dog food, 121
     puppy, 41–43
     quality of, 2, 6, 69, 85
     raw, 56, 67, 103–4
     recipes (see Recipes)
     refusal to eat, 81–83
     signs of a happy, healthy,
          well-fed dog, 52
     to stock up on, 63, 65
     timed feedings, 83
     toxic, 59, 60
     in toys, 41, 50
     when visiting, 158
Food sensitivities
     causes, 84–85
     dealing with, 85–87, 90–91
     ear problems, 99
     gluten, 57, 107
     recipes for
          Beef, Pumpkin, and
               Quinoa Burgers, 98
          Tuna Fish Cakes, 73
     reluctance to eat and, 82
     skin and coat problems, 107
     symptoms, 84
     triggers, 54, 56, 57
Food therapy, 132
For-Bid, 150
Force (The Honest Kitchen)
     Halloween Chicken,
          Pumpkin, and Apple
          Loaf, 177
     Power Pancakes, 186
     Probiotic Mini Chicken
          Meatballs, 130, 131
     Summer No-Cook Probiotic
          Cupcakes, 88, 89
Fruits, 59, 61–66
     in elimination diet, 86
     pet food ingredients, 70
     preparation of, 59
Fun with Paper Bags, 205

G

Games, 205–8
     Duck Hunting, 206, 206
     Fun with Paper Bags, 205
     Goin' Fishin', 207–8
     Hide a Wish, 208
     Smoochie Poochie Race, 207
Gas, 77, 176
Gelsemium, 145
Gifts for Dog Obsessed, 207
Ginger, 164
Glucosamine, 119

Gluten-free recipes
    Bacon Berry Pancakes, <u>3</u>
    Beef, Pumpkin, and Quinoa
        Burgers, <u>98</u>
    Halloween Pumpkin Ginger
        Nibbles, <u>15</u>
    Tuna Fish Cakes, <u>73</u>
Gluten sensitivity, 57, 107
GMO foods, 55, 57, 59, 107
Goat's milk, 59, 91, 110. *See also*
        Pro Bloom (The Honest
        Kitchen)
Goin' Fishin' (game), 207–8
Gorse, 145
Grain(s)
    GMO, 107
    grain-free diet, 57, 99, 107, 109
    sensitivity to, 57, 99, 107
Grain fractions, 107
Grain-free recipes
    Halloween Pumpkin Ginger
        Nibbles, <u>15</u>
    Tuna Fish Cakes, <u>73</u>
    Turkey Frittata with Basil
        and Peaches, <u>108</u>
Grapes, 59, <u>60</u>, 176
Greens, 176
Grief, 82, 83, <u>133</u>
Grooming products, 30
Growling, 188
Guaranteed analysis, 72
Gum disease, 103

H

Halcyon (The Honest Kitchen)
    Autumn Cupcakes, <u>201</u>
    Duck and Ham Dumplings,
        <u>198</u>
    Duck and Orange Cupcakes,
        <u>137</u>
Happiness, oxytocin and, 10
Harness, 29, 30, 31, 51, 191, 193
Health certificate, 165
Health check, home, 96–97
Health issues, 95–125
    diabetes, 62, 91, 105, 120
    ears, 97, 99–102
    first aid, 122, 125
    fleas, 106, 110–12
    heartworm and ticks, 112–14
    home health check, 96–97
    kidney disease, 119
    older dogs, 117, 119
    pancreatitis, 105–6
    paws, 115–17

skin and coat, 106–10
    stools, <u>124</u>
    teeth, 102–5
    urinary tract, 120–22
Hearing loss, 97
Heartworm, 112–13
Herbal tea rinse, 112
Herbal therapy
    anti-itch, 109
    for anxiety, 245
    for bladder health, 121–22
    calming Ruff-n-Tumble
        personality type, 16
    for dealing with grief, <u>133</u>
    digestion aids, 43
    for fleas, 111–12
    veterinary care, 129, 132
Herding dogs, 180–81
Hide-and-seek, 185
Hide a Wish (game), 208
Holding your dog, 101
Holidays, 174–76
Holistic veterinarian, 129
Holly, 147
Homeopathy
    Apis mellifica (bee venom),
        112, <u>118</u>, 122, <u>169</u>
    description of, <u>118</u>
    first aid kit, 125, <u>169</u>
    use for
        anxiety, 245
        bladder health, 121
        fleas, 112
        grief, 83
        nail wounds, 117
        overindulgence, 175
        skin problems, 110
        teething, 40
Honest Kitchen, The. *See also*
        specific products
    ambassador veterinarians,
        xvii
    Dog-Obsessed employees,
        x–xi
    FDA certification, xiv
    origin and growth, xiii–xiv
Honey, 66, 80
Honeysuckle, <u>133</u>, 145
Horoscope, <u>209</u>
Horsetail, 121–22
Hotel, pet-friendly, 166–68
Hot spots, 85, 106, 109
Hounds, 181
Houseguest, being a good,
        158–60
House training, 35–36
Hydration, 105–6, 189

Hyland's Teething Tablets, 40
Hypericum, 117
Hypoallergenic dogs, <u>26</u>

I

ID tags, 163, 167, 171
Ignatia, <u>133</u>
Incontinence, 47, 121
Infectious canine hepatitis
        virus, 39
Ingredients. *See* Food(s),
        ingredients
Ingredient splitting, 70
Insurance, pet, 134–35
Integrative veterinarian, 129
Intelligence, <u>144</u>
Irish Water Spaniel, <u>26</u>
Itching, 84, 87, 106, 110–11

J

Jealousy, 146–47

K

Keen (The Honest Kitchen)
    Picnic Bars, <u>200</u>
    Turkey Cherry Keen Buns, <u>155</u>
Kefir, 60
Kelp, 150
Kerry Blue Terrier, <u>26</u>
K-9 Float Coat (Ruffwear), 193
Kibble
    beef-flavored, 85
    contents of, 67, 70
    description of, 66–67
    fiber in, <u>124</u>
    oral health and, 102, 104
    simple carbohydrates, 102
    transitioning from, 77
    traveling with, 171
    water stores depleted by, 67,
        106, 121
Kidney disease, 119
Kong toys, 30, 40, <u>41</u>, 50, 136,
        142, 143, 160
Kurgo, 31

L

Label, pet food, 69–72
Lagotto Romagnolo, <u>26</u>

Lamb, sensitivity to, 85, 107
Larch, 145
Lavender, 111
Leash
    at campground, 169
    during car travel, 164
    at dog park, 187
    long-line, 169
    for new dog, 29, 30
    teaching dog to swim, 191
Leash laws, 167
Leave it! command, 151, 153
Leaving your dog alone, 141–44
Leftovers, holiday, 175–76
Lemon balm, 111
Life jacket, canine, 193
Lipase, 90, 105
Listening to your dog, 7, 10
Litter box, cat, 151
Liver
    in diet, 56
    fish liver oils, 57
Look at me! command, 153
Louis XV Pet Pavilion, 195
Love dog food (The Honest
        Kitchen)
    Bacon Berry Pancakes, 3
    Halloween Pumpkin Ginger
        Nibbles, 15
    Valentine's Supper Treats, 37
Luggage, 31
Lutein, 62
Lycopene, 61
Lyme disease, 114
Lymph nodes, 96

M

Maltese, 26
Marshmallow, 121–22
Marvel (The Honest Kitchen)
    Turkey and Zucchini Loaf,
        64, 65
Massage, 96
Meal replacements
    Cod and Potato Oven Fritters,
        79
    Tuna Fish Cakes, 73
    Turkey Frittata with Basil
        and Peaches, 108
Meat by-products, 55
Meats
    cooling vs. warming, 85
    effect on anxiety, 145
    fresh, 70
    leftover holiday, 175

organ, 56, 66
pet food ingredients, 69–70
protein in, 72
sensitivity to, 107
sources, 55
Memorializing your dog, 133
Milk, 85
Millet, 86, 87
Mimulus, 145, 147
Minerals, 71–72
Mold, 87, 107
Molly Mutt, 29
Mosquitoes, 112–13
Mouth, examination of, 96
Mucus in stool, 124
Music, calming, 143
Muzzle, 122, 154

N

Nail clipper, 30
Nail clipping, 115–17, 116
Neem oil, 111
Nematodes, 111
Neosporin, 115
Nervous Nellie (dog personality
        type), 14, 16
Neuter, 154
New dog
    boundaries, setting, 34
    bringing home, 33
    crating, 36
    house training, 35–36
    introducing cat to, 48–49
    living together with, 43–45
    veterinary visit, 38–39
Nutrition
    carbohydrates, 57, 59
    dairy products, 59–60
    fats and oils, 56–57
    nuts and seeds, 60
    protein, 55–56
Nuts, 60, 66, 176
Nux vomica, 175
Nuzzles (The Honest Kitchen), 189

O

Oatmeal baths, 109
Oats, 87, 145
Oatstraw, 145
Oils, dietary, 56–57
Older dogs
    care of, 117, 119
    first veterinary visit, 39
Omega-3 fatty acids, 57, 119, 213

Onions, 59, 60, 176
Organ meats, 56, 66
Outdoors, reluctance to go,
        50–51
Overweight dogs, 42, 91–92, 93
Oxytocin, 10

P

Pads, damage to, 115
Pancreatitis, 56, 105–6
Paper bags, 205
Parasites, 38, 39, 148
Parsley, 66, 73, 80, 86, 98, 219,
        227
Passionflower, 145
Patience, 36, 44–45, 139
Paws
    examination of, 96
    health issues, 115–17
Peanut butter, 143
Peanuts, 85
Pecks, 184
Pee pads, 49, 51, 159
Pennyroyal, 111
People Pleaser (dog personality
        type), 23
Perfect Form (The Honest
        Kitchen), 43, 77
Periodontal disease, 102
Personality quirks, 152
Personality types, dog, 14–23
    Baby, 20, 22
    Bossy Britches, 20
    Emo, 17
    Nervous Nellies, 14, 16
    People Pleaser, 23
    Ruff-n-Tumble, 16–17
    Trouble, 19
Peruvian Inca Orchid, 26
Pesticides, 107
PetChatz, 207
Petfinder.com, 28
Pet food. See also Food(s)
    conventional, xii–xiv
    hypoallergenic diet, 85
    labels, 69–72
Pet insurance, 134–35
Pet Plan, 135
Pet stores, 24–25
Phenylalanine, 145
Phosphorus, 42
Phytonutrients, 59, 61–63, 85
Picnic
    recipes, 198–201
        Autumn Cupcakes, 201

Picnic (cont.)
    recipes (cont.)
        Duck and Ham
            Dumplings, 198
        Picnic Bars, 200
        Turkey and Raspberry
            Summer Meatballs, 199
    throwing, 196–97
Planet Dog, 142
Plants, hazardous, 174
Plaque, dental, 103–5
Pollen, 87, 106
Poop
    appearance of, 124
    eating, 148, 150–51, 153
    picking up, 49, 151, 188
Poop bags, 50, 188
Portuguese Water Dog, 26
Possessiveness, 153
Potassium, sources of, 63, 65
Potassium citrate, 121
Potatoes, 85, 176
Potty! command, 35
Preparing for a new dog, 29–31
    for cold climates, 30
    must-have products, 29–30
    for outdoorsy dog, 30
    for travel, 31
Prescription dog food, 121
Prescription medicines, 128–29
    anti-anxiety, 144
    for skin problems, 106
Preservatives, 55, 72, 95, 121,
    169, 175, 211
Primal, 82
Principles of the dog obsessed,
    1–11
    listening to your dog, 7, 10
    one size doesn't fit all, 11
    pets are family, 4–5
    source matters, 6
    trusting your dog, 10
Probiotics
    for older dogs, 119
    for pancreatitis, 105
    Probiotic Mini Chicken
        Meatballs, 130, 131
    in Pro Bloom (The Honest
        Kitchen), 59, 77, 91
    Summer No-Cook Probiotic
        Cupcakes, 88, 89
    for urinary tract infections,
        120
Pro Bloom (The Honest Kitchen),
    43, 59, 77, 91, 150
    Iced Raspberry Latte for
        Pups, 192

Meatless Holiday Cupcakes,
    161
Probiotic Mini Chicken
    Meatballs, 130, 131
Proper Toppers (The Honest
    Kitchen), 82
Protein
    changing source of, 78
    in diet, 55–56
    kidney disease and, 119
    in meats, 72
    single source, 85
Prozyme, 91
Pulex irritans, 112
Pumpkin, 66, 81, 176
Puppy
    feeding, 41–43
    house training, 35–36
    sharing bed with, 45–48
    teething, 39–40
    veterinary visit, 38–39
Puppy mills, 6, 24–25
Purebred dogs, 24, 27, 28
Puzzle toys, 41, 50

Q

Quality, importance of, 2, 6
Quickies (The Honest Kitchen),
    184, 197
Quiet! command, 50
Quinoa, 87
    Beef, Pumpkin, and Quinoa
        Burgers, 98
Quiz (Are You Dog Obsessed),
    xvi

R

Rabies, 39
Radio, 50, 142
Raisins, 59, 60, 176
Raw foods, 56, 67, 103–4
Real Dogs Wine, 207
Recipes
    Autumn Cupcakes, 201
    Bacon Berry Pancakes, 3
    Beef, Flax, and Honey Bars,
        58
    Beef, Pumpkin, and Quinoa
        Burgers, 98
    Beef and Banana Muffins, 22
    Bone Broth Pumpkin
        Surprise, 192
    Chicken and Banana Loaf, 123

Chicken and Cranberry
    Muffins, 68
Cod and Potato Oven Fritters,
    79
Duck and Ham Dumplings,
    198
Duck and Orange Cupcakes,
    137
Halloween Chicken,
    Pumpkin, and Apple
    Loaf, 177
Halloween Pumpkin Ginger
    Nibbles, 15
Holiday Turkey and
    Cranberry Mini
    Muffins, 172, 173
Iced Raspberry Latte for
    Pups, 192
Independence Itty-Bits, 140
Meatless Holiday Cupcakes,
    161
Nourishing Chicken Liver
    Smoothie, 183
Omega Bars, 149
Picnic Bars, 200
Power Pancakes, 186
Probiotic Mini Chicken
    Meatballs, 130, 131
Summer No-Cook Probiotic
    Cupcakes, 88, 89
Summer Seafood Nibblers,
    18
Superfood Cupcakes, 8, 9
Tuna Fish Cakes, 73
Turkey and Raspberry
    Summer Meatballs, 199
Turkey and Zucchini Loaf,
    64, 65
Turkey Cherry Keen Buns,
    155
Turkey Frittata with Basil
    and Peaches, 108
Valentine's Supper Treats, 37
Willow's Decade Delight
    Cake, 204
for you and your dog, 212–27
    Autumn Beef Stew, 217
    Baked Chicken and Kale,
        218
    Beef, Carrot, and Kale
        stew, 216
    Bolognese, 225
    Chicken Stew with
        Tomatoes and Greens,
        219
    Duck with Basil and
        Plums, 212

Grilled Tilapia with Couscous, Lemon, and Capers, **226,** <u>227</u>
Poached Salmon on a Bed of Greens, <u>223</u>
Pumpkin Powwow with Chicken and Snap Peas, **220,** <u>221</u>
Salmon, Chard, and Squash Bake, <u>213</u>
Sort-of-Jamie-Oliver's Summertime Soup, **214,** <u>215</u>
Turkey Soup, <u>222</u>
Whitefish with Summer Vegetables, <u>224</u>
Reclusive dogs, 147–48
Reinforcements, 45, 136
Rendering plants, xii
Rescue groups, 27, 28
Rescue Remedy, 125, 145, 168
Retinol, 62
Rewards. *See also* Treats
  in house training, 35
  introducing new dog to a cat, 48–49
  recipes for
    Duck and Orange Cupcakes, <u>137</u>
    Turkey Cherry Keen Buns, <u>155</u>
Rhus tox, 112
Rice, 57, 63, 85
Ridgeback Rescue, 27
Road trips, 162–64
Rockrose, 145
Rocky Mountain spotted fever, 114
Rosemary, 111
Ruff-n-Tumble (dog personality type), 16–17
Ruffwear, 30, 193, 196
Rugs, <u>31</u>, 50, 168
Rules of dog obsession, <u>21</u>

S

Saliva, 55
Salt, sea, 81
Scent, owner's, <u>160</u>
Schnauzers, <u>26</u>
Seat belts, 163, 165
Sedatives, 166
Seeds, 60
Sense-ation harness, 29, 30, 51
Separation anxiety, 141, 143, 168

Shampoo, 30, 110
Shelters, adopting dog from, 25, 28–29
Shy dogs, 147–48
Skin and coat problems, 85, 106–10
  diet, 107
  fleas, 106, 110–12
  reactions to home environment, 107
  seasonal allergies, 106–7
Skullcap, 145
Sleeping with your dog(s), 45–48
Small Batch, 82
Smoochie Poochie Race, 207
Smoothie
  Nourishing Chicken Liver Smoothie, <u>183</u>
Snacks
  Tuna Fish Cakes, <u>73</u>
  Turkey Frittata with Basil and Peaches, <u>108</u>
Snoring, 47
Sofa, 45, 158
Soft Coated Wheaton Terrier, <u>26</u>
Solid Gold Health Products for Pets, 121, 150
Soy, 57, 85
Spanish Water Dog, <u>26</u>
Sparkle shampoo bars (The Honest Kitchen), 30
Spay, 154
Spirulina, 150
Spoiling, <u>21</u>
Sporting dogs, 180–81
Squash, 176
St. John's wort, 145
Stairs, exercising on, 184–85
Star of Bethlehem, <u>133</u>
Star signs, <u>209</u>
Steroids, xiii, 97, 101–2, 106, 110, 127
Stools, <u>124</u>
Stool sample, 38
Stop! command, 153
Stop Eating Poop, 150
Stress, reducing
  with Rescue Remedy, 125
  during trips to the veterinarian, 136
Struvite crystals, 120
Sugar
  in diets of small dogs, 103
  in grain, 99
  refined carbohydrates, 57
Sulfur, 110, 112

Supplementation, use for
  coprophagia, 150
  crystal, urinary, 120–21
  fleas, 112
  pancreatitis, 105
  skin problems, 109
Sweet chestnut, <u>133</u>
Sweet potatoes, 86, 176
Swimming, 185, 187, 189–91, 193

T

Tag, 187
Tapeworm, 110
Tartar, 102–4
Tea tree, 111
Teeth, 96, 102–5
Teething, 39–40
Tennis balls, <u>41</u>, 182, 191, 197
Terriers, 181
Territorial aggression, 154
Thrive (The Honest Kitchen), <u>98</u>
  Chicken and Banana Loaf, <u>123</u>
  Chicken and Cranberry Muffins, <u>68</u>
Thundershirt, 145
Ticks, 113–14
Tinkle Tonic, 121
Toothbrush, canine, 102–3
Tooth fracture, 104
Toothpaste, 102
Toxic foods, 59, <u>60</u>
Toys
  in bed, 48
  first-time, <u>41</u>
  food in, <u>41</u>, 50
  hard chew, 104
  Kong, 30, 40, <u>41</u>, 50, 136, 142, 143, 160
  for new dog, 30
  travel and, 171
Traditional Chinese veterinary medicine, 129, 145
Travel, 157–71
  being a good houseguest, 158–60
  camping, 168–71
  first aid, <u>169</u>
  flying, 164–66
  hotels, 166–68
  more fun with dog than with human, <u>163</u>
  road trips, 162–64
Travel sickness, 162

Treats
    cutting down on, 91–92
    homemade, 148
    produced in China, 104
    recipes
        Beef, Pumpkin, and
            Quinoa Burgers, 98
        Chicken and Banana Loaf,
            123
        Halloween Chicken,
            Pumpkin, and Apple
            Loaf, 177
        Halloween Pumpkin
            Ginger Nibbles, 15
        Holiday Turkey and
            Cranberry Mini
            Muffins, 172, **173**
        Independence Itty-Bits,
            140
        Summer Seafood Nibblers,
            18
        Turkey Cherry Keen Buns,
            155
        Valentine's Supper Treats,
            37
    in toys, 41
    when teaching dog to swim,
        191, 193
Tree, memorial, 133
Trouble Is My Middle Name (dog
        personality type), 19
Trusting your dog, 10
Trypsin, 90
Tryptophan, 145
Tui na, 132
Turkey
    calming effect of, 145
    in elimination diet, 86
Turmeric, 119, 192
Tweezers, 125

U

Urinary tract health,
        120–22
    crystals, 120–21
    home remedies, 121–22
    incontinence, 47, 121
    infections, 120
Urtica urens, 112

V

Vaccinations, 38–39, 165
Valerian, 145
Vegetables, 59, 61–66
    in elimination diet, 86
    nightshade family, 59
    pet food ingredients, 70
    preparation of, 59
Verve (The Honest Kitchen)
    Beef, Flax, and Honey Bars, 58
    Beef and Banana Muffins, 22
Veterinarian
    aggression, help with, 154
    ambassador, xvii
    checklist for choosing, 135
    ear health and, 99, 101–2
    end-of-life care, 133
    finding, 6, 127, 132, 134
    first visit to, 38–39
    health certificate, 165
    reducing stress during trips
        to, 136
    types, 128–29, 132
        emergency, 134
        holistic/integrative, 129
        specialists, 128
        traditional Chinese
            medicine, 129
        traditionalist, 128–29
Video camera, 41
Vine, 147
Visiting others with your dog,
        158–60
Vitamins
    pet food ingredients, 71–72
    vitamin A, 42, 56, 62, 65
    vitamin B_3, 176
    vitamin B_6, 65, 176
    vitamin B_{12}, 145
    vitamin C, 62, 65, 112, 176
    vitamin D, 42
    vitamin E, 112
Vocalizations, 7, 10, 47, 50, 168

W

Walnut, 145, 147
Water
    house training and, 35
    at picnics, 196–97

Water bottle, 30
Weight, losing, 91–92
Westminister Kennel Club Dog
        Show, 2
Wheat, 57, 85
Wild Planet, 18
Willow, 133
Wine, 207
Wine pairings
    Arneis, 220
    Barolo, 217
    Bordeaux, 219
    Cabernet, 216
    Chardonnay, 213
    Chianti, 225
    Nebbiolo, 217
    Pinot Noir, 212, 223
    Sancerre, 224
    from Santorini, 227
    sauvignon blanc, 215,
        222
    Vermentino, 218
Worms, 38

X

Xoloitzcuintli, 26
Xylitol, 60, 176

Y

Yeast, ear, 80, 99, 101,
        176
Yogurt, 43, 59–60, 66, 78

Z

Zeal (The Honest Kitchen)
    Cod and Potato Oven Fritters,
        79
    Omega Bars, 149
    Tuna Fish Cakes, 73
Zeaxanthin, 62
Zinc-based creams,
        109
Zoonotic diseases,
        38–39